CHIPS FROM A GERMAN WORKSHOP.

VOL. II.

CHIPS

FROM

A GERMAN WORKSHOP.

BY

MAX MÜLLER, M. A.,

FELLOW OF ALL SOULS COLLEGE, OXFORD.

VOLUME II.

ESSAYS ON MYTHOLOGY, TRADITIONS, AND CUSTOMS.

NEW YORK:

CHARLES SCRIBNER AND COMPANY.

1871.

RIVERSIDE, CAMBRIDGE:
STEREOTYPED AND PRINTED BY
H. O. HOUGHTON AND COMPANY

To

JACOB BERNAYS,

PROFESSOR IN THE UNIVERSITY OF BONN

IN MEMORY OF HAPPY HOURS.

τοῦ συμφιλολογεῖν καὶ συμφιλοσοφεῖν.

CONTENTS OF SECOND VOLUME.

XVI.

COMPARATIVE MYTHOLOGY.

Phædros. Dost thou see that very tall plane-tree?

Sokrates. Certainly I do.

Phædros. There is shade there, and the wind is not too strong, and there is grass to sit, or, if we like, to lie down.

Sokrates. Lead on then!

Phædros. Tell me, Sokrates, is it not from some place here they say that Boreas carried away Oreithyia from the Ilissos?

Sokrates. So they say.

Phædros. Should it not be from this spot? for the waters seem so lovely, and pure, and transparent, and as if made for girls to play on the bank.

Sokrates. No; it is two or three stadia further down, where you cross over to the temple of Agra, — and there you find, somewhere, an altar of Boreas.

Phædros. I was not aware of this. But tell me, by Zeus, O Sokrates, — dost *thou* believe this myth to be true?

Sokrates. Well, if I did not believe it, like the wise people, I should not be so very far wrong; and I might set up an ingenious theory and say that a gust of Boreas, the Northwind, carried her down from the rocks in the neighborhood, while she was playing with her friend Pharmakeia; and that, having died in this manner, she was reported to have been carried off by Boreas from thence, or from the Ares peak, — for there goes also this story, that she was carried off from that, and not from this spot. As to myself, Phædros, I think these explanations, on the whole, very pleasant; but they require a man of strong mind and hard work, and a man who, after all, is not much to be envied, if it were only for this, that when he has set right this one fable, he is bound to do the same for the form of the Hippokentaurs, and again for that of the Chimæra. And then a host of such beings rushes in, — Gorgons and Pegasos, and masses of other hopeless beings, and absurdities of monstrous creatures. And if a man, not believing in the existence of these creatures, should try to represent each according to the probable explanation, dealing in a rough kind of philosophy, he would require abundance of leisure. I, at least, have no time to spare for these things, and the reason, my friend, is this, that I cannot yet, according to the Delphic line, know myself; and it seems to me ridiculous that a man who does not yet know this, should trouble himself about what does not concern him. Therefore I leave those things alone, and, believing what other people believe about them, I meditate, as I said just now, not on them, but on myself, — whether I be a monster more complicated and more savage than Typhon, or a tamer and simpler creature, enjoying by nature a blessed and modest lot. But while we are talking, my friend, was not this the tree to which thou wert to lead us?

Phædros. This is the very tree.

THIS passage, from the Introduction of Plato's "Phædros," has been frequently quoted in order to show what the wisest of the Greeks thought about the rationalists of his day. There were at Athens then, as there have been at all times and in all countries, men who had no sense for the miraculous and supernatural, and who, without having the moral courage to deny altogether what they could not bring themselves to believe, endeavored to find some plausible explanation by which the sacred legends which tradition had handed down to them, and which had been hallowed by religious observances, and sanctioned by the authority of the law, might be brought into harmony with the dictates of reason and the laws of nature. That Sokrates, though himself accused of heresy, did not entertain a very high opinion of these speculators, — that he thought their explanations more incredible and absurd than even the most incredible absurdities of Greek mythology, — nay, that at a certain period of his life he treated such attempts as impious, is clear from this and other passages of Plato and Xenophon.

But if Mr. Grote, in his classical work on the "History of Greece," avails himself of this and similar passages, in order to introduce, as it were, Sokrates himself among the historians and critics of our own time, — if he endeavors to make him bear witness "to the uselessness of digging for a supposed basis of truth" in the myths of the Greek world, he makes the ancient philosopher say more than he really said. Our object in considering the myths of the Greeks, or any other nation of antiquity, is so different from that of Sokrates, that the objections which he urged against his rationalizing contemporaries could hardly be said to apply to us. For what is it that makes us at the present day ask the question of the origin of the Greek myths? Why do men study ancient history, acquire a knowledge of dead languages, and decipher illegible inscriptions? What inspires them with an interest not only in the literature of Greece and Rome, but of ancient India and Persia, of Egypt and Babylonia? Why do the puerile and often repulsive legends of savage tribes rivet their attention and engage their thoughts? Have we not been told that there is more wisdom in "The Times" than in Thukydides? Are not the novels of Walter Scott more amusing than Apollodoros? or the works of Bacon more instructive than the cosmogony of the Purâ*n*as? What, then, gives life to the study of antiquity? What compels men, in the midst of these busy times, to sacrifice their leisure to studies apparently so unattractive and useless, if not the conviction, that in order to obey the Delphic commandment, — in order to know *what Man is*, we ought to know *what Man has been?* This is a view as foreign to the mind of Sokrates as any of the principles of inductive philosophy by which men like Columbus, Leonardo da Vinci, Copernicus, Kepler, Bacon, and Galileo regenerated and invigorated the intellectual life of modern Europe. If we grant to Sokrates that the chief object of philosophy is that man should know himself, we should hardly consider his means of arriving at this knowledge adequate to so high an aim. To his mind man was preëminently the individual, without any reference to its being but one manifestation of a power, or, as he might have said, of an idea, realized in and through an endless variety of human souls. He is ever seeking to solve the mystery of human nature by brooding over his own mind, by watching the secret workings of the soul, by analyzing the organs of knowledge, and by trying to determine their proper limits; and thus the last result of his philosophy was, that he knew but one thing, and this was, that he knew nothing. To us, man is no longer this solitary being, complete in itself, and self-sufficient; man to us is a brother among brothers, a member of a class, of a genus, or a kind, and therefore intelligible only with reference to his equals. The earth was unintelligible to the ancients, because looked upon as a solitary being, without a peer in the whole universe; but it assumed a new and true significance as soon as it rose before the eyes of man as one of many planets, all governed by the same laws, and all revolving around the same centre. It is the same with the human soul, and its nature stands before our mind in quite a different light since man has been taught to know and feel himself as a member of one great family, — as one of the myriads of wandering stars, all governed by the same laws, and all revolving around the same centre, and all deriving their light from the same source. The history of the world, or, as it is called, "Universal History," has laid open new avenues of thought, and it has enriched our language with a word which never passed the lips of Sokrates, or Plato, or Aristotle, — *mankind*.[1] Where the Greek saw barbarians, we see brethren; where the Greek saw heroes and demi-gods, we see our parents and ancestors; where the Greek saw nations (ἔθνη), we see mankind, toiling and suffering, separated by oceans, divided by language, and severed by national enmity, — yet evermore tending, under a divine control, towards the fulfillment of that inscrutable purpose for which the world was created, and man placed in it, bearing the image of God. History, therefore, with its dusty and mouldering pages, is to us as sacred a volume as the book of nature. In both we read, or we try to read, the reflex of the laws and thoughts of a Divine Wisdom. As we acknowledge no longer in nature the working of demons or the manifestation of an evil principle, so we deny in history an atomistic conglomerate of chances, or the despotic rule of a mute fate. We believe that there is nothing irrational in either history or nature, and that the human mind is called upon to read and to revere, in both the manifestations of a Divine Power. Hence, even the most ancient and shattered pages of traditions are dear to us, nay dearer, perhaps, than the more copious chapters of modern times. The history of those distant ages and distant men — apparently so foreign to our modern interests — assumes a new charm as soon as we know that it tells us the story of our own race, of our own family, — nay, of our own selves. Sometimes, when opening a desk which we have not opened for many years, — when looking over letters which we have not read for many years, we read on for some time with a cold indifference, and though we see it is our own handwriting, and though we meet

[1] See Cicero, *Tusc. Disp.* v. 37.

with names once familiar to our heart, yet we can hardly believe that we wrote these letters, that we felt those pangs, that we shared in those delights, till at last the past draws near and we draw near to the past, and our heart grows warm, and we feel again as we felt of old, and we know that these letters were our letters. It is the same in reading ancient history. At first it seems something strange and foreign; but the more intensely we read, the more our thoughts are engaged and our feelings warmed; and the history of those ancient men becomes, as it were, our own history, — their sufferings our sufferings, — their joys our joys. Without this sympathy, history is a dead letter, and might as well be burnt and forgotten; while, if it is once enlivened by this feeling, it appeals not only to the antiquarian, but to the heart of every man.

We find ourselves on a stage on which many acts have been acted before us, and where we are suddenly called to act our own part. To know the part which we have to act ourselves, we ought to know the character of those whose place we take. We naturally look back to the scenes on which the curtain of the past has fallen, for we believe that there ought to be one thought pervading the whole drama of mankind. And here History steps in, and gives us the thread which connects the present with the past. Many scenes, it is true, are lost beyond the hope of recovery; and the most interesting, the opening scenes of the childhood of the human race, are known to us by small fragments only. But for this very reason the antiquarian, if he descries a relic of those early times, grasps it with the eagerness of a biographer who finds unexpectedly some scraps written by his hero when yet a child — entirely himself, and before the shadows of life had settled on his brow. In whatever language it may be written, every line, every word, is welcome, that bears the impress of the early days of mankind. In our museums we collect the rude playthings of our hero's boyhood, and we try to guess from their colossal features the thoughts of the mind which they once reflected. Many things are still unintelligible to us, and the hieroglyphic language of antiquity records but half of the mind's unconscious intentions. Yet more and more the image of man, in whatever clime we meet him, rises before us, noble and pure from the very beginning: even his errors we learn to understand, — even his dreams we begin to interpret. As far as we can trace back the footsteps of man, even on the lowest strata of history, we see that the divine gift of a sound and sober intellect belonged to him from the very first; and the idea of a humanity emerging slowly from the depths of an animal brutality can never be maintained again. The earliest work of art wrought by the human mind, — more ancient than any literary document, and prior even to the first whisperings of tradition, — the human language, forms an uninterrupted chain from the first dawn of history down to our own times. We still speak the language of the first ancestors of our race; and this language, with its wonderful structure, bears witness against such gratuitous imputations. The formation of language, the composition of roots, the gradual discrimination of meanings, the systematic elaboration of grammatical forms, — all this working which we can still see under the surface of our own speech, attests from the very first the presence of a rational mind — of an artist as great, at least, as his work.

The period, during which expressions were coined for the most necessary ideas, — such as pronouns, prepositions, numerals, and the household words of the simplest life, — a period to which we must assign the first beginnings of a free and, as yet, hardly agglutinative grammar, — a grammar not impressed with any individual or national peculiarities, yet containing the germs of all the Turanian, as well as the Aryan and Semitic forms of speech, — this period forms the first in the history of man, — the first, at least, to which even the keenest eye of the antiquarian and the philosopher can reach, — and we call it the "Rhematic Period."

This is succeeded by a second period, during which we must suppose that at least two families of language left the simply agglutinative, or nomadic stage of grammar, and received, once for all, that peculiar impress of their formative system which we still find in all the dialects and national idioms comprised under the names of "Semitic" and "Aryan," as distinguished from the "Turanian," the latter retaining to a much later period, and in some instances to the present day, that agglutinative reproductiveness which has rendered a traditional and metamorphic system of grammar impossible, or has at least considerably limited its extent. Hence we do not find in the nomadic or Turanian languages — scattered from China to the Pyrenees, from Cape Comorin, across the Caucasus, to Lapland — that traditional family likeness which enables us to treat the Teutonic, Celtic, Slavonic, Italic, Hellenic, Iranic, and Indic languages on one side, and the Arabian, Aramean, and Hebrew dialects on the other, as mere varieties of two specific forms of speech, in which, at a very early period, and through influences decidedly political, if not individual and personal, the floating elements of grammar have been arrested and made to assume an amalgamated, instead of a merely agglutinative character. This second may be called the "Dialectic Period."

Now, after these two periods, but before the appearance of the first traces of any national literature, there is a period, represented everywhere by the same characteristic features, — a kind of Eocene period, commonly called the "Mythological" or "Mythopœic" Age. It is a period in the history of the human mind, perhaps the most difficult to understand, and the most likely to shake our faith in the regular progress of the human intellect. We can form a tolerably clear idea of the origin of language, of the gradual formation of grammar, and the unavoidable divergence of dialects and languages. We can understand, again, the earliest concentrations of political societies, the establishment of laws and customs, and the first beginnings of religion and poetry. But between the two there is a gulf which it seems impossible for any philosophy to bridge over. We call it the "Mythic Period," and we have accustomed ourselves to believe that the Greeks, for instance, — such as we find them represented to us in the Homeric poems, far advanced in the fine arts, acquainted with the refinements and comforts of life, such as we see at the palaces of Menelaos and Alkinoos, with public meetings and elaborate pleadings, with the mature wisdom of a Nestor and the cunning enterprise of an Odysseus, with the dignity of a Helena and the loveliness of a Nausikaa — could have been preceded by a race of men whose chief amusement consisted in inventing absurd tales about gods and other nondescript beings, — a race of men, in fact, on whose tomb the historian could inscribe no better epigram than that on Bitto and Phainis. Although later poets may have given to some of these fables a charm of beauty, and led us to accept them as imaginative compositions, it is impossible to conceal the fact that, taken by themselves, and in their literal meaning, most of these ancient myths are absurd and irrational, and frequently opposed to the principles of thought, religion, and morality which guided the Greeks as soon as they appear to us in the twilight of traditional history. By whom, then, were these stories invented? — stories, we must say at once, identical in form and character, whether we find them on Indian, Persian, Greek, Italian, Slavonic, or Teutonic soil. Was there a period of temporary insanity, through which the human mind had to pass, and was it a madness identically the same in the south of India and in the north of Iceland? It is impossible to believe that a people who, in the very infancy of thought, produced men like Thales, Herakleitos, and Pythagoras, should have consisted of idle talkers but a few centuries before the time of these sages. Even if we take only that part of mythology which refers to religion, in our sense of the word, or the myths which bear on the highest problems of philosophy, — such as the creation, the relation of man to God, life and death, virtue and vice, — myths generally the most modern in origin, we find that even this small portion, which might be supposed to contain some sober ideas, or some pure and sublime conceptions, is unworthy of the ancestors of the Homeric poets or the Ionic philosophers. When the swineherd Eumæos, unacquainted, perhaps, with the intricate system of the Olympian mythology, speaks of the Deity, he speaks like one of ourselves. "Eat," he says to Odysseus, "and enjoy what is here, for God will grant one thing, but another he will refuse, whatever he will in his mind, for he can do all things."[1] This, we may suppose, was the language of the common people at the time of Homer, and it is simple and sublime, if compared with what has been supposed one of the grandest conceptions of Greek mythology, that, namely, where Zeus, in order to assert his omnipotence, tells the gods, that if they took a rope, and all the gods and goddesses pulled on one side, they could not drag him down from the heaven to the earth; while, if he chose, he could pull them all up, and suspend the earth and the sea from the summit of Olympos. What is more ridiculous than the mythological account of the creation of the human race by Deukalion and Pyrrha throwing stones behind them (a myth which owes its origin to a mere pun on λαός and λᾶας)? while we can hardly expect, among pagans, a more profound conception of the relation between God and man, than the saying of Herakleitos, "Men are mortal gods, and gods are immortal men." Let us think of the times which could bear a Lykurgos and a Solon, — which could found an Areopagos and the Olympic games, and how can we imagine that, a few generations before that time, the highest notions of the Godhead among the Greeks were adequately expressed by the story of Uranos maimed by Kronos, — of Kronos eating his children,

1 *Od.* xiv. 443. Ἔσθιε, δαιμόνιε ξείνων, καὶ τέρπεο τοῖσδε
Οἷα πάρεστι· θεὸς δὲ τὸ μὲν δώσει τὸ δ' ἐάσει,
Ὅττί κεν ᾧ θυμῷ ἐθέλῃ· δύναται γὰρ ἅπαντα.

swallowing a stone, and vomiting out alive his whole progeny? Among the lowest tribes of Africa and America we hardly find anything more hideous and revolting. It is shutting our eyes to the difficulties which stare us in the face, if we say, like Mr. Grote, that this mythology was "a past which was never present;" and it seems blasphemy to consider these fables of the heathen world as corrupted and misinterpreted fragments of a divine revelation once granted to the whole race of mankind — a view so frequently advocated by Christian divines. These myths have been made by man at a certain period of history. There was an age which produced these myths, — an age half-way between the Dialectical Period, presenting the human race gradually diverging into different families and languages, and the National Period, exhibiting to us the earliest traces of nationalized language, and a nationalized literature in India, Persia, Greece, Italy, and Germany. The fact is there, and we must either explain it, or admit in the gradual growth of the human mind, as in the formation of the earth, some violent revolutions, which broke the regularity of the early strata of thought, and convulsed the human mind, like volcanoes and earthquakes arising from some unknown cause, below the surface of history.

Much, however, will be gained if, without being driven to adopt so violent and repugnant a theory, we are able to account in a more intelligible manner for the creation of myths. Their propagation and subsistence in later times, though strange in many respects, is yet a much less intricate problem. The human mind has an inborn reverence for the past, and the religious piety of the man flows from the same natural spring as the filial piety of the child. Even though the traditions of past ages may appear strange, wild, and sometimes immoral or impossible, each generation accepts them, and fashions them so that they can be borne with again, and even made to disclose a true and deeper meaning. Many of the natives of India, though versed in European science, and imbued with the principles of a pure natural theology, yet bow down and worship the images of Vish*n*u and *S*iva. They know that these images are but stone; they confess that their feelings revolt against the impurities attributed to these gods by what they call their sacred writings; yet there are honest Brahmans who will maintain that these stories have a deeper meaning, — that immorality being incompatible with a divine being, a mystery must be supposed to be concealed in these time-hallowed fables, — a mystery which an inquiring and reverent mind may hope to fathom. Nay, even where Christian missionaries have been successful, where the purity of the Christian faith has won the heart of a native, and made the extravagant absurdities of the Purâ*n*as insupportable to him, the faith of his early childhood will still linger on and break out occasionally in unguarded expressions, as several of the myths of antiquity have crept into the legends of the Church of Rome.[1] We find frequent indications in ancient history that the Greeks themselves were shocked by the stories told of their gods; yet as even in our own times faith with most men is not faith in God or in truth, but faith in the faith of others, we may understand why even men like Sokrates were un-

[1] See Grimm's Introduction to his great work on *Teutonic Mythology*, second edition, 1844, p. xxxi.

willing to renounce their belief in what had been believed by their fathers. As their idea of the Godhead became purer, they felt that the idea of perfection, involved in the idea of a divine being, excluded the possibility of immoral gods. Pindar, as pointed out by Otfried Müller,[1] changes many myths because they are not in harmony with his purer conceptions of the dignity of gods and heroes; and, because, according to his opinion, they must be false. Plato [2] argues in a similar spirit when he examines the different traditions about Eros; and in the "Symposium" we see how each speaker maintains that myth of Eros to be the only true one which agrees best with his own ideas of the nature of this god, — Phædros [3] calling him the oldest, Agathon the youngest of the gods; yet each appealing to the authority of an ancient myth. Thus, men who had as clear a conception of the omnipotence and omnipresence of a supreme God as natural religion can reveal, still called him Zeus, forgetting the adulterer and parricide: —

Ζεὺς ἀρχὴ, Ζεὺς μέσσα, Διὸς δ' ἐκ πάντα τέτυκται,

"Zeus is the beginning, Zeus the middle; out of Zeus all things have been made;"

— an Orphic line, but an old one, if, as Mr. Grote supposes, Plato alluded to it.[4] Poets, again, who felt in

[1] See O. Müller's excellent work, *Prolegomena zu einer wissenschaftlichen Mythologie*, 1825, p. 87.

[2] *Phædros*, 242 E.

[3] *Symp.* 178 C. Οὕτως πολλαχόθεν ὁμολογεῖται ὁ Ἔρως ἐν τοῖς πρεσβυτάτ ις εἶναι· πρεσβύτατος δὲ ὢν μεγιστων ἀγαθῶν ἡμῖν αἴτιός ἐστιν· 195 A ἔστι δὲ κάλλιστος ὢν τοιόσδε· πβῶτον μὲν νεώτατος θεῶν ὦ Φαῖδρε.

[4] Lobeck, *Aglaoph.* p. 523, gives

Ζεὺς κεφαλὴ, Ζεὺς μέσσα, Διὸς δ' ἐκ πάντα τέτυκται.

See Preller's *Greek Mythology*, 1854, p 99.

their hearts the true emotion of prayer, a yearning after divine help and protection, still spoke of Zeus, forgetting that at one time Zeus himself was vanquished by Titan, and had to be delivered by Hermes.[1] Æschylos[2] says: "Zeus, whoever he is, if this be the name by which he loves to be called,—by this name I address him. For, pondering on all things except Zeus, I cannot tell whether I may truly cast off the idle burden from my thought."

No, the preservation of these mythic names, the long life of these fables, and their satisfying the religious, poetical, and moral wants of succeeding generations, though strange and startling, is not the real difficulty. The past has its charms, and tradition has a powerful friend in language. We still speak of the sun rising and setting, of rainbows, of thunderbolts, because language has sanctioned these expressions. We use them, though we do not believe in them. The difficulty is how at first the human mind was led to such imaginings,—how the names and tales arose,—and unless this question can be answered, our belief in a regular and consistent progress of the human intellect, through all ages and in all countries, must be given up as a false theory.

Nor can it be said that we know absolutely nothing of this period during which the as yet undivided

1 *Apollod.* 1, 6, 3, Grote, H. G. p. 4.

2 I give the text, because it has been translated in so many different ways:—

Ζεὺς, ὅστις ποτ' ἐστιν, εἰ τόδ' αὐ-
τῷ φίλον κεκλημένῳ,
τοῦτό νιν προσεννέπω·
οὐκ ἔχω προσεικάσαι,
πάντ' ἐπισταθμώμενος
πλὴν Διὸς, εἰ το μάταν ἀπὸ φρόντιδος ἄχθος
χρὴ βαλεῖν ἐτητύμως.

Aryan nations — for it is chiefly of them that we are now speaking — formed their myths. Even if we saw only the deep shadow which lies on the Greek mind from the very beginning of its political and literary history, we should be able to infer from it something of the real character of that age which must have preceded the earliest dawn of the national literature of Greece. Otfried Müller,[1] though he was unacquainted with the new light which comparative philology has shed on this primitive Aryan period, says: "The mythic form of expression which changes all beings into persons, all relations into actions, is something so peculiar that we must admit for its growth a distinct period in the civilization of a people." But comparative philology has since brought this whole period within the pale of documentary history. It has placed in our hands a telescope of such power that, where formerly we could see but nebulous clouds, we now discover distinct forms and outlines; nay, it has given us what we may call contemporary evidence, exhibiting to us the state of thought, language, religion, and civilization at a period when Sanskrit was not yet Sanskrit, Greek not yet Greek, but when both, together with Latin, German, and other Aryan dialects, existed as yet as one undivided language, in the same manner as French, Italian, and Spanish may be said to have at one time existed as one undivided language, in the form of Latin.

This will require a short explanation. If we knew nothing of the existence of Latin; if all historical documents previous to the fifteenth century had been lost; if tradition, even, were silent as to the former

[1] *Prol. Myth.* p. 78.

existence of a Roman empire, a mere comparison of the six Romance dialects would enable us to say, that at some time there must have been a language from which all these modern dialects derived their origin in common; for without this supposition it would be impossible to account for the facts exhibited by these dialects. Let us look at the auxiliary verb. We find: —

	Italian.	Wallachian.	Rhætian.	Spanish.	Portuguese.	French.
I am:	sono,	sum (sunt),	sunt,	soy,	sou,	suis.
Thou art:	sei,	es,	eis,	eres,	es,	es.
He is:	è,	é (este),	ei,	es,	he,	est.
We are:	siamo,	sùntemu,	essen,	somos,	somos,	sommes.
You are:	siete,	sùnteti,	esses,	sois,	sois,	êtes (estes).
They are:	sono,	sùnt,	eân (sun),	son,	sao,	sont.

It is clear, even from a short consideration of these forms, first, that all are but varieties of one common type; secondly, that it is impossible to consider any one of these six paradigms as the original from which the others had been borrowed. To this we may add, thirdly, that in none of the languages to which these verbal forms belong, do we find the elements of which they could have been composed. If we find such forms as *j'ai aimé*, we can explain them by a mere reference to the grammatical materials which French has still at its command, and the same may be said even of compounds like *j'aimerai*, i. e. *je-aimer-ai*, I have to love, I shall love. But a change from *je suis* to *tu es* is inexplicable by the light of French grammar. These forms could not have grown, so to speak, on French soil, but must have been handed down as relics from a former period, — must have existed in some language antecedent to any of the Romance dialects. Now, fortunately, in this case, we are not left to a mere inference, but as we possess the Latin verb, we can prove how by phonetic corruption, and by mistaken analogies, every one of the six paradigms is but a national metamorphosis of the Latin original.

Let us now look at another set of paradigms: —

	Sanskrit.	Lithuanian.	Zend.	Doric.	Old Slav.	Latin.	Gothic.	Armen.
I am:	ásmi,	esmi,	ahmi,	ἐμμί,	yesmĕ,	sum,	im	em.
Thou art:	ási,	essi,	ahi,	ἐσσί,	yesi,	es,	is,	es.
He is;	ásti,	esti,	asti,	ἐστί,	yestŏ,	est,	ist,	ē.
We (two) are:	'svás,	esva,	..	..	yesva,	..	siju,	..
You (two) are:	'sthás,	esta,	stho?	ἐστόν,	yesta,	..	sijuts,	..
They (two) are:	'stás,	(esti),	sto,	ἐστόν,	yesta,	..	..	..
We are:	'smás,	esmi,	hmahi,	ἐσμές,	yesmo,	sumus,	sijum,	emq.
You are:	'sthá,	este,	sta,	ἐστέ,	yeste,	estis,	sijuth,	êq.
They are:	sánti,	(esti),	hĕnti,	ἐντί,	so*m*tĕ,	sunt,	sind,	en.

From a careful consideration of these forms, we ought to draw exactly the same conclusions; first, that all are but varieties of one common type; secondly, that it is impossible to consider any of them as the original from which the others have been borrowed; and thirdly, that, here again, none of the languages in which these verbal forms occur, possess the grammatical materials out of which such forms could have been framed. That Sanskrit cannot be taken as the original from which all the rest were derived (an opinion held by many scholars), is clear, if we see that Greek has, in several instances, preserved a more primitive, or, as it is called, more organic form than Sanskrit. 'Εσ-μές cannot be derived from the Sanskrit "smas," because "smas" has lost the radical *a*, which Greek has preserved, the root being *as*, to be, the termination "mas," we. Nor can Greek be fixed upon as the more primitive language from which others were derived, for not even Latin could be called the daughter of Greek, the language of Rome having preserved some forms more primitive than Greek; for instance, *sunt* instead of ἐντί or ἐνσί or εἰσί. Here Greek has lost the radical *as* altogether, ἐντί standing instead of ἐσεντί, while Latin has at least, like Sanskrit, preserved the radical *s* in *sunt=santi.*

Hence, all these dialects point to some more ancient language which was to them what Latin was to the Romance dialects, — only that at that early period there was no literature to preserve to us any remnants of that mother-tongue that died in giving birth to the modern Aryan dialects, such as Sanskrit, Zend, Greek, Latin, Gothic, Slavonic, and Celtic. Yet, if there is any truth in inductive reasoning, that language was once a living language, spoken in Asia by a small tribe, nay, originally by a small family living under one and the same roof, as the language of Camoens, Cervantes, Voltaire, and Dante, was once spoken by a few peasants who had built their huts on the Seven Hills near the Tibris. If we compare the two tables of paradigms, the coincidences between the language of the Veda and the dialect spoken at the present day by the Lithuanian recruit at Berlin are greater by far than between French and Italian ; and, after Bopp's "Comparative Grammar" has been completed, it will be seen clearly that all the essential forms of grammar had been fully framed and established before the first separation of the Aryan family took place.

But we may learn much more of the intellectual state of the primitive and undivided family of the Aryan nations, if we use the materials which Comparative Philology has placed at our disposal ; and, here again, the Romance languages will teach us the spell by which we may hope to open the archives of the most ancient history of the Aryan race. If we find in all the Romance dialects a word like the French "pont," the Italian "ponte," the Spanish "puente," the Wallachian "pod," identically the same in all, after making allowance for those peculiarities which give to each dialect its national character, we have a right to say that "pons," the name for "bridge," was known *before* these languages separated, and that, therefore, the art of building bridges must have been known at the same time. We could assert, even if we knew nothing of Latin and of Rome, that previous, at least, to the tenth century, books, bread, wine, houses, villages, towns, towers, and gates, etc., were known to those people, whoever they were, from whose language the modern dialects of Southern Europe are derived. It is true, we should not be able to draw a very perfect picture of the intellectual state of the Roman people if we were obliged to construct their history from such scanty materials; yet we should be able to prove that there really was such a people, and, in the absence of any other information, even a few casual glimpses of their work in life would be welcome. But, though we might safely use this method positively, only taking care to avoid foreign terms, we could not invert it or use it negatively. Because each of the Romance dialects has a different name for certain objects, it does not follow that the objects themselves were unknown to the ancestors of the Romance nations. Paper was known at Rome, yet it is called "carta" in Italian, "papier" in French.

Now, as we know nothing of the Aryan race, before it was broken up into different nationalities, such as Indian, German, Greek, Roman, Slavonic, Teutonic, and Celtic, this method of making language itself tell the history of ancient times will become of great value, because it will give a character of historical reality to a period in the history of the human race, the very existence of which had been doubted, — to a period that had been called " a past that was never present." We must not expect a complete history of civilization, exhibiting in full detail a picture of the times when the language of Homer and of the Veda had not yet been formed. But we shall feel by some small but significant traits the real presence of that early period in the history of the human mind — a period which, for reasons that will be clearer hereafter, we identify with the Mythopœic.

	Sanskrit.	Zend.	Greek.	Latin.	Gothic.	Slavonic.	Irish.
Father:	pitár,	patar,	πατήρ,	pater,	fadar,	. .	athair.
Mother:	mâtár,	mâtar,	μήτηρ,	mater,	. .	mati (gen. matere),	mathair.
Brother:	bhrấtar,	brâtar,	(φρατήρ),	frater,	brôthar,	brat',	brathair.
Sister:	svásar,	qanhar,	. .	soror,	svistar,	sestra,	siur.
Daughter:	duhitár,	dughdhar,	θυγάτηρ,	. .	dauhtar,	(Lith.) dukte,	dear.

The mere fact, that the names for *father*, *mother*, *brother*, *sister*, and *daughter* are the same in most of the Aryan languages, might at first sight seem of immaterial significance; yet, even these words are full of import. That the name of father was coined at that early period, shows that the father acknowledged the offspring of his wife as his own, for thus only had he a right to claim the title of father. " Father " is derived from a root Pa, which means not to beget, but to protect, to support, to nourish. The father as progenitor, was called in Sanskrit, "*g*anitár," but as protector and supporter of his offspring he was called "pitár." Hence, in the Veda these two names are used together, in order to express the full idea of father. Thus the poet says (I. 164, 33): —

"Dyaús me pitấ *g*anitấ."
"Jo(vi)s mei pater genitor."
Ζεὺς ἐμοῦ πατὴρ γενετήρ.

In a similar manner, "mâtár," mother, is joined with "*g*anitrî," *genitrix* (Rv. III. 48, 2), which shows that the word "mâtár" must soon have lost its etymological meaning, and have become an expression of respect and endearment. Among the earliest Aryans, "mâtar" had the meaning of maker, from MA, to fashion; and, in this sense, and with the same accent as the Greek μήτηρ, mâ'tar, not yet determined by a feminine affix, it is used in the Veda as a masculine. Thus we read, for instance, Rv. VIII. 41, 4: —

> "Sá*h* mâtâ pûrvyám padám."
> "He, Varu*n*a (Uranos), is the maker of the old place."

Now, it should be observed, that "mâtar," as well as "pitar," is but one out of many names by which the idea of father and mother might have been expressed. Even if we confined ourselves to the root PA, and took the granting of support to his offspring as the most characteristic attribute of father, many words might have been, and actually were formed, all equally fit to become, so to say, the proper names of father. In Sanskrit, protector can be expressed not only by PA, followed by the derivative suffix "tar," but by "pâ-la," "pâ-laka," "pâ-yú," all meaning protector. The fact, that out of many possible forms, *one* only has been admitted into all the Aryan dictionaries, shows that there must have been something like a traditional usage in language long before the separation of the Aryan family took place. Besides, there were other roots from which the name of father might have been formed, such as GAN, from which we have "*g*anitár," *genitor*, γενετήρ; or TAK, from which the Greek τοκεύς; as PAR, from which the Latin *parens;* not to mention many other names equally applicable to express some prominent attribute of a father in his relation to his children. If each Aryan dialect had formed its own name for father, from one of the many roots which all the Aryan dialects share in common, we should be able to say that there was a radical community between all these languages; but we should never succeed in proving, what is most essential, their historical community, or their divergence from one language which had already acquired a decided idiomatical consistency.

It happens, however, even with these, the most essential terms of an incipient civilization, that one or the other of the Aryan dialects has lost the ancient expression, and replaced it by a new one. The common Aryan names for brother and sister, for instance, do not occur in Greek, where brother and sister are called ἀδελφός and ἀδελφή. To conclude from this that at the time when the Greeks started from their Aryan home, the names of brother and sister had not yet been framed, would be a mistake. We have no reason to suppose that the Greeks were the first to leave, and, if we find that nations like the Teutonic or Celtic, who could have had no contact with the natives of India after the first separation had taken place, share the name of brother in common with Sanskrit, it is as certain that this name existed in the primitive Aryan language, as the occurrence of the same word in Wallachian and Portuguese would prove its Latin origin, though no trace of it existed in any other of the other Romance dialects. No doubt, the growth of language is governed by immutable laws, but the influence of accident is more considerable here than in any other branch of natural science; and though in this case it is possible to find a principle which determines the accidental loss[1] of the ancient names for brother and sister in Greek, yet this is not the case always, and we shall frequently find that one or the other Aryan dialect does not exhibit a term which yet, on the strength of our general argument, we shall feel justified in ascribing to the most ancient period of Aryan speech.

The mutual relation between brother and sister had been hallowed at that early period, and it had been sanctioned by names which had become traditional before the Aryan family broke up into different colonies. The original meaning of "bhrâtar" seems to me to have been he who carries or assists; of "savasar," she who pleases or consoles, — "svasti" meaning in Sanskrit joy or happiness.

In "duhitar," again, we find a name which must have become traditional long before the separation took place. It is a name identically the same in all the dialects, except Latin, and yet Sanskrit alone could have preserved a consciousness of its appellative power. "Duhitar," as Professor Lassen was the first to show, is derived from Duh, a root which in Sanskrit means to milk. It is perhaps connected with the Latin *dūco*, and the transition of meaning would be the same as between "trahere," to draw, and "traire," to milk. Now, the name of milkmaid, given to the daughter of the house, opens before our eyes a little idyl of the poetical and pastoral life of the early Aryans. One of the few things by which the daughter, before she was married, might make herself useful in a nomadic household, was the milking of the cattle, and it discloses a kind of delicacy and humor, even in the rudest state of society, if we imagine a father calling his daughter

[1] See *Edinburgh Review*, Oct. 1851, p. 320.

his little milkmaid, rather than "sutâ," his begotten, or "filia," the suckling. This meaning, however, must have been forgotten long before the Aryans separated. "Duhitar" was then no longer a nickname, but it had become a technical term, or, so to say, the proper name of daughter. That many words were formed in the same spirit, and that they were applicable only during a nomadic state of life, we shall have frequent opportunity of seeing, as we go on. But as the transition of words of such special meaning into general terms, deprived of all etymological vitality, may seem strange, we may as well give at once a few analogous cases where, behind expressions of the most general currency, we can discover, by means of etymology, this peculiar background of the ancient nomad life of the Aryan nations. The very word "peculiar" may serve as an illustration, taken from more modern times. Peculiar, now means singular, extraordinary, but originally it meant what was private, *i. e.* not common property; being derived from *peculium.* Now, the Latin *peculium* stands for *pecudium* (like *consilium* for *considium*) ; and being derived from *pecus*, *pecudis*, it expressed originally what we should call cattle and chattel. Cattle constituting the chief personal property of agricultural people, we may well understand how peculiar, meaning originally what refers to one's own property, came to mean not-common, and at last, in our modern conversation, passed into the meaning of strange. I need hardly mention the well-known etymology of *pecunia*, which being derived from the same word, *pecu*, and therefore signifying "flocks," took gradually the meaning of "money," in the same manner as the Anglo-Saxon "feoh," the German "Vieh," cattle (and originally according to Grimm's law, the same word as *pecu*), received in the course of time the sense of a pecuniary remuneration, a fee. What takes place in modern languages, and, as it were, under our own eyes, must not surprise us in more distant ages. Now, the most useful cattle have always been the ox and the cow, and they seem to have constituted the chief riches and the most important means of subsistence among the Aryan nations. Ox and cow are called in Sanskrit "go," plur. "gâvas," which is the same word as the Old High-German "chuo," plur. "chuowi," and with a change from the guttural to the labial media, the classical *βοῦς*, *βόες*, and *bôs*, *bôves*. Some of the Slavonic languages, also, have preserved a few traces of this ancient name: for instance, the Lettish "gôws," cow; the Slavonic "govyado," a herd; Servian "govedar," a cowherd. From *βοῦς*, we have in Greek *βουκόλος*, which meant originally a cowherd, but in the verb *βουκολέω*, the meaning of tending cows has been absorbed by the more general one of tending cattle, nay, it is used in a metaphorical sense, such as *ἐλπίσι βουκολοῦμαι*, I feed myself on vain hopes. It is used with regard to horses, and thus we find for horse-herd, *ἱπποβούκολος*, originally a cowherd of horses, — an expression which we can only compare to Sanskrit "goyuga," meaning a yoke of oxen, but afterwards any pair, so that a pair of oxen would be called "go-go-yuga." Thus, in Sanskrit, "go-pa" means originally a cowherd, but it soon loses this specific meaning, and is used for the head of a cow-pen, a herdsman, and at last, like the Greek *ποιμὴν λαῶν*, for a king. From "gopa" a new verb is formed, "gopayati," and in it all traces of its original meaning are obliterated; it means simply to protect. As "gopa" meant a cow-herd, "go-tra," in Sanskrit, was originally a hurdle, and meant the inclosure by which a herd was protected against thieves, and kept from straying. "Gotra," however, has almost entirely lost its etymological power in the later Sanskrit, where the feminine only, "gotrâ," preserves the meaning of a herd of kine. In ancient times, when most wars were carried on, not to maintain the balance of power of Asia or Europe, but to take possession of good pasture, or to appropriate large herds of cattle,[1] the hurdles grew naturally into the walls of fortresses, the hedges became strongholds; Anglo-Saxon "tûn," a close (German "Zaun"), became a town; and those who lived behind the same walls were called a "gotra," a family, a tribe, a race. In the Veda, "gotra" is still used in the sense of folds or hurdles (III. 39, 4):—

"Náki*h* êshâm ninditấ mártyeshu
Yé asmấkam pitára*h* góshu yodhấ*h*
Indra*h* eshâm dri*m*hitấ mấhinâvân
Út gotrấ*n*i sas*r*i*g*e da*m*sánâvân."

"There is not among men one scoffing at them who were our fathers, who fought among the cows. Indra, the mighty, is their defender; he, the powerful, spread out their hurdles,[2] (*i. e.* their possessions)."

"Fighting among or for the cows," "goshu-yúdh," is used in the Veda as a name for warrior, in general (I. 112, 22); and one of the most frequent words for battle is "gáv-ish*t*i," literally "striving for cows." In the later Sanskrit, however, "gavesha*n*a" means, simply, research (physical or philosophical), "gavesh,"

[1] Ὑπὲρ νομῆς ἢ λείας μαχόμεθα. *Toxar.* 36. Grimm, *History of the German Language*, p. 17.

[2] Hurdle seems to be connected with the Vaidik "*kh*ardis," house, *i. e.* inclosure, and from the same root we have Gothic "hairda," Anglo-Saxon "heord," "hiörò," a herd. The original root would have been "*kh*ard." which stands for "skard," and the initial *s* is dropt. Another explanation is given by Aufrecht in Kuhn's *Zeitschrift*, vol. i. p. 362.

to inquire. Again, "gosh*th*a" means cow-pen or stable (βούσταθμον); but, with the progress of time and civilization, "gosh*th*î" became the name of an assembly, nay, it was used to express discussion and gossip, as gossip in English too meant originally a godfather or godmother, and then took the abstract sense of idle conversation or tattle.

All these words, composed with "go," cattle, to which many more might have been added if we were not afraid of trying the patience of our less skeptical readers, proved that the people who formed them must have led a half nomadic and pastoral life, and we may well understand how the same people came to use "duhitar" in the sense of daughter. Language has been called a map of the science and manners of the people who speak it, and we should probably find, if we examined the language of a maritime people, that instead of cattle and pasture, ships and water would form part of many words which afterwards were applied in a more general sense.

We proceed to examine other terms which indicate the state of society previous to the separation of the Aryan race, and which we hope will give to our distant picture that expression of truth and reality which can be appreciated even by those who have never seen the original.

We pass over the words for son, partly because their etymology is of no interest, their meaning being simply that of *natus*, born,[1] partly because the position of the

[1] For instance, Sansk. "sûnú," Goth. "sunus," Lith. "sunus," all from "su," to beget, whence Greek υἱός, but by a different suffix. Sansk. "putra," son, is of doubtful origin. It was supposed to be shared by the Celtic branch (Bret. "paotr," boy; "paotrez," girl), but it has been shown that the Breton "paotr" comes from "paltr," as "aotrou" is the Corn. "altrou."

son, or the successor and inheritor of his father's wealth and power, would claim a name at a much earlier time than daughter, sister, or brother. All these relations in fact, expressed by father and mother, son and daughter, brother and sister, are fixed, we should say, by the laws of nature, and their acknowledgment in language would not prove any considerable advance in civilization, however appropriately the names themselves might have been chosen. But there are other relations, of later origin, and of a more conventional character, sanctioned, it is true, by the laws of society, but not proclaimed by the voice of nature, — relations which are aptly expressed in English by the addition of *in-law*, as father-in-law, mother, son, daughter, brother, and sister-in-law. If the names for these relations could be vindicated for the earliest period of Aryan civilization, we should have gained something considerable, for though there is hardly a dialect in Africa or Australia in which we do not find words for father, mother, son, daughter, brother, and sister, and hardly a tribe in which these natural degrees of relationship are not hallowed, there are languages in which the degrees of affinity have never received expression, and tribes who ignore their very meaning.[1]

	Sanskrit.	Greek.	Latin.	Gothic.	Slavonic.	Celtic.
Father-in-law:	svásura	ἑκυρός	socer	svaihra	svekr	W. chwegrw
Mother-in law:	svasrú	ἑκυρά	socrus	svaihrô	svekrvj	W. chwegyr
Son-in-law:	gámâtar	γαμβρός	gener	..	..	Bret. gêver
Daughter-in-law:	snushâ	νυός	nurus	O. H.G. snûr	snocha	..
Brother-in-law:	dêvár	δαήρ (ἀνδράδελφος)	levir	A.S. tâcor	Lith. deweri-s	..
Sister-in-law:	(nânandar)	γάλως (ἀνδραδέλφη)	glos	..	O. Bohem. selva	..
	yâtaras (wives of brothers)	εἰνάτερες	janitrices	..	Poln. jatrew	..
	syâlá (wife's brother)	ἀέλιοι and	..	..	..	..
	syâlí (wife's sister)	εἰλιόνες (husbands of sisters).	..	..	..	..

[1] See Sir J. Lubbock, *Transact. of Ethnol. Society*, vi. 337.

The above table shows that, before the separation of the Aryan race, every one of the degrees of affinity had received expression and sanction in language, for, although some spaces had to be left empty, the coincidences, such as they are, are sufficient to warrant one general conclusion. If we find in Sanskrit, the word "putra," son, and in Celtic, again, "paotr," son, root and suffix being the same, we must remember that, although none of the other Aryan dialects has preserved this word in exactly the same form, yet the identity of the Celtic and Sanskrit term can only be explained on the supposition that "putra" was a common Aryan term, well known before any branch of this family was severed from the common stem.

In modern languages we might, if dealing with similar cases, feel inclined to admit a later communication, but fortunately, in ancient languages, no such intercourse was possible, after the southern branch of the Aryan family had once crossed the Himâlaya, and the northern branch set foot on the shores of Europe. Different questions are raised where, as is the case with *g*âmâtar and γαμβρός, originally bridegroom or husband,[1] then son-in-law, we are only able to prove that the same root was taken, and therefore the same radical idea expressed by Greek and Sanskrit, while the derivation is peculiar in each language. Here, no doubt, we must be more careful in our conclusions, but generally we shall find that these formal differences are only such as occur in dialects of the same language, when out of many possible forms, used at first promiscuously, one was chosen by one poet, one by another, and then became popular and traditional. This at least

[1] Γαμβρὸς καλεῖται ὁ γήμας ὑπὸ τῶν οἰκείων τῆς γαμηθείσης.

is more likely than to suppose that to express a relation which might be expressed in such various ways, the Greek should have chosen the same root γαμ to form γαμρός and γαμβρός, independently of the Hindu, who took that root for the same purpose, only giving it a causal form (as in "bhrâtar" instead of "bhartar)," and appending to it the usual suffix, "tar;" thus forming "*g*â'mâtar," instead of "*g*amara" or "yamara." The Latin word *gener* is more difficult still, and if it is the same word as the Greek γαμβρός for γαμρός, the transition of *m* into *n* can only be explained by a process of assimilation and by a desire to give to the ancient word *gemer* a more intelligible form. When, as it happens not unfrequently, one of the Aryan languages has lost a common term, we are sometimes enbled to prove its former existence by means of derivatives. In Greek, for instance, at least in the classical language, there is no trace of *nepos*, grandson, which we have in Sanskrit "nápât," German "nefo"; nor of *neptis*, Sanskrit "náptî," German "nift." Yet there is in Greek ἀ-νεψιός, a first cousin, *i. e.* one with whom we are grandsons together, as the uncle is called the little-grandfather, *avunculus* from *avus*. This word ἀ-νεψιός is formed like Latin *consobrinus*, i. e. *consororinus*, one with whom we are sister-children, our modern cousin, Italian *cugino*, in which there remains very little of the original word *soror*, from which, however, it is derived. Ἀνεψιός therefore proves that in Greek, also, some word like νεπους must have existed in the sense of child or grandchild, and it is by a similar process that we can prove the former presence in Greek, of a term corresponding to Sanskrit "syâla," a wife's brother. In Sanskrit a husband calls his wife's brother "syâla," his wife's sister "syâlî." Therefore, in Greek, Peleus would call Amphitrite, and Poseidon Thetis, their "syâlîs": having married sisters, they would have "syâlîs" in common, — they would be what the Greeks call ἀέλιοι, for "sy" between two vowels is generally dropt in Greek; and the only anomaly consists in the short ε̄ representing the long â in Sanskrit.

There are still a few words which throw a dim light on the early organization of the Aryan family life. The position of the widow was acknowledged in language and in law, and we find no trace that, at that early period, she who had lost her husband was doomed to die with him. If this custom had existed, the want of having a name for widow would hardly have been felt, or, if it had been, the word would most likely have had some reference to this awful rite. Now, husband, or man, in Sanskrit is "dhava," a word which does not seem to exist in the other Aryan languages, for *dea*, which Pictet brings forward as Celtic, in the sense of a man or person, is a word that has never been authenticated. From "dhava," Sanskrit forms the name of the widow by the addition of the preposition "vi," which means without; therefore "vi-dhavâ," husbandless, widow. This compound has been preserved in languages which have lost the simple word "dhava," thus showing the great antiquity of this traditional term. We have it not only in Celtic "feadbh," but in Gothic "viduvo," Slavonic "vdova," Old Prussian "widdewû," and Latin *vidua*. If the custom of widow-burning had existed at that early period, there would have been no "vidhavâs," no husbandless women, because they would all have followed their husband into death. Therefore the very name indicates, what we are further enabled to prove by historical evidence, the late origin of widow-burning in India. It is true, that when the English Government prohibited this melancholy custom, as the Emperor Jehángir had done before, and when the whole of India was said to be on the verge of a religious revolution, the Brahmans were able to appeal to the Veda as the authority for this sacred rite, and as they had the promise that their religious practices should not be interfered with, they claimed respect for the Suttee. Raghunandana and other doctors had actually quoted chapter and verse from the Rig-veda, and Colebrooke,[1]

[1] "On the Duties of a Faithful Widow," *Asiatic Researches*, vol. iv. pp. 209, 219. Calcutta, 1795. The principal authorities of this Essay are to be seen in Colebrooke's *Digest*, book iv. cap. 3, sect. 1, which is a literal translation of a section of *G*agannâtha's "Vivâda-bhangâr*n*ava," to be found in MS. Wilson, 224, vol. iii. p. 62. See some interesting remarks on this subject, and the correction of a mistake in my notes, in the third volume of the *Journal of the Royal Asiatic Society*, Part. I., Art. VII., the source of Colebrooke's Essay, *On the Duties of a Faithful Hindu Widow*, by Fitzedward Hall, Esq., M. A., D. C. L., Oxon. The reasons which I gave at a meeting of the Royal Asiatic Society for my opinion that Colebrooke availed himself of the "Vivâda-bhangâr*n*ava," while writing his Essay on *The Duties of a Faithful Hindu Widow*, were as follows: "On page 117, Colebrooke quotes:—

1. A passage from Vish*n*u;
2. A passage from Pra*k*etas;
3. A passage from the Sm*r*iti.

The same passages, in exactly the same order, are quoted as Nos. 133, 134, 135 of the *Digest*.

This argument has been, if not invalidated, at least modified, by the fact that the same passages occur likewise in the same order in Raghunandana's "*S*uddhitattva," a work which was consulted by *G*agannâtha in the compilation of his *Corpus Juris*.

My second reason was: "On page 119, Colebrooke quotes: —

1. A saying ascribed to Nârada (*i. e.* taken from the "B*r*ihan Nâradíya Purâ*n*a");
2. A passage from B*r*ihaspati, with which, at the end, a line of Raghunandana's commentary is mixed up.
3. A passage supported by the authority of Gotama (or Gautama). The same passages, in exactly the same order, form Nos. 127, 128, 129 of the "Vi-

the most accurate and learned Sanskrit scholar we have ever had, has translated this passage in accordance with their views: —

"Om! let these women, not to be widowed, good wives adorned with collyrium, holding clarified butter, consign themselves to the fire! Immortal, not childless, not husbandless, well adorned with gems, let them pass into the fire, whose original element is water." (From the Rig-veda.)

Now this is perhaps the most flagrant instance of what can be done by an unscrupulous priesthood. Here have thousands and thousands of lives been sacrificed, and a fanatical rebellion been threatened on the authority of a passage which was mangled, mistranslated, and misapplied. If anybody had been able at the time to verify this verse of the Rig-veda, the Brahmans might have been beaten with their own weapons; nay, their spiritual prestige might have been considerably shaken. The Rig-veda, which now hardly one Brahman out of a hundred is able to read, so far from enforcing the burning of widows, shows clearly that this custom was not sanctioned during the earliest period of Indian history. According to the hymns of the Rig-veda and the Vaidik ceremonial contained in the G*r*ihya-sûtras, the wife accompanies the corpse of her

vâda-bhangâr*n*ava." The line from Raghunandana follows in the "Vivâda-bhangâr*n*ava," as in Colebrooke's Essay, immediately after the extract from B*r*ihaspati, and the mistake of mixing the words of Raghunandana with those of B*r*ihaspati could only have arisen because, instead of mentioning Raghunandana's name, the MS. of the "Vivâda-bhangâr*n*ava" reads: "iti Smârtâ*h*." Neither the "Suddhitattva," nor any other work that I have met with, gives these three passages with the extract from Raghunandana in the same order as the "Vivâda-bhangâr*n*ava" and Colebrooke's Essay.

husband to the funeral pile, but she is there addressed with a verse taken from the Rig-veda, and ordered to leave her husband, and to return to the world of the living.[1] "Rise, woman," it is said, "come to the world of life; thou sleepest nigh unto him whose life is gone. Come to us. Thou hast thus fulfilled thy duties of a wife to the husband who once took thy hand, and made thee a mother."

This verse is preceded by the very verse which the later Brahmans have falsified and quoted in support of their cruel tenet. The reading of the verse is beyond all doubt, for there is no various reading, in our sense of the word, in the whole of the Rig-veda. Besides, we have the commentaries and the ceremonials, and nowhere is there any difference as to the text or its meaning. It is addressed to the other women who are present at the funeral, and who have to pour oil and butter on the pile: —

"May these women who are not widows, but have good husbands, draw near with oil and butter. Those who are mothers may go up first to the altar, without tears, without sorrow, but decked with fine jewels."

Now the word, "the mothers may go first to the altar," are in Sanskrit, —

"Â rohantu *g*anayo yonim agre;"

and this the Brahmans have changed into, —

"Â rohantu *g*anayo yonim agne*h*;"

[1] See Grimm's Essay on *The Burning of the Dead;* Roth's article on *The Burial in India*; Professor Wilson's article on *The supposed Vaidik authority for the Burning of Hindu Widows;* and my own translation of the complete documentary evidence published by Professor Wilson at the end of his article, and by myself in the *Journal of the German Oriental Society*, vol. ix. fasc. 4. Professor Wilson was the first to point out the falsification of the text, and the change of "yonim agre" into "yonim agne*h*."

— a small change, but sufficient to consign many lives to the womb (yonim) of fire (agne*h*).[1]

The most important passage in Vedic literature to prove the decided disapproval of widow-burning on the part of the ancient Brahmans, at least as far as their own caste was concerned, occurs in the B*r*ihad-devatâ. There we read: —

> "Udîrshva nârîty anayâ m*r*ita*m* patny anurohati,
> Bhrâtâ kanîyân pretasya nigadya pratishedhati
> Kuryâd etat karma hotâ. devaro na bhaved yadi,
> Pretânugamana*m* na syâd iti brâhma*n*a*s*âsanât.
> Var*n*ânâm itaresh*â*m *k*a strîdharmo 'ya*m* bhaven na vâ."

"With the verse 'Rise, woman,' the wife ascends to follow her dead husband; the younger brother of the departed, repeating the verse, prevents her. The Hot*r*i priest performs that act, if there is no brother-in-law, but to follow the dead husband is forbidden, so says the law of the Brâhmans. With regard to the other castes this law for women may be or may not be."[2]

[1] In a similar manner the custom of widow-burning has been introduced by the Brahmans in an interpolated passage of the "Toy-Cart," an Indian drama of king *S*ûdraka, which was translated by Professor Wilson, and has lately been performed at Paris. *Le Chariot d'Enfant*, Drame en vers en cinq actes et sept tableaux, traduction du Drame Indien du Roi Soudraka, par MM. Méry et Gerard de Nerval. Paris, 1850.

[2] Part of this passage is wanting in MSS. B. b, but it is found in A. C. See also M. M., "Die Todtenbestattung bei den Brahmanen," *Zeitschrift der Deutschen Morgenländischen Gesellschaft*, vol. ix. p. vi. where the ritual is somewhat different.

I add a few extracts from Mr. H. J. Bushby's work on Widow-Burning, p. 21, "Long ago, oriental scholars, both native and European, had shown that the rite of widow-burning was not only unsanctioned, but imperatively forbidden, by the earliest and most authoritative Hindoo scriptures. Nay, Colonel Tod, in his book on Rajpootána (*Annals of Rajasthan*, 1829, vol. i. p. 635), had actually indicated this anomaly in Hindoo doctrine as the best point of attack for abolitionists to select." P. 22, "Scholars, it is true, had proved Suttee to be an innovation and a heresy; but it was an innovation of 2,000 years standing, and a heresy abetted by the priesthood since the

After this digression, we return to the earlier period of history of which language alone can give us any information, and, as we have claimed for it the name of widow, or the husbandless, we need not wonder that the name for husband, also, is to this day in most of the Aryan languages the same which had been fixed upon by the Aryans before their separation. It is "pati" in Sanskrit, meaning originally strong, like Latin *potis* or *potens*. In Lithuanian the form is exactly the same, "patis," and this, if we apply Grimm's law, becomes "faths," as in Gothic "bruth-faths," bridegroom. In Greek, again, we find πόσις instead of πότις. Now, the feminine of "pati" in Sanskrit is "patnî," and there is no doubt that the old Prussian "pattin," in the accusative "wais-pattin," and the Greek πότνια are mere transcripts of it, all meaning the mistress.

What the husband was in his house, the lord, the strong protector, the king was among his people. Now, a common name for people was "vis" in Sanskrit, from which the title of the third caste, the householders, or "Vaisyas" is derived. It comes from the

days of Alexander. Though unnoticed by Manu, the supplementary writings with which the Hindoos, like the Jews, have overlaid their primitive books, are profuse in its praise." P. 29, "Major Ludlow determined, if possible, to induce two or three trustworthy and influential natives to undertake the cause; to ply them with the critical objection drawn from the older Scriptures." For further particulars as to the efforts made for the suppression of Suttee I may refer to the interesting narrative of Mr. H. J. Bushby, on "Widow-Burning," published originally in the *Quarterly Review*, and afterwards as a separate pamphlet. (London: Longmans, 1855.) It shows how much has been done, and therefore, how much more may be done, by appealing to the most ancient and most sacred Sanskrit authorities in discussions with the natives of India. If the fact that Manu never sanctions the burning of widows could produce such an impression on the Vakeels of Râjputâna as described by Mr. Bushby, how much more powerful would be an appeal to the Veda, the authority of which, whenever a discrepancy occurs, invariably overrides that of Manu!

same root from which we have in Sanskrit "vesa," house, οἶκος, *vicus*, Gothic "veihs," German "wich," and the modern English termination of many names of places. Hence "vispati" in Sanskrit meant king, *i. e.* lord of the people, and that this compound had become a title sanctioned by Aryan etiquette before the separation, is confirmed in a strange manner by the Lithuanian "wiêsz-patis," a lord, "wiêsz-patene," a lady, as compared with Sanskrit "vis-patis" and "vispatnì." There was therefore, at that early period, not only a nicely organized family life, but the family began to be absorbed by the state, and here again conventional titles had been fixed, and were handed down perhaps two thousand years before the title of Cæsar was heard of.

Another name for people being "dâsa" or "dasyu," "dâsa-pati" no doubt was an ancient name for king. There is, however, this great difference between "vis" and "dâsa," that the former means people, the latter subjects, conquered races, nay originally enemies. "Dasyu" in the Veda is enemy, but in the Zend-Avesta, where we have the same word, it means provinces or *gentes;* and Darius calls himself, in his mountain records, "king of Persia and king of the provinces" ("kshâyathìya Pârsaiya, kshâyathìya dahyunâm"). Hence it is hardly doubtful that the Greek δεσ-πότης represents a Sanskrit title "dâsa-pati," lord of nations; but we cannot admit that the title of Hospodar, which has lately become so notorious, should, as Bopp says, be the same as Sanskrit "vis-pati" or "dâsa-pati." The word is "gaspadorus" in Lithuanian; in Old Slav. "gospod," "gospodin," and "gospodar;" Pol. "gospodarz;" Boh. "hospodár." A Slavonic *g*, however, does not correspond to Sanskrit *v* or *d*, nor could the *t* of "pati" become *d*.[1] Benfey, who derives "gospod,' from the Vaidik "*g*âspati," avoids the former, but not the latter difficulty; and it is certainly better to state these difficulties than to endeavor to smuggle in some ancient Aryan terms in defiance of laws which can never be violated with impunity.

A third common Aryan word for king is "râ*g*" in the Veda; *rex, regis*, in Latin; "reiks" in Gothic, a word still used in German, as "reich," *regnum*, "Frank-reich," *regnum Francorum;* in Irish "riogh;" Welsh "ri."

A fourth name for king and queen is simply father and mother, "*G*anaka" in Sanskrit means father, from GAN, to beget; it also occurs, as the name of a well-known king, in the Veda. This is the Old German "chuning," the English "king." Mother in Sanskrit is "*g*ani" or "*g*anî," the Greek γυνή, the Gothic "quinô," the Slavonic "*z*ena," the English "queen." Queen, therefore, means originally mother, or lady; and thus, again, we see how the language of family life grew gradually into the political language of the oldest Aryan state, and how the brotherhood of the family became the φρατρία of the state.[2]

We have seen that the name of house was known before the Aryan family broke up towards the south and the north, and we might bring further evidence to this effect by comparing Sanskrit "dama" with Greek δόμος, Latin *domus*, Slav. "domü," Celtic "daimh," and Gothic "timrjan," to build, from which English "tim-

[1] See Schleicher's excellent remarks in his *Formenlehre der Kirchenslawischen Sprache*, 1852, p. 107.

[2] See *Lectures on the Science of Language*, Second Series, p. 255, and particularly the German translation, where objections to this derivation have been answered.

ber," though we may doubt the identity of the Slavonic "grod" and "gorod," the Lithuanian "grod" with the Gothic "gards," Latin *hort-us*, Greek χόρτος, all meaning an inclosed ground. The most essential part of a house, particularly in ancient times, being a door well fastened and able to resist the attacks of enemies, we are glad to find the ancient name preserved in Sanskrit "dvar," "dvâras," Gothic "daur," Lithuanian "durrys," Celtic "dor," Greek θύρα, Latin *fores*. The builder also, or architect, has the same name in Sanskrit and Greek, "takshan" being the Greek τέκτων. The Greek ἄστυ, again, has been compared with Sanskrit "vâstu," house; the Greek κώμη with Gothic "haims," a village; the English "home." Still more conclusive as to the early existence of cities, is the Sanskrit "puri," town, preserved by the Greeks in their name for town, πόλις; and that high-roads also were not unknown, appears from Sanskrit "path," "pathi," "panthan," and "pâthas," all names for "road," the Greek πάτος, the Gothic "fad," which Bopp believes to be identical with Latin *pons*, *pontis*, and Slavonic "ponti."

It would take a volume were we to examine all the relics of language, though no doubt every new word would strengthen our argument, and add, as it were, a new stone from which this ancient and venerable ruin of the Aryan mind might be reconstructed. The evidence, however, which we have gone through must be sufficient to show that the race of men which could coin these words, — words that have been carried down the stream of time, and washed up on the shores of so many nations, — could not have been a race of savages, of mere nomads and hunters. Nay, it should be observed, that most of the terms connected with chase and warfare differ in each of the Aryan dialects, while words connected with more peaceful occupations belong generally to the common heir-loom of the Aryan language. The proper appreciation of this fact in its general bearing will show how a similar remark made by Niebuhr with regard to Greek and Latin, requires a very different explanation from that which that great scholar, from his more restricted point of view, was able to give it. It will show that all the Aryan nations had led a long life of peace before they separated, and that their language acquired individuality and nationality, as each colony started in search of new homes, — new generations forming new terms connected with the warlike and adventurous life of their onward migrations. Hence it is that not only Greek and Latin, but all Aryan languages have their peaceful words in common; and hence it is that they all differ so strangely in their warlike expressions. Thus the domestic animals are generally known by the same name in England and in India, while the wild beasts have different names, even in Greek and Latin. I can only give a list, which must tell its own story, for it would take too much time to enter into the etymological formation of all these words, though no doubt a proper understanding of their radical meaning would make them more instructive as living witnesses to the world of thought and the primitive household of the Aryan race: —

	Sanskrit and Zend.		Greek.	Italian.	Teutonic.	Lithuanian	Slavonic.	Celtic.
Cattle:	pasu	pasu	πῶυ?	pecu	G. faihu, O.H.G. fihu	Pruss. pecku	..	..
Ox and cow:	go (nom. gaus)	gâo	βοῦς	bos	O.H.G. chuo	Lett. gow	govjado	Ir. bó
Ox:	ukshan	ukhshan	..	vacca?	G. auhsan	..	..	W. ych
Steer:	sthûra	staora	ταῦρος	taurus	stiur	taura-s	tour	Ir. tor
Heifer:	stari	..	στεῖρα	(sterilis)	stairo	..	..	..
Horse:	âsu, asva	aspa	ἵππος	equus	A.S. eoh	aszua, fem.	..	Ir. ech, Gaulish, epo-s
Foal:	..	..	πῶλος	pullus	G. fula	..	..	..
Dog:	svan	spa (σπάκα)	κύων	canis	G. hund	szû	R. sobaka, Bulg. kuce	Ir. cu
Sheep:	avi	..	ὄϊς	ovis	G. avi-str, E. ewe	avi-s	Slav. ovjza	Ir. oi
Calf:	vatsa	..	ἴταλος	vitulus	..	..	..	Ir. fithal
He-goat:	..	..	κάπρος	caper	O.H.G. hafr	..	..	Ir. cabha
She-goat:	agâ	..	αἴξ	..	..	ozi-s	..	Ir. aighe
Sow:	sû (kara)	..	ὗς	sus	O.H.G. sû	..	svinia	Ir. suig
Hog:	..	..	πόρκος	porcus	O.H.G. farah	parsza-s	Pol. prosie	Ir. porc
Pig:	ghrishvi	..	χοῖρος	..	O.N. gris, Scotch, gris	..	..	..
Donkey:	..	..	ὄνος	asinus	asilu	asila-s	osilu	W. asyn, Ir. asail
Mouse:	mûsh	..	μῦς	mus	O.H.G. mûs	..	Pol. mysz	..
Fly:	makshikâ	makhshi	μυῖα	musca	O.H.G. micco	muse	R. mucha	..
Goose:	hamsa	..	χὴν	anser	O.H.G. kans	zasi-s	Boh. hus,	G. garira

Of wild animals some were known to the Aryans before they separated, and they happen to be animals which live both in Asia and Europe, the bear and the wolf: —

	Sanskrit.	Greek.	Italian.	Teutonic.	Slavonic.	Celtic.
Bear:	riksha	ἄρκτος	ursus	..	Lith. loky-s	Ir. art
Wolf:	vrika	λύκος	lupus, (v)irpus	G. vulf	Lith. wilka-s	Ir. brech

To them should be added the serpent: —

	Sanskrit.	Greek.	Italian.	Teutonic.	Slavonic.	Celtic.
Serpent:	ahi, sarpa	ἔχις, (ἔγχελυς), ἕρπετον	anguis, (anguilla), serpens	O.H.G. unc, .., ..	Lith. angi-s, (angury-s), ..	.., .., W. sarff

Without dwelling on the various names of those animals which had partly been tamed and domesticated while others were then, as they are now, the natural enemies of the shepherd and his flocks, we proceed at once to mention a few words which indicate that this early pastoral life was not without some of the most primitive arts, such as ploughing, grinding, weaving, and the working of useful and precious metals.

The oldest term for ploughing is Ar, which we find

in Latin *arare*, Greek, ἀροῦν, to ear, Old Slav. "orati," Gothic "arjan," Lithuanian "arti," and Gaelic "ar." From this verb we have the common name of the plough, ἄροτρον, *aratrum*, Old Saxon "erida," Old Norse "ardhr," Old Slavonic "oralo" and "oradlo," Lithuanian "arkla-s," Welsh "aradyr" and "arad," Cornish "aradar." Ἄρουρα and *arvum* come probably from the same root. But a more general name for field is Sanskrit "pada," Greek πέδον, Umbrian "pe*r*um," Latin *pedum* in *oppidum*, Pol. "pole," Saxon "folda," O. H. G. "feld," "field;" or Sanskrit "a*g*ra," ἀγρός, *ager*, and Gothic "akr-s."[1]

The corn which was grown in Asia could not well have been the same which the Aryan nations afterwards cultivated in more northern regions. Some of the names, however, have been preserved, and may be supposed to have had, if not exactly the same, at least a similar botanical character. Such are Sanskrit "yava," Zend "yava," Lithuanian "javai," which in Greek must be changed to ζέα. Sanskrit "*s*veta" means white, and corresponds to Gothic "hveit," O. H. G. "huiz" and "wiz," the Anglo-Saxon "hvît." But the name of the color became also the name of the white grain, and thus we have Gothic "hvaitei," Lith. "kwêty-s," the English "wheat," with which some scholars have compared the Slav. "shito," and the Greek σῖτος. The name of corn signified originally what is crushed or ground. Thus "*k*ûr*n*a" in Sanskrit means ground, *g*îrna," pounded, and from the same radical element we must no doubt derive the Russian "*z*erno," the Gothic "kaurn," the Latin *granum*. In Lithuanian, "girna" is a millstone, and

[1] *Lectures on the Science of Language*, fifth edition, vol. i. p. 283.

the plural "girnôs" is the name of a hand-mill. The Russian word for millstone is, again, "zernov," and the Gothic name for mill, "qvairnus," the later "quirn." The English name for mill is likewise of considerable antiquity, for it exists not only in the O. H. G. "muli," but in the Lithuanian "maluna-s," the Bohemian "mlyn," the Welsh "melin," the Latin *mola*, and the Greek μύλη.

We might add the names for cooking and baking, and the early distinction between flesh and meat, to show that the same aversion which is expressed in later times, for instance, by the poets of the Veda, against tribes eating raw flesh, was felt already during this primitive period. "Kravya-ad" (κρέας-ἔδω) and "âma-ad" (ὠμός-ἔδω) are names applied to barbarians, and used with the same horror in India as ὠμοφάγοι and κρεωφάγοι in Greece. But we can only now touch on these points, and must leave it to another opportunity to bring out in full relief this old picture of human life.

As the name for clothes is the same among all the Aryan nations, being "vastra" in Sanskrit, "vasti" in Gothic, *vestis* in Latin, ἐσθής in Greek, "fassradh" in Irish, "gwisk" in Welsh, we are justified in ascribing to the Aryan ancestors the art of weaving as well as of sewing. To weave in Sanskrit is "ve," and, in a causative form, "vap." With "ve" coincide the Latin *vieo*, and the Greek radical of Fή-τριον; with "vap," the O. H. G. "wab," the English "weave," the Greek ὑφ-αίνω.

To sew in Sanskrit is "siv," from which "sûtra," a thread. The same root is preserved in Latin *suo*, in Gothic "siuja," in O. H. G. "siwu," the English "to sew," Lithuanian "siuv-u," Greek κασσύω for κατασύω.

Another Sanskrit root, with a very similar meaning, is Nah, which must have existed also as "nabh" and "nadh." From "nah" we have Latin *neo* and *necto*, Greek νέω, German "nâhan" and "nâvan," to sew; from "nadh," the Greek νήθω; from "nabh," the Sanskrit "nâbhi" and "nâbha" or "ûr*n*anâbha," the spider, literally the wool-spinner.

There is a fourth root which seems to have had originally the special meaning of sewing or weaving, but which afterwards took in Sanskrit the more general sense of making. This is "ra*k*," which may correspond to the Greek ῥάπτω, to stitch together or to weave; nay, which might account for another name of the spider, ἀράχνη in Greek, and *aranea* in Latin, and for the classical name of woven wool, λάχνος or λάχνη, and the Latin *lana*.

That the value and usefulness of some of the metals was known before the separation of the Aryan race, can be proved only by a few words; for the names of most of the metals differ in different countries. Yet there can be no doubt that iron was known, and its value appreciated, whether for defense or for attack. Whatever its old Aryan name may have been, it is clear that Sanskrit "ayas," Latin *ahes* in *aheneus*, and even the contracted form, *æs*, *æris*, the Gothic "ais," the Old High-German "er," and the English "iron," are names cast in the same mould, and only slightly corroded even now by the rust of so many centuries. The names of the precious metals, such as gold and silver, have suffered more in passing through the hands of so many generations. But, notwithstanding, we are able to discover even in the Celtic "airgiod" the traces of the Sanskrit "ra*g*ata," the Greek ἄργυρος, the

Latin *argentum;* and even in the Gothic "gulth," gold, a similarity with the Slavonic "zlato" and Russian "zoloto," Greek χρύσος and Sanskrit "hira*n*yam," although their formative elements differ widely. The radical seems to have been "har-at," from whence the Sanskrit "harit," the color of the sun and of the dawn, as *aurum* also descends from the same root with *aurora.* Some of the iron implements used, whether for peaceful or warlike purposes, have kept their original name, and it is extremely curious to find the exact similarity of the Sanskrit "para*s*u" and the Greek πέλεκυς, axe, or of Sanskrit "asi," sword, and Latin *ensis.*

New ideas do not gain ground at once, and there is a tendency in our mind to resist new convictions as long as we can. Hence it is only by a gradual and careful accumulation of facts that we can hope, on this linguistic evidence, to establish the reality of a period in the history of mankind previous to the beginning of the most ancient known dialects of the Aryan world; previous to the origin of Sanskrit as well as Greek; previous to the time when the first Greek arrived on the shores of Asia Minor, and looking at the vast expanse of sky and sea and country to the west and north, called it "Europa." Let us examine one other witness, whose negative evidence will be important. During this early period, the ancestors of the Aryan race must have occupied a more central position in Asia, whence the southern branches extended towards India, the northern to Asia Minor, and Europe. It would follow, therefore, that before their separation, they could not have known the existence of the sea, and hence, if our theory be true, the name for sea must be of later growth, and different in the Aryan languages. And this expectation is fully confirmed. We find, indeed, identical names in Greek and Latin, but not in the northern and southern branches of the Aryan family. And even these Greek and Latin names are evidently metaphorical expressions, — names that existed in the ancient language, and were transferred, at a later time, to this new phenomenon. *Pontus* and πόντος mean sea in the same sense as Homer speaks of ὑγρὰ κέλευθα, for *pontus* comes from the same source from which we have *pons*, *pontis*, and the Sanskrit "pantha," if not "pâthas." The sea was not called a barrier, but a high-road, — more useful for trade and travel than any other road, — and Professor Curtius[1] has well pointed out Greek expressions, such as πόντος ἁλὸς πολιῆς and θάλασσα πόντου, as indicating, even among the Greeks, a consciousness of the original import of πόντος. Nor can words like Sanskrit "sara," Latin *sal*, and Greek ἅλς, ἁλός, be quoted as proving an acquaintance with the sea among the early Aryans. "Sara" in Sanskrit means, first, water, afterwards, salt made of water, but not necessarily of sea-water. We might conclude from Sanskrit "sara," Greek ἅλς, and Latin *sal*, that the preparation of salt by evaporation was known to the ancestors of the Aryan family before they separated. But this is all that could be proved by ἅλς, *sal*, and Sanskrit "sara" or "salila;" the exclusive application of these words to the sea belongs to later times; and though the Greek ἐνάλιος means exclusively marine, the Latin *insula* is by no means restricted to an island surrounded by salt water. The same remark applies to words like *æquor* in Latin or πέλαγος in Greek. Θάλασσα has long

[1] See Kuhn's *Journal of Comparative Philology*, i. 34. Professor Curtius gives the equation: πόντος: πάτος=πένθος: πάθος=βένθος; βάθος.

been proved to be a dialectical form of θάρασσα or τάρασσα, expressing the troubled waves of the sea (ἐταραξε δὲ πόντον Ποσειδῶν), and if the Latin *mare* be the same as Sanskrit "vâri," "vâri" in Sanskrit does not mean "sea," but water in general, and could, therefore, only confirm the fact that all the Aryan nations applied terms of a general meaning when they had each to fix their names for the sea. *Mare* is more likely a name for dead or stagnant water, like Sanskrit "maru," the desert, derived from "m*r*i," to die; and though it is identical with Gothic "marei," Slav. "more," Irish "muir," the application of all these words to the ocean is of later date. But, although the sea had not yet been reached by the Aryan nations before their common language branched off into various dialects, navigation was well known to them. The words "oar" and "rudder" can be traced back to Sanskrit, and the name of the ship is identically the same in Sanskrit ("naus," "nâvas"), in Latin (*navis*), in Greek (ναῦς), and in Teutonic (Old High-German "nacho," Anglo-Saxon "naca").

It is hardly possible to look at the evidence hitherto collected, and which, if space allowed, might have been considerably increased,[1] without feeling that these

[1] A large collection of common Aryan words is found in Grimm's *History of the German Language*. The first attempt to use them for historical purposes was made by Eichhof; but the most useful contributions have since been made by Winning in his *Manual of Comparative Philology*, 1838; by Kuhn, Curtius, and Förstemann; and much new material is to be found in Bopp's *Glossarium* and Pott's *Etymologische Forschungen*. Pictet's great work, *Les Origines Indo-Européennes*, 2 vols. 1859 and 1863, brings together the most complete mass of materials, but requires also the most careful sifting. With regard to Sanskrit words in particular, the greatest caution is required, as M. Pictet has not paid to it the same attention as to Celtic, Latin, Greek, and Slavonic.

words are the fragments of a real language, once spoken by a united race at a time which the historian has till lately hardly ventured to realize. Yet here we have in our own hands, the relics of that distant time; we are using the same words which were used by the fathers of the Aryan race, changed only by phonetic influences; nay, we are as near to them in thought and speech as the French and Italians are to the ancient people of Rome. If any more proof was wanted as to the reality of that period which must have preceded the dispersion of the Aryan race, we might appeal to the Aryan numerals, as irrefragable evidence of that long-continued intellectual life which characterizes that period. Here is a decimal system of numeration, in itself one of the most marvelous achievements of the human mind, based on an abstract conception of quantity, regulated by a spirit of philosophical classification, and yet conceived, matured, and finished before the soil of Europe was trodden by Greek, Roman, Slave, or Teuton. Such a system could only have been formed by a very small community, and more than any part of language it seems to necessitate the admission of what might almost be called a conventional agreement among those who first framed and adopted the Aryan names for one to hundred. Let us imagine, as well as we can, that at the present moment we were suddenly called upon to invent new names for one, two, three, and we may then begin to feel what kind of task it was to form and fix such words. We could easily supply new expressions for material objects, because they always have some attributes which language can render either metaphorically or periphrastically. We could call the sea "the salt-water;" the rain, "the water of heaven;" the rivers, "the daughters of the earth." Numbers, however, are, by their very nature, such abstract and empty conceptions, that it tries our ingenuity to the utmost to find any attributive element in them to which expression might be given, and which might in time become the proper name of a merely quantitative idea. There might be less difficulty for one and two; and hence, these two numerals have received more than one name in the Aryan family. But this again would only create a new difficulty, because, if different people were allowed to use different names for the same numeral, the very object of these names would be defeated. If five could be expressed by a term meaning the open hand, and might also be rendered by the simple plural of the word for fingers, these two synonymous terms would be useless for the purpose of any exchange of thought. Again, if a word meaning fingers or toes might have been used to express five as well as ten, all commerce between individuals using the same word in different senses, would have been rendered impossible. Hence, in order to form and fix a series of words expressing one, two, three, four, etc., it was necessary that the ancestors of the Aryan race should have come to some kind of unconscious agreement to use but one term for each number, and to attach but one meaning to each term. This was not the case with regard to other words, as may be seen by the large proportion of synonymous and polyonymous terms by which every ancient language is characterized. The wear and tear of language in literary and practical usage is the only means for reducing the exuberance of this early growth, and for giving to each object but one name, and to each name but one power. And all this must have been achieved with regard to the Aryan numerals before Greek was Greek, for thus only can we account for the coincidences as exhibited in the subjoined table: —

	Sanskrit.	Greek.	Latin.	Lithuanian.	Gothic.
I.	ekas,	εἷς (οἴνη),	unus,	wienas,	ains.
II.	dvau,	δύω,	duo,	du,	tvai.
III.	trayas,	τρεῖς,	tres,	trys,	threis.
IV.	*k*atvâras,	τέτταρες, (Æolic, πίσυρες),	quatuor, (Oscan, petora).	keturi,	fidvôr.
V.	pa*nk*a,	πέντε,	quinque, (Oscan, pomtis).	penki,	fimf.
VI.	shash,	ἕξ,	sex,	szeszi,	saihs.
VII.	sapta,	ἑπτά,	septem,	septyni,	sibun.
VIII.	ash*t*au,	ὀκτώ,	octo,	asztůni,	ahtau.
IX.	nava,	ἐννέα,	novem,	dewyni,	niun.
X.	da*s*a,	δέκα,	decem,	deszimt,	taihun.
XI.	ekâda*s*a,	ἕνδεκα	undecim,	wieno-lika,	ain-lif.
XII.	dvâda*s*a,	δώδεκα,	duodecim,	dwy-lika,	tva-lif.
XX.	vi*n*sati,	εἴκοσι,	viginti,	dwi-deszimti,	tvaitigjus.
C.	*s*atam,	ἑκατόν,	centum,	szimtas,	taihun taihund.
M.	sahasram,	χίλιοι,	mille,	tukstantis,	thusundi.

If we cannot account for the coincidences between the French, Italian, Spanish, Portuguese, and Wallachian numerals, without admitting that all were derived from a common type, the Latin, the same conclusion is forced upon us by a comparison of the more ancient numerals. They must have existed ready made in that language from which Sanskrit as well as Welsh is derived; but only as far as hundred. Thousand had not received expression at that early period, and hence the names for thousand differ, not, however, without giving, by their very disagreement, some further indications as to the subsequent history of the Aryan race. We see Sanskrit and Zend share the name for thousand in common (Sanskrit "sahasra," Zend "hazanra"), which shows, that after the southern branch had been severed from the northern, the ancestors of the Brahmans and Zoroastrians continued united for a time by the ties of a common language. The same conclusion may be drawn from the agreement between the Gothic "thusundi" and the Old Prussian "tûsimtons" (acc.), the Lithuanian "tukstantis," the Old Slavonic "tüisasta;" while the Greeks and the Romans stand apart from all the rest, and seem to have formed, each independently, their own name for thousand.

This earliest period, then, previous to any national separation, is what I call the *mythopœic* period, for every one of these common Aryan words is, in a certain sense, a myth. These words were all originally appellative; they expressed one out of many attributes, which seemed characteristic of a certain object, and the selection of these attributes and their expression in language, represents a kind of unconscious poetry, which modern languages have lost altogether.

Language has been called fossil poetry. But as the artist does not know that the clay which he is handling contains the remnants of organic life, we do not feel that when we address a father, we call him protector, nor did the Greeks, when using the word δαήρ, brother-in-law, know that this term applied originally only to the younger brothers of the husband, who stayed at home with the bride while their elder brother was out in the field or the forests. The Sanskrit "devar" meant originally playmate, — it told its own story, — it was a myth; but in Greek it has dwindled down into a mere name, or a technical term. Yet, even in Greek it is not allowed to form a feminine of δαήρ, as little as we should venture even now to form a masculine of "daughter."

Soon, however, languages lose their etymological

conscience, and thus we find in Latin, for instance, not only *vidua*, husbandless ("Penelope tam diu vidua viro suo caruit"), but *viduus*, a formation which, if analyzed etymologically, is as absurd as the Teutonic "a widower." It must be confessed, however, that the old Latin *viduus*,[1] a name of Orcus, who had temple outside Rome, makes it doubtful whether the Latin *vidua* is really the Sanskrit "vi-dhavâ," however great their similarity. At all events we should have to admit that a verb *viduare* was derived from *vidua*, and that afterwards a new adjective was formed with a more general sense, so that *viduus* to a Roman ear meant nothing more than *privatus*.

But, it may be asked, how does the fact, that the Aryan languages possess this treasure of ancient names in common, or even the discovery that all these names had originally an expressive and poetical power, explain the phenomenon of mythological language among all the members of this family? How does it render intelligible that phase of the human mind which gave birth to the extraordinary stories of gods and heroes, — of gorgons and chimæras, — of things that no human eye had ever seen, and that no human mind in a healthy state could ever have conceived?

Before we can answer this question, we must enter into some more preliminary observations as to the formation of words. Tedious as this may seem, we believe that while engaged in these considerations the mist of mythology will gradually clear away, and enable us to discover behind the floating clouds of the dawn of thought and language, that real nature which mythology has so long veiled and disguised.

1 Hartung, *Die Religion der Römer*, vol. ii. p. 90.

All the common Aryan words which we have hitherto examined referred to definite objects. They are all substantives, they express something substantial, something open to sensuous perception. Nor is it in the power of language to express originally anything except objects as nouns, and qualities as verbs. Hence, the only definition we can give of language during that early state is, that it is the conscious expression in sound, of impressions received by all the senses.

To us, abstract nouns are so familiar that we can hardly appreciate the difficulty which men experienced in forming them. We can scarcely imagine a language without abstract nouns. There are, however, dialects spoken at the present day which have no abstract nouns, and the more we go back in the history of languages, the smaller we find the number of these useful expressions. As far as language is concerned, an abstract word is nothing but an adjective raised into a substantive; but in thought the conception of a quality as a subject, is a matter of extreme difficulty, and, in strict logical parlance, impossible. If we say, "I love virtue," we seldom connect any definite notion with "virtue." Virtue is not a being, however unsubstantial; it is nothing individual, personal, active; nothing that could by itself produce an expressible impression on our mind. The word "virtue" is only a short-hand expression; and when men said for the first time "I love virtue," what they meant by it originally was, "I love all things that become an honest man, that are manly, or virtuous."

But there are other words, which we hardly call abstract, but which, nevertheless, were so originally, and are so still, in form; I mean in words like "day" and "night," "spring" and "winter," "dawn" and "twilight," "storm" and "thunder." For what do we mean if we speak of day and night, or of spring and winter? We may answer, a season, or any other portion of time. But what is time, in our conceptions? It is nothing substantial, nothing individual; it is a quality raised by language into a substance. Therefore if we say "the day dawns," "the night approaches," we predicate actions of things that cannot act, we affirm a proposition which, if analyzed logically, would have no definable subject.

The same applies to collective words, such as "sky" and "earth," "dew" and "rain," — even to "rivers" and "mountains." For if we say, "The earth nourishes man," we do not mean any tangible portion of soil, but the earth, conceived as a whole; nor do we mean by the sky the small horizon which our eye can scan. We imagine something which does not fall under our senses, but whether we call it a whole, a power, or an idea, in speaking of it we change it unawares into something individual.

Now in ancient languages every one of these words had necessarily a termination expressive of gender, and this naturally produced in the mind the corresponding idea of sex, so that these names received not only an individual, but a sexual character. There was no substantive which was not either masculine or feminine; neuters being of later growth, and distinguishable chiefly in the nominative.[1]

[1] "It is with the world, as with each of us in our individual life; for as we leave childhood and youth behind us, we bid adieu to the vivid impressions things once made upon us, and become colder and more speculative. To a little child, not only are all living creatures endowed with human intelligence, but *everything* is *alive*. In *his* Kosmos, Pussy takes rank with

What must have been the result of this? As long as people thought in language, it was simply impossible to speak of morning or evening, of spring and winter, without giving to these conceptions something of an individual, active, sexual, and at last, personal character. They were either nothings, as they are nothings to our withered thought, or they were something; and then they could not be conceived as mere powers, but as beings powerful. Even in our time, though we have the conception of nature as a power, what do we mean by power, except something powerful? Now, in early language, nature was *Natura*, a mere adjective made substantive; she was the Mother always "going to bring forth." Was this not a more definite idea than that which we connect with nature? And let us look to our poets, who still think and feel in language, — that is, who use no word without having really enlivened it in their mind, who do not trifle with language, but use it as a spell to call forth real things, full of light and color. Can they speak of the sun, or the dawn, or the storms as neutral powers, without

Pa and Ma, in point of intelligence. He beats the chair against which he has knocked his head; and afterwards kisses it in token of renewed friendship, in the full belief, that like himself, it is a moral agent amenable to rewards and punishments. The fire that burns his finger is "Naughty Fire," and the stars that shine through his bedroom window are Eyes, like Mamma's, or Pussy's, only brighter.

"The same instinct that prompts the child to *personify* everything remains unchecked in the savage, and grows up with him to manhood. Hence in all simple and early languages, there are but two genders, masculine and feminine. To develop such an idea as that of a *neuter*, requires the slow growth of civilization for its accomplishment. We see the same tendency to class everything as masculine or feminine among even civilized men, if they are uneducated. To a farm laborer, a bundle of hay is "*he*," just as much as is the horse that eats it. He resolutely ignores "*it*," as a pronoun for which there is not the slightest necessity." —*Printer's Register*, Feb. 6, 1868.

doing violence to their feelings? Let us open Wordsworth, and we shall hardly find him use a single abstract term without some life and blood in it: —

Religion.

"Sacred Religion, mother of form and fear,
Dread arbitress of mutable respect,
New rites ordaining when the old are wrecked,
Or cease to please the fickle worshipper."

Winter.

"Humanity, delighting to behold
A fond reflection of her own decay,
Hath painted Winter like a traveller old,
Propped on a staff, and, through the sullen day,
In hooded mantle, limping o'er the plain,
As though his weakness were disturbed by pain:
Or, if a juster fancy should allow
An undisputed symbol of command,
The chosen sceptre is a withered bough,
Infirmly grasped within a palsied hand.
These emblems suit the helpless and forlorn;
But mighty Winter the device shall scorn.
For he it was — dread Winter! — who beset,
Flinging round van and rear his ghastly net,
That host, when from the regions of the Pole
They shrunk, insane Ambition's barren goal, —
That host, as huge and strong as e'er defied
Their God, and placed their trust in human pride!
As fathers prosecute rebellious sons,
He smote the blossoms of their warrior youth;
He called on *Frost's* inexorable tooth
Life to consume in manhood's firmest hold . . . .
And bade the *Snow* their ample backs bestride,
And to the battle ride."

So, again, of *Age and the Hours:* —

"*Age!* twine thy brows with fresh spring flowers,
And call a train of laughing *Hours*,
And bid them dance, and bid them sing;
And thou, too, mingle in the ring!"

Now, when writing these lines, Wordsworth could hardly have thought of the classical *Horæ:* the conception of dancing Hours came as natural to his mind as to the poets of old.

Or, again, of *Storms and Seasons*: —

> "Ye *Storms*, resound the praises of your King!
> And ye mild Seasons, — in a sunny clime,
> Midway, on some high hill, while father *Time*
> Looks on delighted, — meet in festal ring,
> And loud and long of Winter's triumph sing!"

We are wont to call this poetical diction, and to make allowance for what seems to us exaggerated language. But to the poet it is no exaggeration, nor was it to the ancient poets of language. Poetry is older than prose, and abstract speech more difficult than the outpouring of a poet's sympathy with nature. It requires reflection to divest nature of her living expression, to see in the swift-riding clouds nothing but vaporous exhalations, in the frowning mountains masses of stone, and in the lightning electric sparks. Wordsworth feels what he says, when he exclaims, —

> "Mountains, and Vales, and Floods, I call on you
> To share the passion of a just disdain;"

and when he speaks of "the last hill that parleys with the setting sun," this expression came to him as he was communing with nature; it was a thought untranslated as yet into the prose of our traditional and emaciated speech; it was a thought such as the men of old would not have been ashamed of in their common every day conversation.

There are some poems of this modern ancient which are all mythology, and as we shall have to refer to them hereafter, I shall give one more extract, which to a Hindu and an ancient Greek would have been more intelligible than it is to us: —

> "Hail, orient Conqueror of gloomy Night!
> Thou that canst shed the bliss of gratitude
> On hearts, howe'er insensible or rude;
> Whether thy punctual visitations smite

The haughty towers where monarchs dwell,
Or thou, impartial Sun, with presence bright
Cheer'st the low threshold of the peasant's cell!
Not unrejoiced I see thee climb the sky,
In naked splendor, clear from mist and haze,
Or cloud approaching to divert the rays,
Which even in deepest winter testify
  Thy power and majesty,
Dazzling the vision that presumes to gaze.
Well does thine aspect usher in this Day;
As aptly suits therewith that modest pace
  Submitted to the chains
That bind thee to the path which God ordains
  That thou shouldst trace,
Till, with the heavens and earth, thou pass away!
Nor less, the stillness of these frosty plains —
Their utter stillness, and the silent grace
Of yon ethereal summits, white with snow,
(Whose tranquil pomp and spotless purity
  Report of storms gone by
  To us who tread below) —
Do with the service of this day accord.
Divinest object which th' uplifted eye
Of mortal man is suffered to behold;
Thou, who upon these snow-clad Heights has poured
Meek lustre, nor forget'st the humble Vale;
Thou who dost warm Earth's universal mould,
And for thy bounty wert not unadored
  By pious men of old;
Once more, heart-cheering Sun, I bid thee hail!
Bright be thy course to-day, — let not this promise fail!"

Why then, if we ourselves, in speaking of the Sun or the Storms, of Sleep and Death, of Earth and Dawn, connect either no distinct idea at all with these names, or allow them to cast over our mind the fleeting shadows of the poetry of old; why, if we, when speaking with the warmth which is natural to the human heart, call upon the Winds and the Sun, the Ocean and the Sky, as if they would still hear us; why, if plastic thought cannot represent any one of these beings or powers, without giving them, if not a human form, at least human life and human feeling, — why should we wonder at the ancients, with their language throbbing with life and reveling in color, if instead of the gray outlines of our modern thought, they threw out those living forms of nature, endowed with human powers, nay, with powers more than human, inasmuch as the light of the Sun was brighter than the light of a human eye, and the roaring of the Storms louder than the shouts of the human voice. We may be able to account for the origin of rain and dew, of storm and thunder; yet, to the great majority of mankind, all these things, unless they are mere names, are still what they were to Homer, only perhaps less beautiful, less poetical, less real, and living.

So much for that peculiar difficulty which the human mind experiences in speaking of collective or abstract ideas, — a difficulty which, as we shall see, will explain many of the difficulties of Mythology.

We have now to consider a similar feature of ancient languages, — the auxiliary verbs. They hold the same position among verbs, as abstract nouns among substantives. They are of later origin, and had all originally a more material and expressive character. Our auxiliary verbs have had to pass through a long chain of vicissitudes before they arrived at the withered and lifeless form which fits them so well for the purposes of our abstract prose. *Habere*, which is now used in all the Romance languages simply to express a past tense, "j'ai aimé," I loved, was originally, to hold fast, to hold back, as we may see in its derivative, *habenæ*, the reins. Thus *tenere*, to hold, becomes, in Spanish, an auxiliary verb, that can be used very much in the same manner as *habere*. The Greek ἔχω is the Sanskrit "sah," and meant originally, to be strong, to be able, or to can. The Latin *fui*, I was, the Sanskrit "bhû," to be, corresponds to the Greek φύω, and there shows still its original and material power of growing, in an intransitive and transitive sense. "As," the radical of the Sanskrit "as-mi," the Greek ἐμ-μί, the Lithuanian "as-mi," I am, had probably the original meaning of breathing, if the Sanskrit "as-u," breath, is correctly traced back to that root. *Stare*, to stand, sinks down in the Romance dialects to a mere auxiliary, as in "j'ai-été," I have been, i. e. *habeo-statum*, I have stood; "j'ai-été convaincu," I have stood convinced; the phonetic change of *statum* into *été* being borne out by the transition of *status* into *état*. The German "werden," which is used to form futures and passives, the Gothic "varth," points back to the Sanskrit "vrit," the Latin *verto*. "Will," again, in "he will go," has lost its radical meaning of wishing; and "shall" used in the same tense, "I shall go," hardly betrays, even to the etymologist, its original power of legal or moral obligation. "Schuld," however, in German means debt and sin, and "soll," has there not yet taken a merely temporal signification, the first trace of which may be discovered, however, in the names of the three Teutonic Parcæ. These are called "Vurdh," "Verdhandi," and "Skuld," — Past, Present, and Future.[1] But what could be the original conception of a verb which, even in its earliest application, has already the abstract meaning of moral duty or legal obligation? Where could language, which can only draw upon the material world for its nominal and verbal treasures, find something analogous to the abstract idea of he shall pay, or, he ought to yield? Grimm, who has endeavored to

[1] Kuhn, *Zeitschrift für vergleichende Sprachforschung*, vol. iii. p. 449.

follow the German language into its most secret re cesses, proposes an explanation of this verb, which deserves serious consideration, however strange and incredible it may appear at first sight.

Shall, and its preterite *should*, have the following forms in Gothic: —

Present.	Preterite.
Skal,	Skulda.
Skalt,	Skuldês.
Skal,	Skulda.
Skulum,	Skuldedum.
Skuluth,	Skulduduth.
Skulun,	Skuldedun.

In Gothic this verb "skal," which seems to be a present, can be proved to be an old perfect, analogous to Greek perfects like οἶδα, which have the form of the perfect but the power of the present. There are several verbs of the same character in the German language, and in English they can be detected by the absence of the *s*, as the termination of the third person singular of the present. "Skal," then, according to Grimm, means, "I owe," "I am bound;" but originally it meant "I have killed." The chief guilt punished by ancient Teutonic law, was the guilt of manslaughter, — and in many cases it could be atoned for by a fine. Hence, "skal" meant literally, "I am guilty," "ich bin schuldig;" and afterwards, when this full expression had been ground down into a legal phrase, new expressions became possible, such as I have killed a free man, a serf, *i. e.* I am guilty of a free man, a serf; and at last, I owe (the fine for having slain) a free man, a serf. In this manner Grimm accounts for the still later and more anomalous expressions, such as he shall pay, *i. e.* he is guilty to pay ("er ist schuldig zu zahlen"); he shall go, *i. e.* he must go; and last, I shall withdraw, *i. e.* I feel bound to withdraw.

A change of meaning like this seems, no doubt, violent and fanciful, but we should feel more inclined to accept it, if we considered how almost every word we use discloses similar changes as soon as we analyze it etymologically, and then follow gradually its historical growth. The general conception of thing is in Wallachian expressed by "lucru," the Latin *lucrum*, gain. The French "chose" was originally *causa*, or *cause*. If we say, "I am obliged to go," or "I am bound to pay," we forget that the origin of these expressions carries us back to times when men were bound to go, or bound over to pay. *Hoc me fallit* means, in Latin, "it deceives me," "it escapes me." Afterwards, it took the sense of "it is removed from me," I want it, I must have it: and hence, "il me faut," I must. Again, *I may* is the Gothic

Mag, maht, mag, magum, maguth, magun;

and its primary signification was, "I am strong." Now, this verb also was originally a preterite, and derived from a root which meant, "to beget," whence the Gothic "magus," son, *i. e.* begotten, the Scotch "Mac," and Gothic "magath-s," daughter, the English "maid."

In mythological language we must make due allowance for the absence of merely auxiliary words. Every word, whether noun or verb, had still its full original power during the mythopœic ages. Words were heavy and unwieldy. They said more than they ought to say, and hence, much of the strangeness of the mythological language, which we can only understand by watching the natural growth of speech. Where we speak of the sun following the dawn, the ancient poets could only speak and think of the Sun loving and embracing the Dawn. What is with us a sunset, was to them the Sun growing old, decaying, or dying. Our sunrise was to them the Night giving birth to a brilliant child; and in the Spring they really saw the Sun or the Sky embracing the earth with a warm embrace, and showering treasures into the lap of nature. There are many myths in Hesiod, of late origin, where we have only to replace a full verb by an auxiliary, in order to change mythical into logical language. Hesiod calls Nyx (Night) the mother of Moros (Fate), and the dark Kêr (Destruction); of Thanatos (Death), Hypnos (Sleep), and the tribe of the Oneiroi (Dreams). And this her progeny she is said to have borne without a father. Again, she is called the mother of Mômos (Blame), and of the woful Oizys (Woe), and of the Hesperides (Evening Stars), who guard the beautiful golden apples on the other side of the far-famed Okeanos, and the trees that bear fruit. She also bore Nemesis (Vengeance), and Apatê (Fraud), and Philotes (Lust), and the pernicious Geras (Old Age), and the strong-minded Eris (Strife). Now, let us use our modern expressions, such as "the stars are seen as the night approaches," "we sleep," "we dream," "we die," "we run danger during night," "nightly revels lead to strife, angry discussions, and woe," "many nights bring old age, and at last death," "an evil deed concealed at first by the darkness of night will at last be revealed by the day," "Night herself will be revenged on the criminal," and we have translated the language of Hesiod — a language to a great extent understood by the people whom he addressed — into our modern form of thought and speech.[1] All this is hardly mythological language, but rather a poetical and proverbial kind of expression known to all poets, whether modern or ancient, and frequently to be found in the language of common people.

Uranos, in the language of Hesiod, is used as a name for the sky; he is made or born that "he should be a firm place for the blessed gods."[2] It is said twice, that Uranos covers everything (v. 127), and that when he brings the night, he is stretched out everywhere, embracing the earth. This sounds almost as if the Greek myth had still preserved a recollection of the etymological power of Uranos. For "Uranos" is the Sanskrit "Varu*n*a" and this is derived from a root VAR, to cover; "Varu*n*a" being in the Veda also a name of the firmament, but especially connected with the night, and opposed to "Mitra," the day. At all events, the name of "Uranos" retained with the Greek something of its original meaning, which was not the case with names like "Apollo" or "Dionysos;" and when we see him called ἀστερόεις, the starry

[1] As to Philotes being the Child of Night, Juliet understood what it meant when she said: —

> "Spread thy close curtain, love-performing Night!
> That unawares eyes may wink; and Romeo
> Leap to these arms, untalked of and unseen! —
> Lovers can see to do their amorous rites
> By their own beauties; or, if Love be blind,
> It best agrees with Night."

[2] Hesiod, *Theog.* 128: —

> Γαῖα δέ τοι πρῶτον μὲν ἐγείνατο ἶσον ἑαυτῇ
> Οὐρανὸν ἀστερόενθ', ἵνα μιν περὶ πάντα καλύπτοι,
> ὄφρ' εἴη μακάρεσσι θεοῖς ἕδος ἀσφαλὲς αἰεί.

heaven, we can hardly believe, as Mr. Grote says, that to the Greek, "Uranos, Nyx, Hypnos, and Oneiros (Heaven, Night, Sleep, and Dream) are persons, just as much as Zeus and Apollo." We need only read a few lines further in Hesiod, in order to see that the progeny of Gæa, of which Uranos is the first, has not yet altogether arrived at that mythological personification or crystallization which makes most of the Olympian gods so difficult and doubtful in their original character. The poet has asked the Muses in the introduction how the gods and the earth were first born, and the rivers and the endless sea, and the bright stars, and the wide heaven above (οὐρανὸς εὐρὺς ὕπερθεν). The whole poem of the "Theogony" is an answer to this question; and we can hardly doubt therefore that the Greek saw in some of the names that follow, simply poetical conceptions of real objects, such as the earth, and the rivers, and the mountains. Uranos, the first offspring of Gæa, is afterwards raised into a deity,— endowed with human feelings and attributes; but the very next offspring of Gæa, Οὐρέα μακρά, the great Mountains, are even in language represented as neuter, and can therefore hardly claim to be considered as persons like Zeus and Apollo.

Mr. Grote goes too far in insisting on the purely literal meaning of the whole of Greek mythology. Some mythological figures of speech remained in the Greek language to a very late period, and were perfectly understood,— that is to say, they required as little explanation as our expressions of "the sun sets," or "the sun rises." Mr. Grote feels compelled to admit this, but he declines to draw any further conclusions from it. "Although some of the attributes and actions ascribed to these persons," he says, "are often explicable by allegory, the whole series and system of them never are so: the theorist who adopts this course of explanation finds that, after one or two simple and obvious steps, the path is no longer open, and he is forced to clear a way for himself by gratuitous refinements and conjectures." Here, then, Mr. Grote admits what he calls allegory as an ingredient of mythology; still he makes no further use of it and leaves the whole of mythology as a riddle, that cannot and ought not to be solved, as something irrational — as a past that was never present — declining even to attempt a partial explanation of this important problem in the history of the Greek mind. Πλέον ἥμισυ παντός. Such a want of scientific courage would have put a stop to many systems which have since grown to completeness, but which at first had to make the most timid and uncertain steps. In palæontological sciences we must learn to be ignorant of certain things; and what Suetonius says of the grammarian, "boni grammatici est nonnulla etiam nescire," applies with particular force to the mythologist. It is in vain to attempt to solve the secret of every name; and nobody has expressed this with greater modesty than he who has laid the most lasting foundation of Comparative Mythology. Grimm, in the introduction to his "German Mythology," says, without disguise, "I shall indeed interpret all that I can, but I cannot interpret all that I should like." But surely Otfried Müller had opened a path into the labyrinth of Greek mythology, which a scholar of Mr. Grote's power and genius might have followed, and which at least he ought to have proved as either right or wrong. How late mythological language was in vogue among the Greeks has been shown by O. Müller (p. 65) in the myth of Kyrene. The Greek town of Kyrene in Libya was founded about Olymp. 37; the ruling race derived its origin from the Minyans, who reigned chiefly in Iolkos, in Southern Thessaly; the foundation of the colony was due to the oracle of Apollo at Pytho. Hence, the myth, — "The heroic maid Kyrene, who lived in Thessaly, is loved by Apollo and carried off to Libya;" while in modern language we should say, — "The town of Kyrene, in Thessaly, sent a colony to Libya, under the auspices of Apollo." Many more instances might be given, where the mere substitution of a more matter-of-fact verb divests a myth at once of its miraculous appearance.[1]

Kaunos is called the son of Miletos, *i. e.* Kretan colonists from Miletos had founded the town of Kaunos in Lycia. Again, the myth says that Kaunos fled from Miletos to Lycia, and his sister Byblos was changed, by sorrow over her lost brother, into a fountain. Here Miletos in Ionia, being better known than the Miletos in Kreta, has been brought in by mistake, Byblos being simply a small river near the Ionian Miletos. Again, Pausanias tells us as a matter of history, that Miletos, a beautiful boy, fled from Kreta to Ionia, in order to escape the jealousy of Minos, — the fact being, that Miletos in Ionia was a colony of the Miletos of Kreta, and Minos the most famous king of that island. Again, Marpessa is called the daughter of Evenos, and a myth represents her as carried away by Idas, — Idas being the name of a famous hero of the town of Marpessa. The fact, implied by the myth and confirmed by other evidence, is, that colonists started

[1] Kanne's *Mythology*, § 10, p. xxxii.

from the river Evenos, and founded Marpessa in Messina. And here again, the myth adds, that Evenos, after trying in vain to reconquer his daughter from Idas, was changed by sorrow into a river, like Byblos, the sister of Miletos.

If the Hellenes call themselves αὐτόχθονες, we fancy we understand what is meant by this expression. But, if we are informed that πυρρά, the red, was the oldest name of Thessaly, and that Hellen was the son of Pyrrha, Mr. Grote would say that we have here to deal with a myth, and that the Greeks, at least, never doubted that there really was one individual called Pyrrha, and another called Hellen. Now, this may be true with regard to the later Greeks, such as Homer and Hesiod; but was it so — could it have been so originally? Language is always language, — it always meant something originally, and he, whoever it was, who first, instead of calling the Hellenes born of the soil, spoke of Pyrrha, the mother of Hellen, must have meant something intelligible and rational; he could not have meant a friend of his whom he knew by the name of Hellen, and an old lady called Pyrrha; he meant what we mean if we speak of Italy as the mother of Art.

Even in more modern times than those of which Otfried Müller speaks, we find that "to speak mythologically," was the fashion among poets and philosophers. Pausanias complains of those "who genealogize everything, and make Pythis the son of Delphos." The story of Eros in the "Phædros" is called a myth (μῦθος, 254 D; λόγος, 257 B); yet Sokrates says ironically, "that is one of those which you may believe or not" (τούτοις δὴ ἔξεστι μὲν πείθεσθαι, ἔξεστι δὲ μή). Again, when he tells the story of the Egyptian god Theuth, he calls it a "tradition of old" (ἀκοήν γ' ἔχω λέγειν τῶν προτέρων), but Phædros knows at once that it is one of Sokrates' own making, and he says to him, "Sokrates, thou makest easily Egyptian or any other stories" (λόγοι). When Pindar calls Apophasis the daughter of Epimetheus, every Greek understood this mythological language as well as if he had said "an after-thought leads to an excuse."[1] Nay, even in Homer, when the lame Litæ (Prayers) are said to follow Atê (Mischief), trying to appease her, a Greek understood this language as well as we do, when we say that "Hell is paved with good intentions."

When Prayers are called the daughters of Zeus, we are hardly as yet within the sphere of pure mythology. For Zeus was to the Greeks the protector of the suppliants, Ζεὺς ἱκετέσιος, — and hence Prayers are called his daughters, as we might call Liberty the daughter of England, or Prayer the offspring of the soul.

All these sayings, however, though mythical, are not yet myths. It is the essential character of a true myth that it should no longer be intelligible by a reference to the spoken language. The plastic character of ancient language, which we have traced in the formation of nouns and verbs, is not sufficient to explain

[1] O. Müller has pointed out how the different parents given to the "Erinyes" by different poets were suggested by the character which each poet ascribed to them. "Evidently," he says, in his *Essay on the Eumenides*, p. 184, "this genealogy answered better to the views and poetical objects of Æschylos than one of the current genealogies by which the Erinyes are derived from Skotos and Gæa (Sophokles), Kronos and Eurynome (in a work ascribed to Epimenides), Phorkys (Euphorion), Gæa Eurynome (Istron), Acheron and Night (Eudemos), Hades and Persephone (Orphic hymns), Hades and Styx (Athenodoros and Mnaseas). See, however, *Ares*, by H. D. Müller, p. 67.

how a myth could have lost its expressive power or its life and consciousness. Making due allowance for the difficulty of forming abstract nouns and abstract verbs, we should yet be unable to account for anything beyond allegorical poetry among the nations of antiquity; mythology would still remain a riddle. Here, then, we must call to our aid another powerful ingredient in the formation of ancient speech, for which I find no better name than *Polyonymy* and *Synonymy*.[1] Most nouns, as we have seen before, were originally appellatives or predicates, expressive of what seemed at the time the most characteristic attribute of an object. But as most objects have more than one attribute, and as, under different aspects, one or the other attribute might seem more appropriate to form the name, it happened by necessity that most objects, during the early period of language, had more than one name. In the course of time, the greater portion of these names became useless, and they were mostly replaced in literary dialects by one fixed name, which might be called the proper name of such objects. The more ancient a language, the richer it is in synonyms.

Synonyms, again, if used constantly, must naturally give rise to a number of homonyms. If we may call the sun by fifty names expressive of different qualities, some of these names will be applicable to other objects also, which happen to possess the same quality. These different objects would then be called by the same name — they would become homonyms.

In the Veda, the earth is called "urvî" (wide), "p*r*ithvî" (broad), "mahî" (great), and many more

[1] See the Author's letter to Chevalier Bunsen *On the Turanian Languages*, p. 25

names, of which the Nigha*n*tu mentions twenty-one. These twenty-one words would be synonyms. But "urvi" (wide) is not only given as a name of the earth, but also means a river. "P*r*ithvî" (broad) means not only earth, but sky and dawn. "Mahî" (great, strong) is used for cow and speech, as well as for earth. Hence, earth, river, sky, dawn, cow, and speech, would become homonyms. All these names, however, are simple and intelligible. But most of the old terms, thrown out by language at the first burst of youthful poetry, are based on bold metaphors. These metaphors once forgotten, or the meaning of the roots whence the words were derived once dimmed and changed, many of these words would naturally lose their radical as well as their poetical meaning. They would become mere names handed down in the conversation of a family; understood, perhaps, by the grandfather, familiar to the father, but strange to the son, and misunderstood by the grandson. This misunderstanding may arise in various manners. Either the radical meaning of the word is forgotten, and thus what was originally an appellative, or a name, in the etymological sense of the word (*nomen* stands for *gnomen*, "quo gnoscimus res," like *natus* for *gnatus*), dwindled down into a mere sound—a name in the modern sense of the word. Thus ζεύς, being originally a name of the sky, like the Sanskrit "dyâus," became gradually a proper name, which betrayed its appellative meaning only in a few proverbial expressions, such as Ζεὺς ὕει, or "sub Jove frigido."

Frequently it happened that after the true etymological meaning of the word had been forgotten, a new meaning was attached to it by a kind of etymological instinct which exists even in modern languages. Thus, Λυκηγενής, the son of light — Apollo, was changed into a son of Lycia; Δήλιος, the bright one, gave rise to the myth of the birth of Apollo in Delos.

Again, where two names existed for the same object, two persons would spring up out of the two names, and as the same stories could be told of either, they would naturally be represented as brothers and sisters, as parent and child. Thus we find Selene, the moon, side by side with Mene, the moon; Helios (Sûrya), the Sun, and Phœbos (Bhava, a different form of Rudra); and in most of the Greek heroes we can discover humanized forms of Greek gods, with names which, in many instances, were epithets of their divine prototypes. Still more frequently it happened that adjectives connected with a word as applied to one object, were used with the same word even though applied to a different object. What was told of the sea was told of the sky, and the sun once being called a lion or a wolf, was soon endowed with claws and mane, even where the animal metaphor was forgotten. Thus the Sun with his golden rays might be called "golden-handed," *hand* being expressed by the same word as *ray*. But when the same epithet was applied to Apollo or Indra, a myth would spring up, as we find it in German and Sanskrit mythology, telling us that Indra lost his hand, and that it was replaced by a hand made of gold.

Here we have some of the keys to mythology, but the manner of handling them can only be learnt from comparative philology. As in French it is difficult to find the radical meaning of many a word, unless we compare it with its corresponding forms in Italian, Spanish, or Provencal; we should find it impossible to discover the origin of many a Greek word, without comparing it with its more or less corrupt relatives in German, Latin, Slavonic, and Sanskrit. Unfortunately we have in this ancient circle of languages nothing corresponding to Latin, by which we can test the more or less original form of a word in French, Italian, and Spanish. Sanskrit is not the mother of Latin and Greek, as Latin is the mother of French and Italian. But although Sanskrit is but one among many sisters, it is, no doubt, the eldest, in so far as it has preserved its words in their most primitive state; and if we once succeed in tracing a Latin and Greek word to its corresponding form in Sanskrit, we are generally able at the same time to account for its formation, and to fix its radical meaning. What should we know of the original meaning of *πατήρ*, *μήτηρ*, and *θυγάτηρ*,[1] if we were reduced to the knowledge of one language like Greek? But as soon as we trace these words to Sanskrit, their primitive power is clearly indicated. O. Müller was one of the first to see and acknowledge that classical philology must surrender all etymological research to comparative philology, and that the origin of Greek words cannot be settled by a mere reference to Greek. This applies with particular force to mythological names. In order to become mythological, it was necessary that the radical meaning of certain names should have been obscured and forgotten in the language to which they belong. Thus what is mythological in one language, is frequently natural and intelligible in another. We say, "the sun sets," but in our

[1] Here is a specimen of Greek etymology, from tl e *Etymologicum Magnum*: Θυγάτηρ παρὰ τὸ θύειν καὶ ὁρμᾶν κατὰ γαστρός· ἐκ τοῦ θύω καὶ τοῦ γαστήρ· λέγεται γὰρ τα θήλεα τάχιον κινεῖσθαι ἐν τῇ μήτρᾳ.

own Teutonic mythology, a seat or throne is given to the sun on which he sits down, as in Greek "Eos" is called χρυσόθρονος, or as the modern Greek speaks of the setting sun as ἥλιος βασιλεύι. We doubt about "Hekate," but we understand at once Ἕκατος and Ἑκατήβολος. We hesitate about *Lucina*, but we accept immediately what is a mere contraction of *Lucna*, the Latin *Luna*.

What is commonly called Hindu mythology is of little or no avail for comparative purposes. The stories of *S*iva, Vish*n*u, Mahâdeva, Pârvati, Kali, K*r*ish*n*a, etc., are of late growth, indigenous to India, and full of wild and fanciful conceptions. But while this late mythology of the Purâ*n*as and even of the Epic poems, offers no assistance to the comparative mythologist, a whole world of primitive, natural, and intelligible mythology has been preserved to us in the Veda. The mythology of the Veda is to comparative mythology what Sanskrit has been to comparative grammar. There is, fortunately, no system of religion or mythology in the Veda. Names are used in one hymn as appellatives, in another as names of gods. The same god is sometimes represented as supreme, sometimes as equal, sometimes as inferior to others. The whole nature of these so-called gods is still transparent; their first conception, in many cases, clearly perceptible. There are as yet no genealogies, no settled marriages between gods and goddesses. The father is sometimes the son, the brother is the husband, and she who in one hymn is the mother, is in another the wife. As the conceptions of the poet varied, so varied the nature of these gods. Nowhere is the wide distance which separates the ancient poems of India from the most ancient literature of Greece more clearly felt than when we compare the growing myths of the Veda with the full-grown and decayed myths on which the poetry of Homer is founded. The Veda is the real Theogony of the Aryan races, while that of Hesiod is a distorted caricature of the original image. If we want to know whither the human mind, though endowed with the natural consciousness of a divine power, is driven necessarily and inevitably by the irresistible force of language as applied to supernatural and abstract ideas, we must read the Veda; and if we want to tell the Hindus what they are worshipping, — mere names of natural phenomena, gradually obscured, personified, and deified, — we must make them read the Veda. It was a mistake of the early Fathers to treat the heathen gods[1] as demons or evil spirits, and we must take care not to commit the same error with regard to the Hindu gods. Their gods have no more right to any substantive existence than Eos or Hemera, — than Nyx or Apatê. They are masks without an actor, — the creations of man, not his creators; they are *nomina*, not *numina;* names without being, not beings without names.

In some instances, no doubt, it happens that a Greek, or a Latin, or a Teutonic myth, may be explained from the resources which each of these languages still possesses, as there are many words in Greek which can be explained etymologically without any reference to San-

[1] Aristotle has given an opinion of the Greek gods in a passage of the *Metaphysics.* He is attacking the Platonic ideas, and tries to show their contradictory character, calling them αἰσθητὰ ἀΐδια, eternal uneternals, *i. e.* things that cannot have any real existence; as men, he continues, maintain that there are gods, but give them a human form, thus making them really "immortal mortals," *i. e.* nonentities.

skrit or Gothic. We shall begin with some of these myths, and then proceed to the more difficult, which must receive light from more distant regions, whether from the snowy rocks of Iceland and the songs of the "Edda," or from the borders of the "Seven Rivers," and the hymns of the Veda.

The rich imagination, the quick perception, the intellectual vivacity, and ever-varying fancy of the Greek nation, make it easy to understand that, after the separation of the Aryan race, no language was richer, no mythology more varied, than that of the Greeks. Words were created with wonderful facility, and were forgotten again with that carelessness which the consciousness of inexhaustible power imparts to men of genius. The creation of every word was originally a poem, embodying a bold metaphor or a bright conception. But like the popular poetry of Greece, these words, if they were adopted by tradition, and lived on in the language of a family, of a city, of a tribe, in the dialects, or in the national speech of Greece, soon forgot the father that had given them birth, or the poet to whom they owed their existence. Their genealogical descent and native character were unknown to the Greeks themselves, and their etymological meaning would have baffled the most ingenious antiquarian. The Greeks, however, cared as little about the etymological individuality of their words as they cared to know the name of every bard that had first sung the "Aristeia" of Menelaos or Diomedes. One Homer was enough to satisfy their curiosity, and any etymology that explained any part of the meaning of a word was welcome, no historical considerations being ever allowed to interfere with ingenious guesses. It is known how Sokrates changes, on the spur of the moment, Eros into a god of wings, but Homer is quite as ready with etymologies, and they are useful, at least so far as they prove that the real etymology of the names of the gods had been forgotten long before Homer.

We can best enter into the original meaning of a Greek myth when some of the persons who act in it have preserved names intelligible in Greek. When we find the names of Eos, Selene, Helios, or Herse, we have words which tell their own story, and we have a ποῦ στῶ for the rest of the myth. Let us take the beautiful myth of Selene and Endymion. Endymion is the son of Zeus and Kalyke, but he is also the son of Æthlios, a king of Elis, who is himself called a son of Zeus, and whom Endymion is said to have succeeded as king of Elis. This localizes our myth, and shows, at least, that Elis is its birthplace, and that, according to Greek custom, the reigning race of Elis derived its origin from Zeus. The same custom prevailed in India, and gave rise to the two great royal families of ancient India, — the so-called Solar and the Lunar races: and Purûravas, of whom more by and by, says of himself, —

> 'The great king of day
> And monarch of the night are my progenitors;
> Their grandson I." . . . .

There may, then, have been a king of Elis, Æthlios, and he may have had a son, Endymion; but what the myth tells of Endymion could not have happened to the king of Elis. The myth transfers Endymion to Karia, to Mount Latmos, because it was in the Latmian cave that Selene saw the beautiful sleeper, loved him and lost him. Now about the meaning of Selene, there can be no doubt; but even if tradition had only preserved her other name, Asterodia, we should have had to translate this synonym, as Moon, as "Wanderer among the stars." But who is Endymion? It is one of the many names of the sun, but with special reference to the setting or dying sun. It is derived from ἐνδύω, a verb which, in classical Greek, is never used for setting, because the simple verb δύω had become the technical term for sunset. Δυσμαὶ ἡλίου, the setting of the sun, is opposed to ἀνατολαί, the rising. Now, δύω meant originally, to dive into; and expressions like ἠέλιος δ' ἄρ' ἔδυ, the sun dived, presuppose an earlier conception of ἔδυ πόντον, he dived into the sea. Thus Thetis addresses her companions ("Il." xviii. 140): —

'Υμεῖς μὲν νῦν δῦτε θαλάσσης εὐρέα κόλπον.

"You may now dive into the broad bosom of the sea."

Other dialects, particularly of maritime nations, have the same expression. In Latin we find,[1] "Cur mergat seras æquore flammas." In Old Norse, "Sôl gengr i ægi." Slavonic nations represent the sun as a woman stepping into her bath in the evening, and rising refreshed and purified in the morning; or they speak of the Sea as the mother of the Sun (the "apâm napât"), and of the Sun as sinking into her mother's arms at night. We may suppose, therefore, that in some Greek dialect ἐνδύω was used in the same sense; and that from ἐνδύω, ἔνδυμα was formed to express sunset. From this was formed ἐνδυμίων,[2] like οὐρανίων from οὐρανός, and like most of the names of the Greek

1 Grimm's *Deutsche Mythologie*, p 704.

2 Lauer, in his *System of Greek Mythology*, explains Endymion as the Diver. Gerhard, in his *Greek Mythology*, gives, 'Ενδυμίων as ὁ ἐν δύμῃ ὤν.

months. If ἔνδυμα had become the commonly received name for sunset, the myth of Endymion could never have arisen. But the original meaning of Endymion being once forgotten, what was told originally of the setting sun was now told of a name, which, in order to have any meaning, had to be changed into a god or a hero. The setting sun once slept in the Latmian cave, the cave of night — "Latmos" being derived from the same root as "Leto," "Latona," the night; — but now he sleeps on Mount Latmos, in Karia. Endymion, sinking into eternal sleep after a life of but one day, was once the setting sun, the son of Zeus, the brilliant Sky, and of Kalyke, the covering Night (from καλύπτω); or, according to another saying, of Zeus and Protogeneia, the first-born goddess, or the Dawn, who is always represented, either as the mother, the sister, or the forsaken wife of the Sun. Now he is the son of a king of Elis, probably for no other reason except that it was usual for kings to take names of good omen, connected with the sun, or the moon, or the stars, — in which case a myth, connected with a solar name, would naturally be transferred to its human namesake. In the ancient poetical and proverbial language of Elis, people said "Selene loves and watches Endymion," instead of "it is getting late;" "Selene embraces Endymion," instead of "the sun is setting and the moon is rising;" "Selene kisses Endymion into sleep," instead of "it is night." These expressions remained long after their meaning had ceased to be understood; and as the human mind is generally as anxious for a reason as ready to invent one, a story arose by common consent, and without any personal effort, that Endymion must have been a young lad loved by a young lady, Selene; and, if children were anxious to know still more, there would always be a grandmother happy to tell them that this young Endymion was the son of the Protogeneia, — she half meaning and half not meaning by that name the dawn who gave birth to the sun; or of Kalyke, the dark and covering Night. This name, once touched, would set many chords vibrating; three or four different reasons might be given (as they really were given by ancient poets) why Endymion fell into this everlasting sleep, and if any one of these was alluded to by a popular poet, it became a mythological fact, repeated by later poets; so that Endymion grew at last almost into a type, no longer of the setting sun, but of a handsome boy beloved of a chaste maiden, and therefore a most likely name for a young prince. Many myths have thus been transferred to real persons, by a mere similarity of name, though it must be admitted that there is no historical evidence whatsoever that there ever was a prince of Elis, called by the name of Endymion.

Such is the growth of a legend, originally a mere word, a μῦθος, probably one of those many words which have but a local currency, and lose their value if they are taken to distant places, words useless for the daily interchange of thought, spurious coins in the hands of the many, — yet not thrown away, but preserved as curiosities and ornaments, and deciphered at last by the antiquarian, after the lapse of many centuries. Unfortunately, we do not possess these legends as they passed originally from mouth to mouth in villages or mountain castles, — legends such as Grimm has collected in his "Mythology," from the language of the poor people in Germany. We do not know them, as they were told by the older members of a family, who spoke a language half intelligible to themselves and strange to their children, or as the poet of a rising city embodied the traditions of his neighborhood in a continuous poem, and gave to them their first form and permanence. Unless where Homer has preserved a local myth, all is arranged as a system; with the "Theogony" as its beginning, the "Siege of Troy" as its centre, and the "Return of the Heroes" as its end. But how many parts of Greek mythology are never mentioned by Homer! We then come to Hesiod — a moralist and theologian, and again we find but a small segment of the mythological language of Greece. Thus our chief sources are the ancient chroniclers, who took mythology for history, and used of it only so much as answered their purpose. And not even these are preserved to us, but we only believe that they formed the sources from which later writers, such as Apollodoros and the scholiasts, borrowed their information. The first duty of the mythologist is, therefore, to disentangle this cluster, to remove all that is systematic, and to reduce each myth to its primitive unsystematic form. Much that is unessential has to be cut away altogether, and after the rust is removed, we have to determine first of all, as with ancient coins, the locality, and, if possible, the age, of each myth, by the character of its workmanship; and as we arrange ancient medals into gold, silver, and copper coins, we have to distinguish most carefully between the legends of gods, heroes, and men. If, then, we succeed in deciphering the ancient names and legends of Greek or any other mythology, we learn that the past which stands before our eyes in Greek mythology, has had its present, that there are traces of organic thought in these petrified relics, and that they once formed the surface of the Greek language. The legend of Endymion was present at the time when the people of Elis understood the old saying of the Moon (or Selene) rising under the cover of Night (or in the Latmian cave), to see and admire, in silent love, the beauty of the setting Sun, the sleeper Endymion, the son of Zeus, who had granted to him the double boon of eternal sleep and everlasting youth.

Endymion is not the Sun in the divine character of Phoibos Apollon, but a conception of the Sun in his daily course, as rising early from the womb of Dawn, and after a short and brilliant career, setting in the evening, never to return again to this mortal life. Similar conceptions occur in most mythologies. In Betshuana, an African dialect, "the sun sets" is expressed by "the sun dies."[1] In Aryan mythology the Sun viewed in this light is sometimes represented as divine, yet not immortal; sometimes as living, but sleeping; sometimes as a mortal beloved by a goddess, yet tainted by the fate of humanity. Thus, "Tithonos," a name that has been identified with the Sanskrit "dîdhyâna*h*,"[2] brilliant, expressed originally the idea of the Sun in his daily or yearly character. He also, like Endymion, does not enjoy the full immortality of Zeus and Apollon. Endymion retains his youth, but is doomed to sleep. Tithonos is made immortal, but as Eos forgot to ask for his eternal youth, he pines away as a decrepit old man, in the arms of his ever youthful wife, who loved him when he was young, and

[1] See Pott, Kuhn's *Zeitschrift*, vol. ii. p. 109.

[2] See Sonne, "On Charis," in Kuhn's *Zeitschrift*, vol. x. p. 178.

is kind to him in his old age. Other traditions, careless about contradictions, or ready to solve them sometimes by the most atrocious expedients, call Tithonos the son of Eos and Kephalos, as Endymion was the son of Protogeneia, the Dawn; and this very freedom in handling a myth seems to show, that at first, a Greek knew what it meant if Eos was said to leave every morning the bed of Tithonos. As long as this expression was understood, I should say that the myth was present; it was passed when Tithonos had been changed into a son of Laomedon, a brother of Priamos, a prince of Troy. Then the saying, that Eos left his bed in the morning, became mythical, and had none but a conventional or traditional meaning. Then, as Tithonos was a prince of Troy, his son, the Ethiopian Memnon, had to take part in the Trojan war. And yet how strange! — even then the old myth seems to float through the dim memory of the poet! — for when Eos weeps for her son, the beautiful Memnon, her tears are called "morning-dew," — so that the past may be said to have been still half-present.

As we have mentioned Kephalos as the beloved of Eos, and the father of Tithonos, we may add, that Kephalos also, like Tithonos and Endymion, was one of the many names of the Sun. Kephalos, however, was the rising sun — the head of light, — an expression frequently used of the sun in different mythologies. In the Veda, where the sun is addressed as a horse, the head of the horse is an expression meaning the rising sun. Thus, the poet says (Rv. I. 163, 6), "I have known through my mind thyself when it was still far — thee, the bird flying up from below the sky; I saw a head with wings, toiling on smooth and dustless paths." The Teutonic nations speak of the sun as the eye of Wuotan, as Hesiod speaks of—

Πάντα ἰδὼν Διὸς ὀφθαλμὸς καὶ πάντα νοήσας;

and they also call the sun the face of their god.[1] In the Veda, again, the sun is called (I. 115, 1) "the face of the gods," or "the face of Aditi" (I. 113, 19); and it is said that the winds obscure the eye of the sun by showers of rain (V. 59, 5).

A similar idea led the Greeks to form the name of Kephalos; and if Kephalos is called the son of Herse — the Dew, — this patronymic meant the same in mythological language that we should express by the sun rising over dewy fields. What is told of Kephalos is, that he was the husband of Prokris, that he loved her, and that they vowed to be faithful to one another. But Eos also loves Kephalos; she tells her love, and Kephalos, true to Prokris, does not accept it. Eos, who knows her rival, replies, that he might remain faithful to Prokris, till Prokris had broken her vow. Kephalos accepts the challenge, approaches his wife disguised as a stranger, and gains her love. Prokris, discovering her shame, flies to Kreta. Here Diana gives her a dog and a spear, that never miss their aim, and Prokris returns to Kephalos disguised as a huntsman. While hunting with Kephalos, she is asked by him to give him the dog and the spear. She promises to do so only in return for his love, and when he has assented, she discloses herself, and is again accepted by Kephalos. Yet Prokris fears the charms of Eos; and while jealously watching her husband, she is killed by him unintentionally, by the spear that never misses its aim.

[1] Grimm, *Deutsche Mythologie*, p. 666.

Before we can explain this myth, which, however, is told with many variations by Greek and Latin poets, we must dissect it, and reduce it to its constituent elements.

The first is "Kephalos loves Prokris." Prokris we must explain by a reference to Sanskrit, where "prush" and "p*r*ish" mean to sprinkle, and are used chiefly with reference to rain-drops. For instance (Rv. I. 168, 8): "The lightnings laugh down upon the earth, when the winds shower forth the rain."

The same root in the Teutonic languages has taken the sense of "frost;" and Bopp identifies "prush" with O. H. G. "frus," "frigere." In Greek we must refer to the same root πρώξ, πρωκός, a dew-drop, and also "Prŏkris," the dew.[1] Thus, the wife of Kephalos is only a repetition of Herse, her mother, — "Herse," dew, being derived from Sanskrit "v*r*ish,"[2] to sprinkle;

[1] I see no reason to modify this etymology of "Prokris." "P*r*ish" in Sanskrit means to sprinkle, and "p*r*ishita" occurs in the sense of shower, in "vidyut-stanayitnu-p*r*ishiteshu," "during lightning, thunder, and rain," *Gobh.* 3, 3, 15, where Professor Roth ingeniously, but without necessity, suspects the original reading to have been "prushita." "P*r*ishat," fem. "p*r*ishatî," means sprinkled, and is applied to a speckled deer, a speckled cow, a speckled horse. "P*r*ishata," too, has the same meaning, but is likewise used in the sense of drops. "Prush," a cognate root, means in Sanskrit to sprinkle, and from it we have "prushva," the rainy season, and "prushvâ," a drop, but more particularly a frozen drop, or frost. Now, it is perfectly true, that the final *sh* of "p*r*ish" or "prush" is not regularly represented in Greek by a guttural consonant. But we find that in Sanskrit itself the lingual *sh* of this root varies with the palatal *s*, for instance, in "p*r*is-ni," speckled; and Professor Curtius has rightly traced the Greek περκ-νός, spotted, back to the same root as the Sanskrit "p*r*is-ni," and has clearly established for πρόξ and προκάς, the original meaning of a speckled deer. From the same root, therefore, not only πρώξ, a dew-drop, but προκ-ρίς also may be derived, in the sense of dew or hoar-frost, the derivative syllable being the same as in νεβ-ρίς, or ἴδ-ρις, gen. ιος or ιδος.

[2] This derivation of ἕρση, dew, from the Sanskrit root "v*r*ish" has been questioned, because Sanskrit *v* is generally represented in Greek by the

"Prokris," dew, from a Sanskrit root "prush," having the same sense. The first part of our myth, therefore, means simply, "the Sun kisses the Morning Dew."

The second saying is "Eos loves Kephalos." This requires no explanation; it is the old story, repeated a hundred times in Aryan mythology, "The Dawn loves the Sun."

The third saying was, "Prokris is faithless; yet her new lover, though in a different guise, is still the same Kephalos." This we may interpret as a poetical expression for the rays of the sun being reflected in various colors from the dew-drops, — so that Prokris may be said to be kissed by many lovers; yet they are all the same Kephalos, disguised, but at last recognized.

The last saying was, "Prokris is killed by Kephalos," *i. e.* the dew is absorbed by the sun. Prokris dies for her love to Kephalos, and he must kill her because he loves her. It is the gradual and inevitable absorption of the dew by the glowing rays of the sun which is expressed, with so much truth, by the unerring shaft of Kephalos thrown unintentionally at Prokris hidden in the thicket of the forest.[1]

We have only to put these four sayings together, and every poet will at once tell us the story of the love and jealousy of Kephalos, Prokris, and Eos. If

digamma, or the spiritus lenis. But in Greek we find both ἕρση and ἔρση, a change of frequent occurrence, though difficult to explain. In the same manner the Greek has ἵστωρ and ἴστωρ, from the root "vid," ἑστία from a root "vas"; and the Attic peculiarity of aspirating unaspirated initial vowels was well known even to ancient grammarians (Curtius, *Grundzüge*, p. 617). Forms like ἐέρση and ἄερσα clearly prove the former presence of a digamma (Curtius, *Grundzüge*, p. 509).

[1] "La rugiada
Pugna col sole." — Dante, *Purgatorio*, i. 121.

anything was wanted to confirm the solar nature of Kephalos, we might point out how the first meeting of Kephalos and Prokris takes place on Mount Hymettos, and how Kephalos throws himself afterwards, in despair, into the sea, from the Leukadian mountains. Now, the whole myth belongs to Attika, and here the sun would rise, during the greater part of the year, over Mount Hymettos like a brilliant head. A straight line from this, the most eastern point, to the most western headland of Greece, carries us to the Leukadian promontory, — and here Kephalos might well be said to have drowned his sorrows in the waves of the ocean.

Another magnificent sunset looms in the myth of the death of Herakles. His twofold character as a god and as a hero is acknowledged even by Herodotos; and some of his epithets are sufficient to indicate his solar character, though, perhaps, no name has been made the vehicle of so many mythological and historical, physical and moral stories, as that of Herakles. Names which he shares with Apollo and Zeus are Δαφνηφόρος, Ἀλεξίκακος, Μάντις, Ἰδαῖος, Ὀλύμπιος, Παγγενέτωρ.

Now, in his last journey, Herakles also, like Kephalos, proceeds from east to west. He is performing his sacrifice to Zeus, on the Kenæon promontory of Eubœa, when Deianeira (" dâsya-narî "=" dâsa-patnî ") sends him the fatal garment. He then throws Lichas into the sea, who is transformed into the Lichadian islands. From thence Herakles crosses over to Trachys, and then to Mount Oeta, where his pile is raised, and the hero is burnt, rising through the clouds to the seat of the immortal gods — himself henceforth immortal and wedded to Hebe, the goddess of youth. The coat which Deianeira sends to the solar hero is an expression frequently used in other mythologies; it is the coat which in the Veda, "the mothers weave for their bright son,"—the clouds which rise from the waters and surround the sun like a dark raiment. Herakles tries to tear it off; his fierce splendor breaks through the thickening gloom, but fiery mists embrace him, and are mingled with the parting rays of the sun, and the dying hero is seen through the scattered clouds of the sky, tearing his own body to pieces, till at last his bright form is consumed in a general conflagration, his last-beloved being Iole, — perhaps the violet-colored evening clouds, — a word which, as it reminds us also of ἰός, poison (though the ι is long), may perhaps have originated the myth of a poisoned garment.

In these legends the Greek language supplies almost all that is necessary in order to render these strange stories intelligible and rational, though the later Greeks — I mean Homer and Hesiod — had certainly in most cases no suspicion of the original import of their own traditions. But as there are Greek words which find no explanation in Greek, and which, without a reference to Sanskrit and the other cognate dialects, would have forever remained to the philologist mere sounds with a conventional meaning, there are also names of gods and heroes inexplicable from a Greek point of view, and which cannot be made to disclose their primitive character, unless confronted with contemporary witnesses from India, Persia, Italy, or Germany. Another myth of the dawn will best explain this: —

"Ahan" in Sanskrit is a name of the day, and is said to stand for "dahan," like "asru," tear, for "dasru," Greek δάκρυ. Whether we have to admit an actual loss of this initial *d*, or whether the *d* is to be considered rather as a secondary letter, by which the root "ah" was individualized to "dah," is a question which does not concern us at present. In Sanskrit we have the root "dah," which means to burn, and from which a name of the day might have been formed in the same manner as "dyu," day, is formed from "dyu," to be brilliant. Nor does it concern us here, whether the Gothic "daga," nom. "dag-s," day, is the same word or not. According to Grimm's law, "daha," in Sanskrit should in Gothic appear as "taga," and not as "daga." However, there are several roots in which the aspiration affects either the first or the last letter or both. This would give us "dhah" as a secondary type of "dah," and thus remove the apparent irregularity of the Gothic "daga."[1] Bopp seems inclined to consider "daga" and "daha" identical in origin. Certain it is that the same root from which the Teutonic words for day are formed, has also given rise to the name for dawn. In German we say, "der Morgen tagt;" and in Old English day was "dawe;" while to dawn was in Anglo-Saxon "dagian." Now, in the Veda, one of the names of the dawn is "Ahanâ." It occurs only once (Rv. I. 123, 4): —

"G*r*ihám g*r*iham Ahanấ yâti á*kk*h*a
Divé dive ádhi nấma dádhânâ
Sísâsantî Dyotanấ sâsvat ấ agât
A′gram agram ít bha*g*ate vásûnâm."

"Ahanâ (the dawn) comes near to every house, — she who makes every day to be known.

"Dyotanâ (the dawn), the active maiden, comes

[1] This change of aspiration has been fully illustrated, and well explained by Grassmann, in Kuhn's *Zeitschrift*, vol. xii. p. 110.

back for evermore, — she enjoys always the first of all goods."

We have already seen the Dawn in various relations to the Sun, but not yet as the beloved of the Sun, flying before her lover, and destroyed by his embrace. This, however, was a very familiar expression in the old mythological language of the Aryans. The Dawn has died in the arms of the Sun, or the Dawn is flying before the Sun, or the Sun has shattered the car of the Dawn, were expressions meaning simply, the sun has risen, the dawn is gone. Thus, we read in the Rv. IV. 30, in a hymn celebrating the achievements of Indra, the chief solar deity of the Veda: —

"And this strong and manly deed also thou hast performed, O Indra, that thou struckest the daughter of Dyaus (the Dawn), a woman difficult to vanquish.

"Yes, even the daughter of Dyaus, the magnified, the Dawn, thou, O Indra, a great hero, hast ground to pieces.

"The Dawn rushed off from her crushed car, fearing that Indra, the bull, might strike her.

"This her car lay there well ground to pieces; she went far away."

In this case, Indra behaves rather unceremoniously to the daughter of the sky; but, in other places, she is loved by all the bright gods of heaven, not excluding her own father. The Sun, it is said (Rv. I. 115, 2), follows her from behind, as a man follows a woman. "She, the Dawn, whose cart is drawn by white horses, is carried away in triumph by the two Asvins," as the Leukippides are carried off by the Dioskuroi.

If now we translate, or rather transliterate, "Dahanâ" into Greek, Dáphne stands before us, and her whole history is intelligible. Daphne is young and beautiful, — Apollo loves her, — she flies before him, and dies as he embraces her with his brilliant rays. Or, as another poet of the Veda (X. 189) expresses it, "The Dawn comes near to him, — she expires as soon as he begins to breathe, — the mighty one irradiates the sky." Any one who has eyes to see and a heart to feel with nature like the poets of old, may still see Dahne and Apollo, — the dawn rushing and trembling through the sky, and fading away at the sudden approach of the bright sun. Thus even in so modern a poet as Swift, the old poetry of nature breaks through when, in his address to Lord Harley on his marriage, he writes: —

"So the bright Empress of the Morn
Chose for her spouse a mortal born:
The Goddess made advances first,
Else what aspiring hero durst?
Though like a maiden of fifteen
She blushes when by mortals seen:
Still blushes, and with haste retires
When Sol pursues her with his fires."

The metamorphosis of Daphne into a laurel-tree is a continuation of the myth of peculiarly Greek growth. Daphne, in Greek, meant no longer the dawn, but it had become the name of the laurel.[1] Hence the

[1] Professor Curtius admits my explanation of the myth of Daphne as the dawn, but he says, "If we could but see why the dawn is changed into a laurel!" I have explained before the influence of homonymy in the growth of early myths, and this is only another instance of this influence. The dawn was called δάφνη, the burning, so was the laurel, as wood that burns easily. Afterward the two, as usual, were supposed to be one, or to have some connection with each other, for how, the people would say, could they have the same name? See *Etym. M.* p. 250, 20, δαυχμόν· εὔκαυστον ξύλον; Hesych. δαυχμόν· ἔνκαυστον ξύλον δάφνης (l. εὔκαυστον ξύλον δάφνην, Ahrens, *Dial. Græc.* ii. 532). Legerlotz, in Kuhn's *Zeitschrift*, vol. vii. p. 292. *Lectures on the Science of Language*, Second Series, p. 502.

tree Daphne was considered sacred to the lover of Daphne, the dawn, and Daphne herself was fabled to have been changed into a tree when praying to her mother to protect her from the violence of Apollo.

Without the help of the Veda, the name of Daphne and the legend attached to her, would have remained unintelligible, for the later Sanskrit supplies no key to this name. This shows the value of the Veda for the purpose of comparative mythology, a science which, without the Veda, would have remained mere guess-work, without fixed principles and without a safe basis.[1]

In order to show in how many different ways the same idea may be expressed mythologically, I have confined myself to the names of the dawn. The dawn is really one of the richest sources of Aryan mythology; and another class of legends, embodying the strife between winter and summer, the return of spring, the revival of nature, is in most languages but a reflection and amplification of the more ancient stories telling of the strife between night and day, the return of the morn, the revival of the whole world. The stories, again, of solar heroes fighting through a thunder-storm against the powers of darkness, are borrowed from the same source; and the cows, so frequently alluded to in the Veda, as carried off by V*r*itra and brought back by Indra, are in reality the same bright cows which the Dawn drives out every morning to their pasture ground; sometimes the clouds, which, from their heavy udders, send down refreshing and fertilizing rain or

[1] For another development of the same word "Ahanâ," leading ultimately to the myth of Athene, see *Lectures on the Science of Language*, Second Series, p. 502.

dew upon the parched earth; sometimes the bright days themselves, that seem to step out one by one from the dark stable of the night, and to be carried off from their wide pasture by the dark powers of the West. There is no sight in nature more elevating than the dawn even to us, whom philosophy would wish to teach that *nil admirari* is the highest wisdom. Yet in ancient times the power of admiring was the greatest blessing bestowed on mankind; and when could man have admired more intensely, when could his heart have been more gladdened and overpowered with joy, than at the approach of—

> "the Lord of light,
> Of life, of love, and gladness!"

The darkness of night fills the human heart with despondency and awe, and a feeling of fear and anguish sets every nerve trembling. There is man like a forlorn child, fixing his eye with breathless anxiety upon the East, the womb of day, where the light of the world has flamed up so many times before. As the father waits the birth of his child, so the poet watches the dark heaving Night who is to bring forth her bright son, the sun of the day. The doors of heaven seem slowly to open, and what are called the bright flocks of the Dawn step out of the dark stable, returning to their wonted pastures. Who has not seen the gradual advance of this radiant procession,—the heaven like a distant sea tossing its golden waves,—when the first rays shoot forth like brilliant horses racing round the whole course of the horizon,—when the clouds begin to color up, each shedding her own radiance over her more distant sisters! Not only the east, but the west, and the south, and the north, the whole temple of heaven is illuminated, and the pious worshipper lights in response his own small light on the altar of his hearth, and stammers words which express but faintly the joy that is in nature and in his own throbbing heart: —

"Rise! Our life, our spirit has come back! the darkness is gone, the light approaches!"

If the people of antiquity called these eternal lights of heaven their gods, their bright ones ("deva"), the Dawn was the first-born among all the gods, — Protogeneia, — dearest to man, and always young and fresh. But if not raised to an immortal state, if only admired as a kind being, awakening every morning the children of man, her life would seem to be short. She soon fades away, and dies when the fountain-head of light rises in naked splendor, and sends his first swift glance through the vault of heaven. We cannot realize that sentiment with which the eye of antiquity dwelt on these sights of nature. To us all is law, order, necessity. We calculate the refractory power of the atmosphere, we measure the possible length of the dawn in every climate, and the rising of the sun is to us nc greater surprise than the birth of a child. But if we could believe again, that there was in the sun a being like our own, that in the dawn there was a soul open to human sympathy, — if we could bring ourselves to look for a moment upon these powers as personal, free, and adorable, how different would be our feelings at the blush of day! That Titanic assurance with which we say, the sun *must* rise, was unknown to the early worshippers of nature, or if they also began to feel the regularity with which the sun and the other stars perform their daily labor, they still thought of free beings kept in temporary servitude, chained for a time, and bound to obey a higher will, but sure to rise, like Herakles, to a higher glory at the end of their labors. It seems to us childish when we read in the Veda such expressions as, "Will the Sun rise?" "Will our old friend, the Dawn, come back again?" "Will the powers of darkness be conquered by the God of light?" And when the Sun rose, they wondered how, but just born, he was so mighty, and strangled, as it were, in his cradle, the serpents of the night. They asked how he could walk along the sky? why there was no dust on his road? why he did not fall backward? But at last they greeted him like the poet of our own time,—

"Hail, orient Conqueror of gloomy Night!"

and the human eye felt that it could not bear the brilliant majesty of him whom they call "the Life, the Breath, the brilliant Lord and Father."

Thus sunrise was the revelation of nature, awakening in the human mind that feeling of dependence, of helplessness, of hope, of joy and faith in higher powers, which is the source of all wisdom, the spring of all religion. But if sunrise inspired the first prayers, called forth the first sacrificial flames, sunset was the other time when, again, the heart of man would tremble, and his mind be filled with awful thoughts. The shadows of night approach, the irresistible power of sleep grasps man in the midst of his pleasures, his friends depart, and in his loneliness his thoughts turn again to higher powers. When the day departs, the poet bewails the untimely death of his bright friend, nay, he sees in his short career the likeness of his own life. Perhaps, when he has fallen asleep, his sun may never rise again, and thus the place to which the setting sun withdraws in the far West rises before his mind as the abode where he himself would go after death, where "his fathers went before him," and where all the wise and the pious rejoice in a "new life with Yama and Varu*n*a." Or he might look upon the sun, not as a short-lived hero, but as young, unchanging, and always the same, while generations after generations of mortal men were passing away. And hence, by the mere force of contrast, the first intimation of beings which do not wither and decay — of immortals, of immortality! Then the poet would implore the immortal sun to come again, to vouchsafe to the sleeper a new morning. The god of day would become the god of time, of life and death. Again, the evening twilight, the sister of the dawn, repeating, though with a more sombre light, the wonders of the morning, how many feelings must it have roused in the musing poet — how many poems must it have elicited in the living language of ancient times! Was it the Dawn that came again to give a last embrace to him who had parted from her in the morning? Was she the immortal, the always returning goddess, and he the mortal, the daily dying sun? Or was she the mortal, bidding a last farewell to her immortal lover, burnt, as it were, on the same pile which would consume her, while he would rise to the seat of the gods?

Let us express these simple scenes in ancient language, and we shall find ourselves surrounded on every side by mythology full of contradictions and incongruities, the same being represented as mortal or immortal, as man or woman, as the poetical eye of man shifts its point of view, and gives its own color to the mysterious play of nature.

One of the myths of the Veda which expresses this

correlation of the Dawn and the Sun, this love between the immortal and the mortal, and the identity of the Morning Dawn and the Evening Twilight, is the story of Urvasî and Purûravas. The two names "Urvasî" and "Purûravas," are to the Hindu mere proper names, and even in the Veda their original meaning has almost entirely faded away. There is a dialogue in the Rig-veda between Urvasî and Purûravas, where both appear personified in the same manner as in the play of "Kalidâsa." The first point, therefore, which we have to prove is that "Urvasî" was originally an appellation, and meant dawn.

The etymology of "Urvasî" is difficult. It cannot be derived from "urva" by means of the suffix "sa,[1]" because there is no such word as "urva," and because derivatives in "sa," like "romasá," "yuvasá," etc., have the accent on the last syllable.[2] I therefore accept the common Indian explanation by which this name is derived from "uru," wide (εὐρυ), and a root "as," to pervade, and thus compare "uru-asî" with another frequent epithet of the Dawn, "urûkî," the feminine of "uru-ak," far-going. It was certainly one of the most striking features, and one by which the Dawn was distinguished from all the other dwellers in the heavens, that she occupies the wide expanse of the sky, and that her horses ride, as it were, with the swiftness of thought round the whole horizon. Hence we find that names beginning with "uru" in Sanskrit, and with εὐρυ in Greek, are almost invariably old mythological names of the Dawn or the Twilight. The earth also, it is true,

[1] Pânini, V. 2, 100.

[2] Other explanations of "Urvasî" may be seen in Professor Roth's edition of the Nirukta, and in the Sanskrit Dictionary published by him and Professor Boehtlingk.

claims this epithet, but in different combinations from those which apply to the bright goddess. Names of the Dawn are Euryphaessa, the mother of Helios; Eurykyde or Eurypyle, the daughter of Endymion; Eurymede, the wife of Glaukos; Eurynome, the mother of the Charites; and Eurydike, the wife of Orpheus, whose character as an ancient god will be discussed hereafter. In the Veda the name of Ushas or Eos is hardly ever mentioned without some allusion to her far and wide-spreading splendor; such as "urviyâ vibhâti," she shines wide; "urviyâ vi*k*âkshe," looking far and wide; "varîyasî," the widest[1], whereas the light of the Sun is not represented as wide-stretching, but rather as far-darting.

But there are other indications beside the mere name of Urva*s*î, which lead us to suppose that she was originally the goddess of the dawn. "Vasish*t*ha," though best known as the name of one of the chief poets of the Veda, is the superlative of "vasu," bright; and as such also a name of the Sun. Thus it happens that expressions which apply properly to the sun only, were transferred to the ancient poet. He is called the son of Mitra and Varu*n*a, night and day, an expression which has a meaning only with regard to Vasish*t*ha, the sun; and as the sun is frequently called the off-

[1] The name which approaches nearest to "Urva*s*î" in Greek might seem to be "Europe," because the palatal *s* is occasionally represented by a Greek π, as *a*s*va*=ἵππος. The only difficulty is the long ω in Greek; otherwise Europe, carried away by the white bull ("v*r*ishan," man, bull, stallion, in the Veda a frequent appellation of the sun, and "*s*veta," white, applied to the same deity), carried away on his back (the sun being frequently represented as behind or below the dawn, see p. 92 and the myth of Eurydike on p. 127); again carried to a distant cave (the gloaming of the evening); and mother of Apollo, the god of daylight, or of Minos (Manu, a mortal Zeus), — all this would well agree with the goddess of the dawn.

spring of the dawn, Vasish*t*ha, the poet, is said to owe his birth to Urva*s*î (Rv. VII. 33, 11). The peculiarity of his birth reminds us strongly of the birth of Aphrodite, as told by Hesiod.

Again, we find that in the few passages where the name of Urva*s*î occurs in the Rig-veda, the same attributes and actions are ascribed to her which usually belong to Ushas, the Dawn.

It is frequently said of Ushas, that she prolongs the life of man, and the same is said of Urva*s*î (V. 41, 19; X. 95, 10). In one passage (Rv. IV. 2, 18) Urva*s*î is even used as a plural, in the sense of many dawns or days increasing the life of man, which shows that the appellative power of the word was not yet quite forgotten. Again, she is called "antarikshaprâ," filling the air, a usual epithet of the sun, "b*r*ihaddivâ," with mighty splendor, all indicating the bright presence of the dawn. However, the best proof that "Urva*s*î" was the dawn is the legend told of her and of her love to Purûravas, a story that is true only of the Sun and the Dawn. That "Purûravas" is an appropriate name of a solar hero requires hardly any proof. "Purûravas" meant the same as πολυδευκής, endowed with much light; for though "rava" is generally used of sound, yet the root "ru," which means originally to cry, is also applied to color,[1] in the sense of a loud or crying color, *i. e.* red (cf. *ruber*, *rufus*, Lith. "rauda,"

[1] Thus it is said (Rv. VI. 3, 6) the fire cries with light, "*so*k*ishâ* *rârapîti*;" the two Spartan Charites are called Κλητά (κλητά, *incluta*) and Φαεννά, *i. e.* Clara, clear shining (see Sonne, in Kuhn's *Zeitschrift*, vol. x. p. 363). In the Veda the rising sun is said to cry like a new-born child (Rv. IX. 74, 1). Professor Kuhn himself has evidently misunderstood my argument. I do not derive "ravas" from "rap," but I only quote "rap" as illustrating the close connection between loudness of sound and brightness of light. See also Justi, *Orient und Occident*, vol. ii. p. 69.

O. H. G. "rôt," "rudhira," ἐρυθρός; also Sanskrit "ravi," sun). Besides, Purûravas calls himself "Vasish*th*a," which, as we know, is a name of the Sun; and if he is called "Ai*d*a," the son of "I*d*â," the same name is elsewhere (Rv. III. 29, 3) given to "Agni," the fire.

Now the story, in its most ancient form, is found in the Brâhma*n*a of the Ya*g*ur-veda. There we read: —

"Urva*s*î, a kind of fairy, fell in love with Purûravas, the son of I*d*â, and when she met him, she said: 'Embrace me three times a day, but never against my will, and let me never see you without your royal garments, for this is the manner of women.' In this manner she lived with him a long time, and she was with child. Then her former friends, the Gandharvas, said: 'This Urva*s*î has now dwelt a long time among mortals; let us see that she come back.' Now, there was a ewe, with two lambs, tied to the couch of Urva*s*î and Purûravas, and the Gandharvas stole one of them. Urva*s*î said: 'They take away my darling, as if I lived in a land where there is no hero and no man.' They stole the second, and she upbraided her husband again. Then Purûravas looked and said: 'How can that be a land without heroes or men where I am?' And naked, he sprang up; he thought it too long to put on his dress. Then the Gandharvas sent a flash of lightning, and Urva*s*î saw her husband naked as by daylight. Then she vanished; 'I come back,' she said — and went. Then he bewailed his vanished love in bitter grief; and went near Kurukshetra. There is a lake there, called "Anyata*h*plaksha," full of lotus flowers, and while the king walked along its border, the fairies were playing there in the water, in the shape of birds. And Urvasî discovered him, and said: —

"'That is the man with whom I dwelt so long.' Then her friends said: 'Let us appear to him.' She agreed, and they appeared before him. Then the king recognized her and said: —

"'Lo! my wife! stay, thou cruel in mind! let us now exchange some words! Our secrets, if they are not told now, will not bring us luck on any later day.'

"She replied: 'What shall I do with thy speech? I am gone like the first of the dawns. Purûravas, go home again! I am hard to be caught, like the wind.'

"He said, in despair: 'Then may thy former friend now fall down, never to rise again; may he go far, far away! May he lie down on the threshold of death, and may rabid wolves there devour him!'

"She replied: 'Purûravas, do not die! do not fall down! let not evil wolves devour thee! there is no friendship with women, their hearts are the hearts of wolves. When I walked among mortals under a different form — when I dwelt with thee, four nights of the autumn, I ate once a day a small piece of butter — and even now I feel pleasure from it.'

"Thus, at last, her heart melted, and she said: 'Come to me the last night of the year, and thou shalt be with me for one night, and a son will be born to thee.' He went the last night of the year to the golden seats, and while he was alone, he was told to go up, and then they sent Urvasî to him. Then she said: 'The Gandharvas will to-morrow grant thee a wish; choose!' He said: 'Choose thou for me.' She replied: 'Say to them, let me be one of you.' Early the next morn, the Gandharvas gave him his choice;

but when he said 'Let me be one of you,' they said: 'That kind of sacred fire is not yet known among men, by which he could perform a sacrifice, and become one of ourselves.' They then initiated Purûravas in the mysteries of a certain sacrifice, and when he had performed it, he became himself one of the Gandharvas."

This is the simple story, told in the Brâhma*n*a, and it is told there in order to show the importance of a peculiar rite, the rite of kindling the fire by friction, which is represented as the one by which Purûravas obtained immortality.[1] The verses quoted in the story are taken from the Rig-veda, where we find, in the last book, together with many strange relics of popular poetry, a dialogue between the two celestial lovers. It consists of seventeen verses, while the author of the Brâhma*n*a knew only fifteen. In one of the verses which he quotes, Urvasî says, "I am gone forever, like the first of the dawns," which shows a strange glimmering of the old myth in the mind of the poet, and reminds us of the tears which the mother of Memnon shed over the corpse of her son, and which even by later poets are called morning dew. Again, in the fourth verse, Urvasî addressing herself, says: "This person (that is to say I), when she was wedded to him, O Dawn! she went to his house, and was embraced by him day and night." Again, she tells Purûravas that he was created by the gods in order to slay the powers of darkness ("dasyuhatyâya"), a task invariably ascribed to Indra and other solar beings.

[1] A most interesting and ingenious explanation of this ceremony is given by Professor Kuhn, in his Essay, *Die Herabkunft, des Feuers*, p. 79. The application of that ceremony to the old myth of Urvasî and Purûravas belongs clearly to a later age: it is an after-thought that could only arise with people who wished to find a symbolical significance in every act of their traditional ritual.

Even the names of the companions of Urvasi point to the dawn, and Purûravas says: —

"When I, the mortal, threw my arms around those flighty immortals, they trembled away from me like a trembling doe, like horses that kick against the cart."

No goddess is so frequently called the friend of man as the Dawn. "She goes to every house" (I. 123, 4); "she thinks of the dwelling of man" (I. 123, 1); "she does not despise the small or the great" (I. 124, 6); "she brings wealth" (I. 48, 1); "she is always the same, immortal, divine" (I. 124, 4; I. 123, 8); "she does not grow old" (I. 113, 15); "she is the young goddess, but she makes man grow old" (I. 92, 11). Thus Purûravas called Urvasî "the immortal among the mortals;" and, in his last verse, he addressed his beloved in the following words: —

"I, the brightest Sun, I hold Urvasî, her who fills the air (with light), who spreads the sky. May the blessing of thy kind deed be upon thee! Come back, the heart burns me."

Then the poet says: —

"Thus the gods spake to thee, O son of I*d*â; in order that thou, bound to death, mayest grow to be this (immortal), thy race should worship the gods with oblations! Then thou also wilt rejoice in heaven."

We must certainly admit, that even in the Veda, the poets were as ignorant of the original meaning of Urvasî and Purûravas as Homer was of Tithonos, if not of Eos. To them they were heroes, indefinite beings, men yet not men, gods yet not gods. But to us, though placed at a much greater distance, they disclose their true meaning. As Wordsworth says: —

"Not unrejoiced, I see thee climb the sky
In naked splendor, clear from mist and haze" —

Antiquity spoke of the naked Sun, and of the chaste Dawn hiding her face when she had seen her husband. Yet she says she will come again. And after the Sun has travelled through the world in search of his beloved, when he comes to the threshold of death, and is going to end his solitary life, she appears again in the gloaming, the same as the dawn,—as Eos in Homer begins and ends the day, — and she carries him away to the golden seats of the immortals.[1]

I have selected this myth chiefly in order to show how ancient poetry is only the faint echo of ancient language, and how it was the simple story of nature which inspired the early poet, and held before his mind that deep mirror in which he might see reflected the passions of his own soul. For the heart of man, as long as it knows but its own bitterness, is silent and sullen. It does not tell its love and its loss. There may be a mute poetry in solitary grief, but "Mnemosyne," the musing goddess of recollection, is not a muse herself, though she is the mother of the Muses. It is the sympathy with the grief of others which first gives utterance to the poet's grief, and opens the lips of a silent despair. And if his pain was too deep and too sacred, if he could not compare it to the suffering of any other human heart, the ancient poet had still the heart of nature to commune with, and in her silent suffering he saw a noble likeness of what he felt and suffered within himself. When, after a dark night, the light of the day returned, he thought of his own light that would never rise again. When he saw the

1 *Od.* v. 390. ἀλλ' ὅτε δὴ τρίτον ἦμαρ ἐϋπλόκαμος τέλεσ' Ἠώς. For different explanations of this and similar verses, see Völcker, *Über homerische Geographie und Weltkunde*, Hannover, 1830, p. 31.

Sun kissing the Dawn, he dreamt of days and joys gone forever. And when the Dawn trembled, and grew pale, and departed, and when the Sun seemed to look for her, and to lose her the more his brilliant eye sought her, an image would rise in his mind, and he would remember his own fate and yet forget it, while telling in measured words the love and loss of the Sun. Such was the origin of poetry. Nor was the evening without its charms. And when, at the end of a dreary day, the Sun seemed to die away in the far West, still looking for his Eastern bride, and suddenly the heavens opened, and the glorious image of the Dawn rose again, her beauty deepened by a gloaming sadness — would not the poet gaze till the last ray had vanished, and would not the last vanishing ray linger in his heart, and kindle there a hope of another life, where he would find again what he had loved and lost on earth?

> "There is a radiant, though a short-lived flame,
> That burns for poets in the dawning east;
> And oft my soul has kindled at the same,
> When the captivity of sleep had ceased."

There is much suffering in nature to those who have eyes for silent grief, and it is this tragedy — the tragedy of nature — which is the life-spring of all the tragedies of the ancient world. The idea of a young hero, whether he is called "Baldr," or "Sigurd," or "Sîfrit," or "Achilles," or "Meleager," or "Kephalos," dying in the fullness of youth, a story so frequently told, localized, and individualized, was first suggested by the Sun, dying in all his youthful vigor, either at the end of a day, conquered by the powers of darkness, or at the end of the sunny season, stung by the thorn of Winter. Again, that fatal spell by which these sunny heroes must leave their first love, become unfaithful to her or she to them, was borrowed from nature. The fate of these solar heroes was inevitable, and it was their lot to die by the hand or by the unwilling treachery of their nearest friends or relatives. The Sun forsakes the Dawn, and dies at the end of the day according to an inexorable fate, and bewailed by the whole of nature. Or the Sun is the Sun of Spring, who woos the Earth, and then forsakes his bride and grows cold, and is killed at last by the thorn of Winter. It is an old story, but it is forever new in the mythology and the legends of the ancient world. Thus Baldr, in the Scandinavian "Edda," the divine prototype of Sigurd and Sîfrit, is beloved by the whole world. Gods and men, the whole of nature, all that grows and lives, had sworn to his mother not to hurt the bright hero. The mistletoe alone, that does not grow on the earth, but on trees, had been forgotten, and with it Baldr is killed at the winter solstice: —

> "So on the floor lay Balder, dead; and round
> Lay thickly strewn, swords, axes, darts, and spears,
> Which all the gods in sport had idly thrown
> At Balder, whom no weapon pierced or clove:
> But in his breast stood fixt the fatal bough
> Of mistletoe, which Lok, the accuser, gave
> To Hoder, and unwitting Hoder threw:
> 'Gainst that alone had Balder's life no charm."

Thus Isfendiyar, in the Persian epic, cannot be wounded by any weapon, yet it is his fate to be killed by a thorn, which, as an arrow, is thrown into his eye by Rustem. Rustem, again, can only be killed by his brother; Herakles, by the mistaken kindness of his wife; Sîfrit, by the anxious solicitude of Kriemhilt, or by the jealousy of Brunhilt, whom he had forsaken. He is vulnerable in one spot only, like Achilles, and it is there where Hagene (the thorn) strikes him. All these are fragments of solar myths. The whole of nature was divided into two realms — the one dark, cold, wintry, and deathlike, the other bright, warm, vernal, and full of life. Sigurd, as the solar hero is called in the "Edda," the descendant of Odin, slays the serpent Fafnir, and conquers the treasure on which Andvari, the dwarf, had pronounced his curse. This is the treasure of the Niflungs or Nibelungs, the treasure of the earth, which the nebulous powers of winter and darkness had carried away like robbers. The vernal sun wins it back, and like Demeter, rich in the possession of her restored daughter, the earth becomes for a time rich with all the treasures of spring.[1] He then, according to the "Edda," delivers Brynhild, who had been doomed to a magic sleep after being wounded with a thorn by Odin, but who is now, like the spring after the sleep of winter, brought back to new life by the love of Sigurd. But he, the lord of the treasure ("vasupati"), is driven onward by his fate. He plights his troth to Brynhild, and gives her the fatal ring he had taken from the treasure. But he must leave her, and when he arrives at the castle of Gunnar, Gunnar's wife, Grimhild, makes him forget Brynhild, and he marries her daughter, Gudrun. Already his course begins to decline. He is bound to Gunnar, nay, he must conquer for him his own former bride, Brynhild, whom Gunnar now marries. Gunnar Gjukason seems to signify darkness, and thus we see that

[1] Cf. Rig-veda V. 47, 1: "Prayuñ*g*atî diva*h* eti bruvâ*n*â mahî mâtâ duhitu*h* bodhayantî, âvivâsantî yuvati*h* manîshâ pit*r*ibhya*h* â sadane *g*ohuvânâ." On "mahî mâtâ"=*Magna Mater*, see Grassmann, in Kuhn's *Zeitschrift*, vol. xvi. p. 169. "Duhitur bodhayantî," inquiring for or finding her daughter.

the awakening and budding spring is gone, carried away by Gunnar, like Proserpina by Pluto; like Sîtâ by Râva*n*a. Gudrun, the daughter of Grimhild, and sometimes herself called Grimhild, whether the latter name meant summer (cf. "gharma" in Sanskrit) or, the earth and nature in the latter part of the year, is a sister of the dark Gunnar, and though now married to the bright Sigurd, she belongs herself to the nebulous regions. Gunnar, who has forced Sigurd to yield him Brynhild, is now planning the death of his kinsman, because Brynhild has discovered in Sigurd her former lover, and must have her revenge. Högni dissuades his brother Gunnar from the murder; but at last the third brother Hödr, stabs Sigurd while he is asleep at the winter solstice. Brynhild has always loved him, and when her hero is killed she distributes the treasure, and is burnt, like Nanna, on the same pile with Sigurd, a sword being placed between the two lovers. Gudrun also bewails the death of her husband, but she forgets him, and marries Atli, the brother of Brynhild. Atli now claims the treasure from Gunnar and Högni, by right of his wife, and when they refuse to give it up, he invites them to his house, and makes them prisoners. Gunnar still refuses to reveal the spot where the treasure is buried till he sees the heart of Högni, his brother. A heart is brought him, but it quivers, and he says, "This is not the heart of my brother." The real heart of Högni is brought at last, and Gunnar says, "Now I alone know where the treasure lies, and the Rhine shall rather have it than I will give it up to thee." He is then bound by Atli, and thrown among serpents. But even the serpents he charms by playing on the harp with his teeth, till at last one viper crawls up to him, and kills him.

How much has this myth been changed, when we find it again in the poem of the "Nibelunge" as it was written down at the end of the twelfth century in Germany! All the heroes are Christians, and have been mixed up with historical persons of the fourth, fifth, and sixth centuries. Gunther is localized in Burgundy, where we know that, in 435, a Gundicarius or Gundaharius happened to be a real king, the same who, according to Cassiodorus, was vanquished first by Aetius, and afterwards by the Huns of Attila. Hence Atli, the brother of Brynhild, and the second husband of Gudrun (or Kriemhilt), is identified with Attila, the king of the Huns (453); nay, even the brother of Attila, Bleda, is brought in as Blödelin, the first who attacked the Burgundians, and was killed by Dankwart. Other historical persons were drawn into the vortex of the popular story, persons for whom there is no precedent at all in the "Edda." Thus we find in the "Nibelunge" Dietrich von Bern, who is no other but Theodoric the Great (455–525), who conquered Odoacer in the battle of Ravenna (the famous Rabenschlacht), and lived at Verona, in German, Bern. Irenfried, again, introduced in the poem as the Landgrave of Thuringia, has been discovered to be Hermanfried, the king of Thuringia, married to Amalaberg, the niece of Theodoric. The most extraordinary coincidence, however, is that by which Sigurd, the lover of Brynhild, has been identified with Siegbert, king of Austrasia from 561 to 575, who was actually married to the famous Brunehault, who actually defeated the Huns, and was actually murdered under the most tragical circumstances by Fredegond, the mistress of his brother Chilperic. This coincidence between myth and history is so great, that it has induced some euhemeristic critics to derive the whole legend of the "Nibelunge" from Austrasian history, and to make the murder of Siegbert by Brunehault the basis of the murder of Sîfrit or Sigurd by Brynhild. Fortunately, it is easier to answer these German than the old Greek euhemerists, for we find in contemporary history that Jornandes, who wrote his history at least twenty years before the death of the Austrasian Siegbert, knew already the daughter of the mythic Sigurd, Swanhild, who was born, according to the "Edda," after the murder of his father, and afterwards killed by Jörmunrek, whom the poem has again historicized in Hermanricus, a Gothic king of the fourth century.

Let us now apply to the Greek myths what we have learned from the gradual growth of the German myth. There are evidently historical facts round which the myth of Herakles has crystallized, only we cannot substantiate them so clearly as in the myth of the "Nibelunge," because we have there no contemporaneous historical documents. Yet as the chief Herakles is represented as belonging to the royal family of Argos, there may have been a Herakles, perhaps the son of a king called Amphitryo, whose descendants, after a temporary exile, reconquered that part of Greece which had formerly been under the sway of Herakles. The traditions of the miraculous birth, of many of his heroic adventures, and of his death, were as little based on historical facts as the legends of Sîfrit. In Herakles killing the Chimæra and similar monsters, we see the reflected image of the Delphian Apollo killing the worm, or of Zeus, the god of the brilliant sky, with whom Herakles shares in common the names of Idæos,

Olympios, and Pangenetor. As the myth of Sigurd and Gunnar throws its last broken rays on the kings of Burgundy, and on Attila and Theodoric, the myth of the solar Herakles was realized in some semi-historical prince of Argos and Mykenæ. Herakles may have been the name of the national god of the Heraklidæ, and this would explain the enmity of Hêrê, whose worship flourished in Argos before the Dorian immigration. What was formerly told of a god was transferred to Herakles, the leader of the Heraklidæ, the worshippers or sons of Herakles, while, at the same time, many local and historical facts connected with the Heraklidæ and their leaders may have been worked up with the myth of the divine hero. The idea of Herakles being, as it were, the bond-servant of Eurystheus, is of solar origin — it is the idea of the sun fettered to his work, and toiling for men, his inferiors in strength and virtue.[1] Thus Sîfrit is toiling for Gunther, and even Apollo is for one year the slave of Laomedon — pregnant expressions, necessitated by the absence of more abstract verbs, and familiar even to modern poets: —

> "As aptly suits therewith that modest pace
> Submitted to the chains
> That bind thee to the path which God ordains
> That thou shouldst trace."

The later growth of epic and tragical poetry may be Greek, or Indian, or Teutonic; it may take the dif-

[1] The Peruvian Inca, Yupanqui, denied the pretension of the sun to be the doer of all things, for if he were free, he would go and visit other parts of the heavens where he had never been. "He is," said the Inca, "like a tied beast who goes ever round and round in the same track." *Garcilaso de la Vega*, part I. viii. 8. Acosta, *Historia del Nuevo Orbe*, cap. v. Tylor, *Early History of Mankind*, p. 343. Brinton, *The Myths of the New World*, p. 55.

ferent colors of the different skies, the different warmth of the different climes; nay, it may attract and absorb much that is accidental and historical. But if we cut into it and analyze it, the blood that runs through all the ancient poetry is the same blood; it is the ancient mythical speech. The atmosphere in which the early poetry of the Aryans grew up was mythological, it was impregnated with something that could not be resisted by those who breathed in it. It was like the siren voice of the modern rhyme, which has suggested so many common ideas to poets writing in a common language.

We know what Greek and Teutonic poets have made of their epic heroes; let us see now whether the swarthy Hindu has been able to throw an equally beautiful haze around the names of his mythical traditions.

The story of the loves of Purûravas and Urvasî has frequently been told by Hindu poets. We find it in their epic poems, in their Purâ*n*as, and in the B*r*ihatkathâ, the "Great Story," a collection of the popular legends of India. It has suffered many changes, yet even in Kalidâsa's[1] play, of which I shall give a short abstract, we recognize the distant background, and we may admire the skill with which this poet has breathed new life and human feeling into the withered names of a language long forgotten.

The first act opens with a scene in the Himâlaya mountains. The nymphs of heaven, on returning from an assembly of the gods, have been attacked, and are

[1] Professor Wilson has given the first and really beautiful translation of this play in his *Hindu Theatre*. The original was published first at Calcutta, and has since been reprinted several times. The best edition is that published by Professor Bollensen.

mourning over the loss of Urvasî, who has been carried off by a demon. King Purûravas enters on his chariot, and on hearing the cause of their grief, hastens to the rescue of the nymph. He soon returns, after having vanquished the robber, and restores Urvasî to her heavenly companions. But while he is carrying the nymph back to her friends in his chariot, he falls in love with her and she with him. He describes how he saw her slowly recovering from her terror: —

"She recovers, though but faintly.
So gently steals the moon upon the night,
Retiring tardily; so peeps the flame
Of coming fires through smoky wreaths; and thus
The Ganges slowly clears her troubled wave,
Engulfs the ruin that the crumbling bank
Has hurled across her agitated course,
And flows a clear and stately stream again."

When they part, Urvasî wishes to turn round once more to see Purûravas. She pretends that "a straggling vine has caught her garland," and while feigning to disengage herself, she calls one of her friends to help her. Her friend replies, —

"No easy task, I fear: you seem entangled
Too fast to be set free: but, come what may,
Depend upon my friendship."

The eye of the king then meets that of Urvasî, and he exclaims, —

"A thousand thanks, dear plant, to whose kind aid
I owe another instant, and behold
But for a moment, and imperfectly,
Those half-averted charms."

In the second act we meet the king at Allahabad, his residence. He walks in the garden of the palace, accompanied by a Brahman, who acts the part of the gracioso in the Indian drama. He is the confidential companion of the king, and knows his love for Urvasî. But he is so afraid of betraying what must remain a secret to everybody at court, and in particular to the queen, that he hides himself in a retired temple. There a female servant of the queen discovers him, and "as a secret can no more rest in his breast than morning dew upon the grass," she soon finds out from him why the king is so changed since his return from the battle with the demon, and carries the tale to the queen. In the mean time, the king is in despair, and pours out his grief, —

> "Like one contending with the stream,
> And still borne backwards by the current's force."

But Urvasî also is sighing for Purûravas, and we suddenly see her, with her friend, descending through the air to meet the king. Both are at first invisible to him, and listen to the confession of his love. Then Urvasî writes a verse on a birch-leaf, and lets it fall near the bower where her beloved reclines. Next, her friend becomes visible; and, at last, Urvasî herself is introduced to the king. After a few moments, however, both Urvasî and her friend are called back by a messenger of the gods, and Purûravas is left alone with his jester. He looks for the leaf on which Urvasî had first disclosed her love, but it is lost, carried away by the wind: —

> "Breeze of the south, the friend of love and spring,
> Though from the flower you steal the fragrant down
> To scatter perfume, yet why plunder me
> Of these dear characters, her own fair hand,
> In proof of her affection, traced? Thou knowest,
> The lonely lover that in absence pines,
> Lives on such fond memorials."

But worse than this, the leaf is picked up by the

queen, who comes to look for the king in the garden. There is a scene of matrimonial upbraiding, and, after a while, her majesty goes off in a hurry, like a river in the rainy season. The king is doubly miserable, for though he loves Urva*s*î, he acknowledges a respectful deference for his queen. At last he retires: —

> "'Tis past midday: exhausted by the heat,
> The peacock plunges in the scanty pool
> That feeds the tall tree's root; the drowsy bee
> Sleeps in the hollow chamber of the lotus,
> Darkened with closing petals; on the brink
> Of the now tepid lake the wild duck lurks
> Amongst the sedgy shades; and, even here,
> The parrot from his wiry bower complains,
> And calls for water to allay his thirst."

At the beginning of the third act we are first informed of what befell Urva*s*î, when she was recalled to Indra's heaven. She had to act before Indra — her part was that of the goddess of beauty, who selects Vish*n*u for her husband. One of the names of Vish*n*u is Purushottama, and poor Urva*s*î, when called upon to confess whom she loves, forgetting the part she has to act, says, "I love Purûravas," instead of "I love Purushottama." The author of the play was so much exasperated by this mistake, that he pronounced a curse upon Urva*s*î, that she should lose her divine knowledge. But when the performance was over, Indra observing her as she stood apart, ashamed and disconsolate, called her. The mortal who engrossed her thoughts, he said, had been his friend in the hours of peril; he had aided him in conflict with the enemies of the gods, and was entitled to his acknowledgments. She must, accordingly, repair to the monarch, and remain with him "till he beholds the offspring she shall bear him."

A second scene opens, in the garden of the palace. The king has been engaged in the business of the state, and retires as the evening approaches: —

> "So ends the day, the anxious cares of state
> Have left no interval for private sorrow.
> But how to pass the night? its dreary length
> Affords no promise of relief."

A messenger arrives from the queen, apprising his majesty that she desires to see him on the terrace of the pavilion. The king obeys — and ascends the crystal steps while the moon is just about to rise, and the east is tinged with red.

> "*King.* — 'Tis even so; illumined by the rays
> Of his yet unseen orb, the evening gloom
> On either hand retires, and in the midst
> The horizon glows, like a fair face that smiles
> Betwixt the jetty curls on either brow
> In clusters pendulous. I could gaze forever."

As he is waiting for the queen, his desire for Urvasî is awakened again: —

> "In truth, my fond desire
> Becomes more fervid as enjoyment seems
> Remote, and fresh impediments obstruct
> My happiness — like an impetuous torrent,
> That, checked by adverse rocks, awhile delays
> Its course, till high with chafing waters swollen
> It rushes past with aggravated fury.
> As spreads the moon its lustre, so my love
> Grows with advancing night."

On a sudden Urvasî enters on a heavenly car, accompanied by her friend. They are invisible again, and listen to the king; but the moment that Urvasî is about to withdraw her veil, the queen appears. She is dressed in white, without any ornaments; and comes to propitiate her husband, by taking a vow.

> "*King.* — In truth she pleases me. Thus chastely robed
> In modest white, her clustering tresses decked

With sacred flowers alone, her haughty mien
Exchanged for meek devotion: thus arrayed
She moves with heightened charms.

"*Queen.* — My gracious lord, I would perform a rite,
Of which you are the object, and must beg you
Bear with the inconvenience that my presence
May for brief time occasion you.

"*King.* — You do me wrong; your presence is a favor,
. . . . Yet trust me, it is needless
To wear this tender form, as slight and delicate
As the lithe lotus stem, with rude austerity.
In me behold your slave, whom to propitiate
Claims not your care, — your favor is his happiness.

"*Queen.* — Not vain my vow, since it already wins me
My lord's complacent speech."

Then the queen performs her solemn vow; she calls upon the god of the moon —

"Hear, and attest
The sacred promise that I make my husband!
Whatever nymph attract my lord's regard,
And share with him the mutual bonds of love,
I henceforth treat with kindness and complacency."

"*The Brahman, the confidential friend of the king,* (apart to Purûravas). The culprit that escapes before his hand is cut off determines never to run such a risk again. (*Aloud.*) What then; is his majesty indifferent to your grace?

"*Queen.* — Wise sir, how think you, — to promote his happiness
I have resigned my own. Does such a purpose
Prove him no longer dear to me?

"*King.* — I am not what you doubt me; but the power
Abides with you; do with me as you will.
Give me to whom you please, or if you please,
Retain me still your slave.

'*Queen.*—Be what you list;
My vow is plighted — nor in vain the rite,
If it afford you satisfaction. Come
Hence, girls; 'tis time we take our leave.

"*King.* — Not so:
So soon to leave me is no mark of favor.

"*Queen.* — You must excuse me; I may not forego
The duties I have solemnly incurred."

It does not bring out the character of the king under a very favorable light, that this scene of matrimonial reconciliation, when the queen acts a part which we should hardly expect on an oriental stage, should be followed immediately by the apparition of Urvasî. She has been present, though invisible, during the preceding conversation between him and his queen, and she now advances behind the king, and covers his eyes with her hands.

> "It must be Urvasî (the king says);
> No other hand could shed such ecstasy
> Through this emaciate frame. The solar ray
> Wakes not the night's fair blossom; that alone
> Expands when conscious of the moon's dear presence." [1]

Urvasî takes the resignation of the queen in good earnest, and claims the king as granted her by right. Her friend takes leave, and she now remains with Purûravas as his beloved wife.

> "*Urvasî.* — I lament
> I caused my lord to suffer pain so long.

> "*King.* — Nay, say not so! The joy that follows grief
> Gains richer zest from agony foregone.
> The traveller who, faint, pursues his track
> In the fierce day alone can tell how sweet
> The grateful shelter of the friendly tree."

The next act is the gem of the whole play, though it is very difficult to imagine how it was performed without a *mise en scène* such as our modern theatres would hardly be able to afford. It is a melo-dramatic intermezzo, very different in style from the rest of the play. It is all in poetry, and in the most perfect and

[1] This refers to a very well-known legend. There is one lotus which expands its flower at the approach of the sun and closes them during night: while another, the beloved of the moon, expands them during night and closes them during day-time. We have a similar myth of the *daisy*, the Anglo-Saxon "dæges eâge," day's eye, Wordsworth's darling.

highly elaborate metres. Besides, it is not written in Sanskrit, but in Prâkrit, the *lingua vulgaris* of India, poorer in form, but more melodious in sound than Sanskrit. Some of the verses are like airs to be performed by a chorus, but the stage directions which are given in the MSS. are so technical as to make their exact interpretation extremely difficult.

We first have a chorus of nymphs, deploring the fate of Urva*s*î. She had been living with the king in the groves of a forest, in undisturbed happiness.

" Whilst wandering pleasantly along the brink
Of the Mandâkinî, a nymph of air,
Who gamboled on its sandy shore, attracted
The monarch's momentary glance, — and this
Aroused the jealous wrath of Urvasî.
Thus incensed
She heedlessly forgot the law that bars
All female access from the hateful groves
Of Kârtikeya. Trespassing the bounds
Proscribed, she suffers now the penalty
Of her transgression, and, to a slender vine
Transformed, there pines till time shall set her free.'

Mournful strains are heard in the air —

" Soft voices low sound in the sky,
Where the nymphs a companion deplore,
And lament, as together they fly,
The friend they encounter no more.

" So sad and melodious awakes
The plaint of the swan o'er the stream
Where the red lotus blossoms, as breaks
On the wave the day's orient beam.

" Amidst the lake where the lotus, shining,
Its flowers unfold to the sunny beam.
The swan, for her lost companion pining,
Swims sad and slow o'er the lonely stream."

The king now enters, his features expressing insanity — his dress disordered. The scene represents a wild forest, clouds gathering overhead, elephants, deer, peacocks, and swans are seen. Here are rocks and waterfalls, lightning and rain. The king first rushes frantically after a cloud which he mistakes for a demon that carried away his bride.

"Hold, treacherous fiend; suspend thy flight — forbear:
Ah! whither wouldst thou bear my beauteous bride?
And now his arrows sting me; thick as hail,
From yonder peak, whose sharp top pierces heaven,
They shower upon me.

[*Rushes forward as to the attack, then pauses, and looks upwards.*

It is no demon, but a friendly cloud, —
No hostile quiver, but the bow of Indra;
The cooling rain-drops fall, not barbed shafts, —
And I mistake the lightning for my love."

These raving strains are interrupted by airs, bewailing the fate of the separated lovers; but it is impossible to give an idea of the real beauty of the whole, without much fuller extracts than we are able to give. The following passages may suffice: —

"Ah me! whatever I behold but aggravates
My woe. These bright and pendulous flowers,
Surcharged with dew, resemble those dear eyes,
Glistening with starting tears. How shall I learn
If she have passed this way?"

He addresses various birds, and asks them whether they have seen his love: the peacock, "the bird of the dark blue throat and eye of jet," — the cuckoo, "whom lovers deem Love's messenger," — the swans, "who are sailing northward, and whose elegant gait betrays that they have seen her," — the "*k*akravâka," "a bird who, during the night, is himself separated from his mate," — but none give answer. Neither he, nor the bees who murmur amidst the petals of the lotus, nor the royal elephant, that reclines with his mate under the kadamba-tree, has seen the lost one.

"*King.* — From his companion he accepts the bough
Her trunk has snapped from the balm-breathing tree —
How rich with teeming shoots and juicy fragrance.
He crushes it.
Deep on the mountain's breast
A yawning chasm appears — such shades are ever
Haunts of the nymphs of air and earth. Perchance,
My Urvasî now lurks within the grotto,
In cool seclusion. I will enter. — All
Is utter darkness. Would the lightning's flash
Now blaze to guide me — No, the cloud disdains —
Such is my fate perverse — to shed for me
Its many-channeled radiance. Be it so.
I will retire — but first the rock address.

Air.

"With horny hoofs and a resolute breast,
The boar through the thicket stalks;
He ploughs up the ground, as he plies his quest
In the forest's gloomiest walks.

"Say, mountain, whose expansive slope confines
The forest verge, — O tell me, hast thou seen
A nymph, as beauteous as the bride of love,
Mounting, with slender frame, thy steep ascent,
Or, wearied, resting in thy crowning woods?
How! no reply? remote, he hears me not, —
I will approach him nearer.

Air.

"From the crystal summits the glistening springs
Rush down the flowery sides,
And the spirit of heaven delightedly sings,
As among the peaks he hides.
Say, mountain so favored, — have the feet
Of my fair one pressed this calm retreat?

"Now, by my hopes, he answers! He has seen her:
Where is she? — say. Alas! again deceived.
Alone I hear the echo of my words,
As round the cavern's hollow mouth they roll,
And multiplied return. Ah, Urvasî!
Fatigue has overcome me. I will rest
Upon the borders of this mountain torrent,
And gather vigor from the breeze that gleans
Refreshing coolness from its gelid waves.

Whilst gazing on the stream whose new swoln waters
Yet turbid flow, what strange imaginings
Possess my soul, and fill it with delight.
The rippling wave is like her arching brow;
The fluttering line of storks, her timid tongue;
The foamy spray, her white loose floating robe;
And this meandering course the current tracks,
Her undulating gait. All these recall
My soon-offended love. I must appease her . . . .
I'll back to where my love first disappeared.
Yonder the black deer couchant lies; of him
I will inquire. O, antelope, behold . . . .
How! he averts his gaze, as if disdaining
To hear my suit! Ah no, he, anxious, marks
His doe approach him; tardily she comes,
Her frolic fawn impeding her advance."

At last the king finds a gem, of ruddy radiance; it is the gem of union, which, by its mighty spell, should restore Urvasî to her lover. He holds it in his hands, and embraces the vine, which is now transformed into Urvasî. The gem is placed on Urvasî's forehead, and the king and his heavenly queen return to Allahabad.

"Yonder cloud
Shall be our downy car, to waft us swift
And lightly on our way; the lightning's wave
Its glittering banners; and the bow of Indra (the rainbow)
Hangs as its overarching canopy
Of variegated and resplendent hues."
[*Exeunt on the cloud. Music.*

The fifth and last act begins with an unlucky incident. A hawk has borne away the ruby of reunion. Orders are sent to shoot the thief, and, after a short pause, a forester brings the jewel and the arrow by which the hawk was killed. An inscription is discovered on the shaft, which states that it belonged to Âyus, the son of Urvasî and Purûravas. The king is not aware that Urvasî has ever borne him a son; but while he is still wondering, a female ascetic enters, leading a boy with a bow in his hand. It is Âyus, the son of Urvasî, whom his mother confided to the pious *K*yavana, who educated him in the forest, and now sends him back to his mother. The king soon recognizes Âyus as his son. Urvasî also comes to embrace him: —

"Her gaze intent
Is fixed upon him, and her heaving bosom
Has rent its veiling scarf."

But why has she concealed the birth of this child? and why is she now suddenly bursting into tears? She tells the king herself, —

"When for your love I gladly left the courts
Of heaven, the monarch thus declared his will:
'Go, and be happy with the prince, my friend;
But when he views the son that thou shalt bear him,
Then hitherward direct thy prompt return.' . . . .
The fated term expires, and to console
His father for my loss, he is restored.
I may no longer tarry.

"*King.* — The tree that languished in the summer's blaze
Puts forth, reviving, as young rain descends,
Its leafy shoots, when lo! the lightning bursts
Fierce on its top, and fells it to the ground.

"*Urvasî.* — But what remains for me? my task on earth
Fulfilled. Once gone, the king will soon forget me.

"*King.* — Dearest, not so. It is no grateful task
To tear our memory from those we love.
But we must bow to power supreme; do you
Obey your lord; for me, I will resign
My throne to this my son, and with the deer
Will henceforth mourn amidst the lonely woods."

Preparations are made for the inauguration of the young king, when a new *deus ex machina* appears — Narada, the messenger of Indra.

"*Messenger.* — May your days be many! King, attend:
The mighty Indra, to whom all is known,
By me thus intimates his high commands.

Forego your purpose of ascetic sorrow,
And Urvasî shall be through life united
With thee in holy bonds."

After this all concludes happily. Nymphs descend from heaven with a golden vase containing the water of the heavenly Ganges, a throne, and other paraphernalia, which they arrange. The prince is inaugurated as partner of the empire, and all go together to pay their homage to the queen, who had so generously resigned her rights in favor of Urvasî, the heavenly nymph.

Here, then, we have the full flower whose stem we trace through the Purânas and the Mahâbhârata to the Brâhmanas and the Veda, while the seed lies buried deep in that fertile stratum of language from which all the Aryan dialects draw their strength and nourishment. Mr. Carlyle had seen deep into the very heart of mythology when he said, "Thus, though tradition may have but one root, it grows, like a banian, into a whole overarching labyrinth of trees." The root of all the stories of Purûravas and Urvasî were short proverbial expressions, of which ancient dialects are so fond. Thus: "Urvasî loves Purûravas," meant "the sun rises;" "Urvasî sees Purûravas naked," meant "the dawn is gone;" "Urvasî finds Purûravas again," meant "the sun is setting." The names of Purûravas and Urvasî are of Indian growth, and we cannot expect to find them identically the same in other Aryan dialects. But the same ideas pervade the mythological language of Greece. There one of the many names of the dawn was Eurydike (p. 102). The name of her husband is, like many Greek words, inexplicable, but Orpheus is the same word as the

Sanskrit "*R*ibhu" or "Arbhu," which, though it is best known as the name of the three *R*ibhus, was used in the Veda as an epithet of Indra, and a name of the sun. The old story then, was this: "Eurydike is bitten by a serpent (*i. e.* by the night), she dies, and descends into the lower regions. Orpheus follows her, and obtains from the gods that his wife should follow him if he promised not to look back. Orpheus promises, — ascends from the dark world below; Eurydike is behind him as he rises, but, drawn by doubt or by love, he looks round; the first ray of the sun glances at the dawn, — and the dawn fades away." There may have been an old poet of the name of Orpheus, — for old poets delight in solar names; but, whether he existed or not, certain it is, that the story of Orpheus and Eurydike was neither borrowed from a real event, nor invented without provocation. In India also, the myth of the *R*ibhus has taken a local and historical coloring by a mere similarity of names. A man, or a tribe of the name of Bribu (Rv. VI. 45, 31–33),[1] was admitted into the Brahmanic community. They were carpenters, and had evidently rendered material assistance to the family of a Vedic chief, Bharadvâ*g*a. As they had no Vaidik gods, the *R*ibhus were made over to them, and many things were ascribed to these gods which originally applied only to the mortal Bribus. These historical realities will never yield to a mythological analysis, while the truly mythological answers at once if we only know how to test it. There is a grammar by which that ancient dialect can be retranslated into the common language of the Aryans.

[1] This explains the passage in Manu X. 107, and shows how it ought to be corrected.

I must come to a close ; but it is difficult to leave a subject in which, as in an arch, each stone by itself threatens to fall, while the whole arch would stand the strongest pressure. One myth more. — We have seen how the sun and the dawn have suggested so many expressions of love, that we may well ask, did the Aryan nations, previous to their separation, know the most ancient of the gods, the god of love ? Was Eros known at that distant period of awakening history, and what was meant by the name by which the Aryans called him ? The common etymology derives "Eros" from a Sanskrit root, "v*r*i" or "var," which means to choose, to select,

Now, if the name of love had first been coined in our ball-rooms, such an etymology might be defensible, but surely the idea of weighing, comparing, and prudently choosing could not have struck a strong and genuine heart as the most prominent feature of love. Let us imagine, as well as we can, the healthy and strong feelings of a youthful race of men, free to follow the call of their hearts, — unfettered by the rules and prejudices of a refined society, and controlled only by those laws which Nature and the Graces have engraved on every human heart. Let us imagine such hearts suddenly lighted up by love, — by a feeling of which they knew not either whence it came and whither it would carry them ; an impulse they did not even know how to name. If they wanted a name for it, where could they look ? Was not love to them like an awakening from sleep ? Was it not like a morn radiating with heavenly splendor over their souls, pervading their hearts with a glowing warmth, purifying their whole being like a fresh breeze, and illuminating the whole world around them with a new light? If it was so, there was but one name by which they could express love, — there was but one similitude for the roseate bloom that betrays the dawn of love — it was the blush of the day, the rising of the sun. "The sun has risen," they said, where we say, "I love;" "The sun has set," they said, where we say, "I have loved."

And this, which we might have guessed, if we could but throw off the fetters of our own language, is fully confirmed by an analysis of ancient speech. The name of the dawn in Sanskrit is "ushas," the Greek Ἕως, both feminine. But the Veda knows also a masculine dáwn, or rather a dawning sun ("Agni aushasya," Ἑῷος), and in this sense Ushas might be supposed to have taken in Greek the form of Ἔρως. *S* is frequently changed into *r*. In Sanskrit it is a general rule that *s* followed by *a* media becomes *r*. In Greek we have the Lakonic forms in ορ instead of ος (Ahrens, "D. D." § 8); in Latin an *r* between two vowels often exists in ancient inscriptions under the more original form of *s* (*asa* = *ara*). The very word "ushas" has in Latin taken the form of *aurora*, which is derived from an intermediate *auros*, *auroris*, like *flora*, from *flos*, *floris*.

But, however plausible such analogies may seem, it is only throwing dust in our eyes if comparative philologists imagine they can establish in this manner the transition of a Sanskrit *sh* into a Greek *r*. No, whatever analogies other dialects may exhibit, no Sanskrit *sh* between two vowels has ever as yet been proved to be represented by a Greek *r*. Therefore Eros cannot be Ushas.

And yet the name of Eros was originally that of the

dawning sun. The Sun in the Veda is frequently called the runner, the quick racer, or simply the horse, while in the more humanized mythology of Greece, and also in many parts of the Veda, he is represented as standing on his cart, which in the Veda is drawn by two, seven, or ten horses, while in Greek we also have the quadriga: —

῞Αρματα μὲν τάδε λαμπρὰ τεθρίππων
῞Ηλιος ἤδη λάμπει κατὰ γῆν

These horses are called "haritas;" they are always feminine. They are called "bhadrâs," happy or joyful (I. 115, 3); "*k*itrâs," many-colored (I. 115, 3); "gh*r*itâ*k*is" and "gh*r*itasnâs," bathed in dew (IV. 6, 9); "sva*nk*as," with beautiful steps; "vîtap*r*ish*th*âs," with lovely backs (V. 45, 10). Thus we read: —

Rv. IX. 63, 9. "The Sun has yoked the ten Harits for his journey."

Rv. I. 50, 8. "The seven Harits bring thee, O bright Sun, on thy cart."

Rv. IV. 13, 3. "The seven Harits bring him, the Sun, the spy of the world."

In other passages, however, they take a more human form, and as the Dawn which is sometimes called simply "a*s*vâ," the mare, is well known by the name of the sister, these Harits also are called the Seven Sisters (VII. 66, 15); and in one passage (IX. 86, 37) they appear as "the Harits with beautiful wings." After this I need hardly say that we have here the prototype of the Grecian "Charites."[1]

I should like to follow the track which this recognition of the Charites, as the Sanskrit "Haritas," opens

[1] This point has been more fully discussed in the Second Series of my *Lectures on the Science of Language*, p. 368.

to comparative mythology; but I must return to Eros, in whose company they so frequently appear. If, according to the laws which regulate the metamorphosis of common Aryan words adopted in Greek or Sanskrit, we try to transliterate ἔρως into Sanskrit, we find that its derivative suffix ως, ωτος, is the same as the termination of the participle of the perfect. This termination is commonly represented in Sanskrit by "vas," nom. masc. "vân," fem. "ushi," neut. "vat," and this, though very different grammatically, may etymologically be considered as a modified form of the originally possessive suffix "vat," nom. masc. "vân," fem. "vatî," neut. "vat." There being no short *e* in Sanskrit, and a Greek ρ corresponding to a Sanskrit *r*, ἔρως, ἔρωτος, if it existed at all in Sanskrit, would have had the form of "ar-vas," nom. "árvân," gen. "árushas." Now it is true that we do not find in Sanskrit "ár-vân," gen. "ár-ushas," with any meaning that approaches the Greek ἔρως. But we find "ár-vat," gen. "ár-vatas," which in the later Sanskrit means a horse, and which in the Veda has retained traces of its radical power, and still displays the sense of quick, running, vehement. This very word is applied to the Sun, so that in some passages it stands as the name of the Sun, while in others it is used as a substantive, meaning horse or rider. Thus, through the irresistible influence of the synonymous character of ancient language, and without any poetical effort on the part of the speaker, those who spoke of the sun as "arvat," spoke and thought at the same time of a horse or rider. The word "arvat," though intended only to express the rapid sun, set other ideas vibrating which gradually changed the sun into a horse or a horseman.

"Arvat" means simply horse in passages like I. 91, 20: —

"The god Soma gives us the cow; Soma gives us the quick horse; Soma gives a strong son."

It means horseman or runner (Rv. I. 152, 5): —

"The rider is born without a horse, without a bridle."

The rider who is meant here is the rising sun, and there is a whole hymn addressed to the sun as a horse. Nay, the growth of language and thought is so quick that in the Veda the myth turns, so to speak, back upon itself; and one of the poets (I. 163, 2) praises the bright Vasus, because "out of the sun they have wrought a horse." Thus "árvat" becomes by itself, without any adjective or explanation, the name for sun, like "sûrya," "âditya," or any other of his old titles. Rv. I. 163, 3, the poet tells the sun, "Thou, O Arvat (horse), art Âditya" (the sun); and (VI. 12, 6), Agni, or the fire of the sun, is invoked by the same name: "Thou, O Arvat, keep us from evil report! O Agni, lighted with all the fires! thou givest treasures, thou sendest away all evils; let us live happy for hundred winters; let us have good offspring."

Before we can show how the threads of this name of the sun in India enter into the first woof of the god of love in Greece, we have still to observe that sometimes the horses, *i. e.* the rays of the sun, are called not only "harítas," but "rohítas" (or "róhitâs") and "árushîs" (or "arushâ's"). Rv. I. 14, 12: "Yoke the A'rushîs to thy cart, O bright Agni! the Haríts, the Rohits! with them bring the gods to us!" These names may have been originally mere adjectives, meaning red, bright, or brown,[1] but they soon grew into names of certain animals belonging to certain gods, according to their different color and character. Thus we read: —

Rv. II. 10, 2. "Hear thou, the brilliant Agni, my prayer; whether the two black horses ('syâvâ') bring thy cart, or the two ruddy ('róhitâ'), or the two red horses ('arushấ')."

And again: —

Rv. VII. 42, 2. "Yoke the Haríts and the Rohíts, or the Arushás which are in thy stable."

"A'rushî," by itself, is also used for cow; for instance (VIII. 55, 3), where a poet says that he has received four hundred cows ("árushî*n*âm *k*ätu*h*-satm"). These "árushîs," or bright cows, belong more particularly to the Dawn, and instead of saying "the day dawns," the old poets of the Veda say frequently, "the bright cows return" (Rv. I. 92, 1). We found that the Harits were sometimes changed into seven sisters, and thus the A'rushîs also, originally the bright cows, underwent the same metamorphosis: —

Rv. X. 5, 5. "He brought the Seven Sisters, the A'rushîs (the bright cows);" or (X. 8, 3), "When the sun flew up, the A'rushîs refreshed their bodies in the water."

Sanskrit scholars need hardly be told that this "árushî" is in reality the feminine of a form "árvas," nom. "árvân," gen. "árushas," while "árvatî" is the feminine of "ár-vat," nom. "árvâ," gen. "árvatas." As

1 "Poi chè l'altro mattin la bella Aurora
L'aer seren fè bianco e rosso e giallo." — Ariosto, xxiii. 52.
"Sì, che le bianche e le vermiglie guance,
Là dove io era, della bella Aurora,
Per troppa etate divenivan rance." — Dante, *Purgatorio*, ii. 7.

"vidvâ'n," knowing, forms its feminine "vidúshî" ("*k*ikitvâ'n," "*k*ikitúshî"), so "árvâ(*n*)" leads to "árushî," a form which fully explains the formation of the feminine of the past participle in Greek. This may be shown by the following equation: vidvâ'n : vidúshî= εἰδώς : εἰδυῖα. This feminine "árushî" is important for our purpose, because it throws new light on the formation of another word, namely, "arushá," a masculine, meaning bright or red, and in the Veda a frequent epithet of the sun. "Arushá," gen. "ásya," follows the weak declension, and "árushî" is by Sanskrit grammarians considered as the regular feminine of "arushá." "Arushá," as compared with the participial form "ar-vas," is formed like διάκτορος, ου, instead of διάκτωρ, ορος; like Latin *vasum*, *i*, instead of *vas*, *vasis;* like Prâkrit "*k*aranteshu," instead of "*k*aratsu;" like Modern Greek ἡ νύκτα, instead of ἡ νύξ.

This "arushá," as applied in the Veda to bright and solar deities, brings us as near to the Greek Eros as we can expect. It is used in the sense of bright: —

Rv. VII. 75, 6. "The red bright horses are seen bringing to us the brilliant Dawn."

The horses[1] of Indra, of Agni, of B*r*ihaspati, as quick as the wind, and as bright as suns, who lick the udder of the dark cow, the Night, are called "arushá;" the smoke which rises from the burning sun at daybreak, the limbs of the Sun with which he climbs the sky, the thunderbolt which Indra throws, the fire which is seen by day and by night, all are called "arushá." "He who fills heaven and earth with light, who runs across

[1] "Arusha, si voisin d'Aru*n*a (cocher du soleil), et d'Arus (le soleil), se retrouve en Zend sous la forme d'Aurusha (dont Anquetil fait Eorosh, l'oiseau). les chevaux qui traînent Serosh." Burnouf, Bhâgavata-Purâ*n*a p. LXXIX.

the darkness along the sky, who is seen among the black cows of the night," he is called "arushá" or the bright hero ("arushó vríshâ").

But this bright solar hero, whether Agni[1] or Sûrya, is in the Veda, as in Greek mythology, represented as a child.

Rv. III. 1, 4. "The Seven Sisters have nursed him, the joyful, the white one, as he was born, the red one (Arusha), by growth; the horses came as to a foal that is born; the gods brought up Agni when he was born."

"Arusha" is applied to the young sun in the Veda; the sun who drives away the dark night, and sends his first ray to awaken the world: —

Rv. VII. 71, 1. "Night goes away from her sister, the Dawn; the dark one opens the path for Arusha."

Though in some of his names there is an unintentional allusion to his animal character, he soon takes a purely human form. He is called "Nri*k*akshâs" (III. 15, 3), "having the eyes of a man;" and even his wings, as Grimm[2] will be glad to learn, have begun to grow in the Veda, where once, at least (V. 47, 3), he is called "Arushá*h* supar*n*ás," "the bright sun with beautiful wings:" —

Τὸν δ' ἤτοι θνητοὶ ηὲν Ἔρωτα καλοῦσι ποτηνόν,
Ἀθάνατοι δὲ Πτέρωτα, διὰ πτεροφύτορ ἀνάγκην.

As Eros is the child of Zeus, Arusha is called the child of Dyaus ("Divá*h* *sísus*").

Rv. IV. 15, 6. "Him, the god Agni, they adorn and purify every day like a strong horse, — like Arushá (the bright sun), the child of Dyaus (heaven)."

[1] How the god Kâma was grafted on Agni, may be seen from later passages in the Atharva-veda, the Taittirîya-sanhitâ, and some of the Grihya-sûtras.— *Indische Studien*, vol. v. pp. 224-226.

[2] See Jacob Grimm's *Essay on the God of Love*.

Rv. VI. 49, 2. "Let us worship Agni, the child of Dyaus, the son of strength, Arushá, the bright light of the sacrifice."

This deity is the first of the gods, for he comes (V. 1, 5) "agre ahnâm," "at the point of the days;" "ushasâm agre" (VII. 8, 1; X. 45, 5) "at the beginning of the dawns;" but in one passage two daughters are ascribed to him, different in appearance, — the one decked with the stars, the other brilliant by the light of the sun, — Day and Night, who are elsewhere called the daughters of the Sun. As the god of love, in the Greek sense of the word, Arusha does not occur, neither has love, as a mere feeling, been deified in the Veda under any name. Kâma, who is the god of love in the later Sanskrit, never occurs in the Veda with personal or divine attributes, except in one passage of the tenth book, and here love is rather represented as a power of creation than as a personal being. But there is one other passage in the Veda, where "Kâma," love, is clearly applied to the rising sun. The whole hymn (II. 38, 6) is addressed to Savitar, the sun. It is said, "He rises as a mighty flame, — he stretches out his wide arms, — he is even like the wind. When he stops his horses, all activity ceases, and the night follows in his track. But before the Night has half finished her weaving, the sun rises again. Then Agni goes to all men and to all houses; his light is powerful, and his mother, the Dawn, gives him the best share, the first worship among men." Then the poet goes on: —

"He came back with wide strides, longing for victory; the love of all men came near. The eternal approached, leaving the work (of Night) half-done; he followed the command of the heavenly Savitar."

"The love of all men," may mean he who is loved by all men, or who grants their wishes to all men; yet I do not think it is by accident that "Kâma," love, is thus applied to the rising sun.

Even in the latest traditions of the Purâ*n*as, the original solar character of the god of love, the beloved of the Dawn, was not quite forgotten. For we find that one of the names given to the son of Kâma, to Aniruddha, the irresistible (ἀνίκατος μάχαν), is Ushâpati, the lord of the Dawn.

If we place clearly before our mind all the ideas and allusions which have clustered round the names of "Arvat" and "Arusha" in the Veda, the various myths told of Eros, which at first seem so contradictory, become perfectly intelligible. He is in Hesiod the oldest of the gods, born when there exist as yet only Chaos and Earth. Here we have "Arusha born at the beginning of all the days." He is the youngest of the gods, the son of Zeus, the friend of the Charites, also the son of the chief Charis, Aphrodite, in whom we can hardly fail to discover a female Eros (an "Ushâ" instead of an "Agni aushasya"). Every one of these myths finds its key in the Veda. Eros or Arusha is the rising sun, and hence the child, the son of Dyaus; he yokes the Harits, and is, if not the son,[1] at least the beloved of the dawn. Besides, in Greek mythology also, Eros has many fathers and many mothers; and one pair of parents given him by Sappho, Heaven and Earth, is identical with his Vaidik parents, Dyaus and I*d*â.[2]

[1] Cf. *Maxim. Tyr.* XXIV. τὸν Ἔρωτά φησιν ἡ Διοτίμα τῷ Σωκράτει οὐ παῖδα, ἀλλ' ἀκόλουθον τῆς Ἀφροδίτης, καὶ θεράποντα εἶναι. See Preller, *Greek Mythology*, p. 238.

[2] The objections raised by Professor Curtius (*Grundzüge der Griechischen Etymologie*, p. 114) against the common origin of ἔρως and "arvat"

India, however, is not Greece; and though we may trace the germs and roots of Greek words and Greek

deserve careful attention. "How can we separate Ἔρως," he says, "from ἔρος, ἔραμαι, ἐράω, ἐρατός, ἐρατεινός, and other words, all of ancient date, and even Homeric? They cannot have sprung from the name ἔρως, and if we suppose that they sprang from the same root *ar*, to which we have to assign the sense of going, running, striving, ἔρος would mean striving, or desire, and it would be difficult to prove that the cognate Ἔρως started from the meaning of horse, or solar horse, which in Sanskrit was assigned to 'arvat.'" Professor Curtius then proceeds to urge the same objections against the etymology of Charis: "For what shall we do," he says, "with χαρά, χαίρω, χαρίζομαι, χαρίεις?" With regard to Charis, I may refer to the explanations which I have given in the Second Series of my Lectures, page 368, where I hope I have proved that Charis cannot be placed, as Professor Curtius proposes, in the same category of deities as Δειμός or Φόβος; and that there is nothing in the least improbable in certain derivatives of an ancient Aryan root taking a mythological character, while others retain an analogous appellative meaning. From the root "dyu," to shine, we have Dyaus and Ζεύς: but we also have in Sanskrit "diva" and "dina," day; and in Greek ἔνδιος, at noon-day, δῆλος, bright. From the root "vas" or "ush," to glow, to burn, we have Ἑστία, Vesta, Ushas, Eos, Aurora: but likewise Sanskrit "usra," early, "ush*na*," hot; Latin *uro, aurum;* Greek αὔω, αὔριον, ἦρι. Unless we suppose that roots, after having given rise to a single mythological name, were struck by instantaneous sterility, or that Greek mythological names can only be derived from roots actually employed in that language, what we observe in the case of Eros and Charis is the natural and almost inevitable result of the growth of language and myth, such as we now understand it. Greek scholars have asked, "how can we separate ἑρμηνεύω from Ἑρμῆς (*Grundzüge*, p. 312), or ἐριννύειν from Ἐριννύς (Welcker)?" Yet few have questioned Kuhn's etymology of Ἑρμῆς and Ἐριννύς, whatever difference of opinion may prevail as to the exact process by which these two deities came to be what they are. But, on the other hand, I cannot protest too strongly against the opinion which has been ascribed to me, that the Greeks were in any way conscious of the secondary or idiomatic meaning which "arvat" and "harit," had assumed in India. In India both "arvat," running, and "harit," bright, became recognized names for horse. As "arvat" was also applied to the sun, the heavenly runner, the conception of the sun as a horse became almost inevitable, and required no poetical effort on the part of people speaking Sanskrit. Nothing of the kind happened in Greek. In Greek ἔρως was never used as an appellative in the sense of horse, as little as ζεύς was used, except in later times, to signify the material sky. But unless we are prepared to look upon Eros, "the oldest of the Greek gods," as a mere abstraction, as, in fact, a kind of Cupid, I thought, and I still think, that we have to admit among the earliest worshippers of Eros, even on Greek soil, a faint ideas to the rich soil of India, the full flower of Aryan language, of Aryan poetry and mythology, belongs to Hellas, where Plato has told us what Eros is, and where Sophokles sang his —

Ἔρως ἀνίκατε μάχαν,
Ἔρως, ὃς ἐν κτήμασι πίπτεις,
ὃς ἐν μαλακαῖς παρειαῖς
νεάνιδος ἐννυχεύεις·
φοιτᾷς δ' ὑπερπόντιος, ἔν τ'
ἀγρονόμοις αὐλαῖς·
καί σ' οὔτ' ἀθανάτων φύξιμος οὐδείς,
οὔθ' ἁμερίων ἐπ' ἀν-
θρώπων· ὁ δ' ἔχων μέμηνεν.[1]

recollection of the ancient Aryan mythology in which the same word as Eros had been applied to the sun, and especially the rising sun. All the rest is simple and easy. The root *ar*, no doubt, had the sense of running or rushing, and might have yielded, therefore, names expressive of quick motion as well as of strong desire. Not every shoot, however, that springs from such a seed, lives on, when transferred to a different soil. "Eros" might have been the name for horse in Greece as "arvat" was in India, but it was not: "arvat," or some other derivative like "artha," might have expressed desire in Sanskrit as it did in Greek, but this, too, was not the case. Why certain words die, and others live on, why certain meanings of words become prominent so as to cause the absorption of all other meanings, we have no chance of explaining. We must take the work of language as we find it, and in disentangling the curious skein, we must not expect to find one continuous thread, but rest satisfied if we can separate the broken ends, and place them side by side in something like an intelligible order. Greek mythology was not borrowed from Vedic mythology any more than Greek words were taken from a Sanskrit dictionary. This being once understood and generally admitted, offense should not be taken if here and there a Vedic deity or a Sanskrit word is called a prototype. The expression, I know, is not quite correct, and cannot be defended, except on the plea that almost everybody knows what is meant by it. The Greek Charites are certainly not a mere modification of the Vedic Haritas, nor the Greek Eros of the Vedic Arvat. There was no recollection of an equine character in the Greek Eros or the Charites, just as, from a purely Greek point of view, no traces of a canine character could be discovered in Ἑλένη =Saramâ, or Ἑρμείας=Sârameya. Arvat and Eros are radii starting from a common central thought, and the angle of the Vedic radius is less obtuse than that of the Greek. This is all that could be meant, and I believe this is the sense in which my words have been understood by the majority of my readers.

[1] *Antigone*, ed. Dindorf, Oxford 1859, v. 781.

If Hegel calls the discovery of the common origin of Greek and Sanskrit the discovery of a new world, the same may be said with regard to the common origin of Greek and Sanskrit mythology. The discovery is made, and the science of comparative mythology will soon rise to the same importance as that of comparative philology. I have here explained but a few myths, but they all belong to one small cycle, and many more names might have been added. I may refer those who take an interest in this geology of language to the "Journal of Comparative Philology," published by my learned friend, Dr. Kuhn, at Berlin, who, in his periodical, has very properly admitted comparative mythology as an integral part of comparative philology, and who has himself discovered some of the most striking parallelisms between the traditions of the Veda and the mythological names of other Aryan nations. The very "Hippokentaurs and the Chimæra, the Gorgons and Pegasos, and other monstrous creatures," have apparently been set right; and though I differ from Dr. Kuhn on several points, and more particularly with regard to the elementary character of the gods, which he, like Lauer, the lamented author of the "System of Greek Mythology," seems to me to connect too exclusively with the fleeting phenomena of clouds, and storms, and thunder, while I believe their original conception to have been almost always solar, yet there is much to be learnt from both. Much, no doubt, remains to be done, and even with the assistance of the Veda, the whole of Greek mythology will never be deciphered and translated. But can this be urged as an objection? There are many Greek words of which we cannot find a satisfactory etymology, even by the help of Sanskrit. Are we therefore to say that the whole Greek language has no etymological organization? If we find a rational principle in the formation of but a small portion of Greek words, we are justified in inferring that the same principle which manifests itself in part, governed the organic growth of the whole; and though we cannot explain the etymological origin of all words, we should never say that language had no etymological origin, or that etymology "treats of a past which was never present." That the later Greeks, such as Homer and Hesiod, ignored the origin and purport of their myths, I fully admit, but they equally ignored the origin and purport of their words. What applies to etymology, therefore, applies with equal force to mythology. It has been proved by comparative philology that there is nothing irregular in language, and what was formerly considered as irregular in declension and conjugation is now recognized as the most regular and primitive stratum in the formation of grammar. The same, we hope, may be accomplished in mythology, and instead of deriving it, as heretofore, "ab ingenii humani imbecillitate et a dictionis egestate," it will obtain its truer solution, "ab ingenii humani sapientia et a dictionis abundantia." Mythology is only a dialect, an ancient form of language. Mythology, though chiefly concerned with nature, and here again mostly with those manifestations which bear the character of law, order, power, and wisdom impressed on them, was applicable to all things. Nothing is excluded from mythological expression; neither morals nor philosophy, neither history nor religion, have escaped the spell of that ancient sibyl. But mythology is neither philosophy, nor history, nor religion, nor ethics. It is, if we may use a scholastic expression, a *quale*, not a *quid* — something formal, not something substantial, and, like poetry, sculpture, and painting, applicable to nearly all that the ancient world could admire or adore.

April, 1856.

XVII.

GREEK MYTHOLOGY.[1]

It does not happen very often that we take up a German book of more than eight hundred pages, closely printed, and bristling with notes and quotations, and feel unwilling to put it down again before having finished the whole of it. However, this is what has happened to us, and will happen to many a reader of Professor Welcker's "Greek Mythology," if he is capable of entering with a real and human interest into the life, and thoughts, and feelings of the ancient Greeks, and more particularly into the spirit of their religion, their worship, and sacred traditions. To those who require any preliminary information respecting the author, we may say, first of all, that Welcker is a very old man, a man belonging almost to an age gone by, one of the few men remaining of the heroic age of German scholarship. The present generation, a race not quite contemptible in itself, looks up to him as the Greeks looked up to Nestor. He knew old Voss, the translator of Homer, when he was a young man fighting the battle of rational mythology against the symbolic school of Creuzer. He was the friend of Zoëga. He speaks of

1 *Griechische Götterlehre.* Von F. G. Welcker. Erster Band. Gottingen, 1857.

Buttmann, of Lexilogus Buttmann, as a scholar who had felt the influence of his teaching; and he looks upon Otfried Müller, the Dorian Müller, as belonging originally to his school, though afterwards carrying out the views of his master in an independent, and sometimes too independent spirit. Welcker has been lecturing and writing on mythology for many years, and he finds, not without satisfaction, that many of the views which he first propounded in his lectures, lectures open to any one who liked to listen, have become current, and, as it were, public property, long before his book was published. He is not a man to put forward any claims of priority; and if he dwells at all on the subject, it is rather in self-defense. He wishes to remind his readers that if he propounds certain views with the warmth of a discoverer, if he defends them strenuously against all possible objections, it is because he has been accustomed to do so for years, and because it was necessary for him to do so, at the time when he first elaborated his system, and explained it in his lectures. Welcker's "Mythology" has been expected for many years. It has been discussed long before it appeared. "It is to my great regret, and certainly without my fault," the author says, "that so great expectations have been raised." However, if the expectations have been great among the professors in Germany, they will admit that they have not been disappointed, and that the promise given by young Welcker has been fulfilled by the veteran.

"The Science of the Greek Gods" ("die Griechische Götterlehre"), which is the title of the book, though it carries the reader along most rapidly, exciting curiosity at every page, and opening new views in every chapter, is nevertheless a book which requires more than one perusal. It may be read, with the exception of some less finished chapters, for pleasure ; but it deserves to be studied, to be thought over, examined, and criticized, and it is then only that its real value is discovered. There have been many books published lately on mythology. Preller, Gerhard, Schelling, Maury, have followed each other in rapid succession. Preller's "Greek Mythology" is a useful and careful compendium. Gerhard's "Greek Mythology" is a storehouse, only sometimes rather a labyrinth, of mythological lore. On Schelling's "Philosophy of Mythology," published in his posthumous works, we hardly dare to pronounce an opinion. And yet, with all due respect for his great name, with a sincere appreciation of some deep thoughts on the subject of mythology too, and more particularly with a full acknowledgment of his merits in having pointed out more strongly than anybody else the inevitable character of mythological thought and language in the widest sense of the word, we must say, as critics, that his facts and theories defy all rules of sound scholarship, and that his language is so diffuse and vague, as to be unworthy of the century we live in. To one who knows how powerful and important an influence Schelling's mind exercised on Germany at the beginning of this century, it is hard to say this. But if we could not read his posthumous volumes without sadness, and without a strong feeling of the mortality of all human knowledge, we cannot mention them, when they must be mentioned, without expressing our conviction that though they are interesting on account of their author, they are disappointing in every other respect. Maury's "Histoire des Religions de la Grèce Antique " is, like all the works of that industrious writer, lucid and pleasing. It does not profess to add many results of independent research to what was known before on the various subjects on which he writes. Thus the gifted author escapes criticism, and only carries away the thanks of all who read his careful manuals.

What distinguishes Welcker from all his predecessors is this, that with him mythology is not only a collection of fables, to be described, sifted, and arranged, but a problem to be solved, and a problem as important as any in the history of the world. His whole heart is in his work. He wants to know, and wants to explain what mythology means, how such a thing as Greek mythology could ever have existed. It is the origin of every god which he tries to discover, leaving everything else to flow naturally from the source once opened and cleared.

A second feature, which is peculiar to his treatment of mythology, is that he never looks on the Greek fables as a system. There were myths before there was a mythology, and it is in this, their original and unsystematic form alone, that we may hope to discover the genuine and primitive meaning of every myth.

A third distinguishing feature of Welcker's book consists in the many things he leaves out. If a myth had once been started, poets, artists, philosophers, and old women might do with it whatever they pleased. If there was once a Herakles travelling all over the earth, killing monsters, punishing wickedness, and doing what no one else could do, the natural result would be that, in every town and village, whatever no one else could have done would be ascribed to Herakles. The little stories invented to account for all these Heraklean doings may be very interesting to the people of the village, but they have as little right to a place in Greek mythology as the Swiss legends of the Devil's bridges have to a place in a work on Swiss theology or history. To be able to distinguish between what is essential and what is not, requires a peculiar talent, and Professor Welcker possesses it.

A fourth point which is of characteristic importance in Welcker's manner of handling Greek mythology, is the skill with which he takes every single myth to pieces. When he treats of Apollo, he does not treat of him as one person, beginning with his birth, detailing his various exploits, accounting for his numerous epithets, and removing the contradictory character of many of his good or bad qualities. The birth of the god is one myth, his association with a twin sister another, his quarrel with Hermes a third, — each intelligible in itself, though perplexing when gathered up into one large web of Apollonic theology.

Nowhere, again, have we seen the original character of the worship of Zeus, as the God, or, as he is called in later times, as the Father of the gods, as the God of gods, drawn with so sure and powerful a hand as in Welcker's "Mythology." When we ascend with him to the most distant heights of Greek history the idea of God, as the supreme Being, stands before us as a simple fact. Next to this adoration of One God, the father of heaven, the father of men, we find in Greece a worship of nature. The powers of nature, originally worshipped as such, were afterwards changed into a family of gods, of which Zeus became the king and father.

This third phase is what is generally called Greek mythology; but it was preceded in time, or at least rendered possible in thought, by the two prior conceptions, a belief in a supreme God, and a worship of the powers of nature. The Greek religions, says Welcker, if they are analyzed and reduced to their original form, are far more simple than we think. It is so in all great things. And the better we are acquainted with the variety and complications of all that has grown up around them, the more we feel surprised at the smallness of the first seeds, the simplicity of the fundamental ideas. The divine character of Zeus, as distinct from his mythological character, is most carefully brought out by Welcker. He avails himself of all the discoveries of comparative philology in order to show more clearly how the same idea which found expression in the ancient religions of the Brahmans, the Slaves, and the Germans, had been preserved under the same simple, clear, and sublime name by the original settlers of Hellas. We are not inclined to be too critical when we meet with a classical scholar who avails himself of the works of Sanskrit philologists. It does him credit if he only acknowledges that the beginnings of Greek language, Greek thought and tradition, lie beyond the horizon of the so-called classical world. It is surprising to find, even at the present day, men of the highest attainments in Greek and Latin scholarship, intentionally shutting their eyes to what they know to be the light of a new day. Unwilling to study a new subject, and unable to confess their ignorance on any subject, they try to dispose of the works of a Humboldt, Bopp, or Bunsen, by pointing out a few mistakes, perhaps a wrong accent or a false quantity, — which "any schoolboy would be ashamed of." They might as well scoff at Wyld's Globe because it has not the accuracy of an Ordnance survey. So, if we find in a work like Welcker's little slips, such as "devas," sky, instead of god, "dyavî," a Sanskrit dative, instead of "divê," the dative, or "dyavi," the locative, we just mark them on the margin, but we do not crow over them like schoolmasters, or rather schoolboys. We should sometimes like to ask a question: for instance, how Professor Welcker could prove that the German word God has the same meaning as good? He quotes Grimm's "History of the German Language," p. 571, in support of this assertion, but we have looked in vain for any passage where Grimm gives up his former opinion, that the two words *God* and *good*, run parallel in all the Teutonic dialects, but never converge towards a common origin. However, Welcker's example, we hope, will have its good effect among classical scholars. What could have been a greater triumph for all who take an interest in comparative philology and in a more comprehensive study of ancient humanity, than to find in a work on Greek mythology, written by one of the most famous classical scholars, the fundamental chapter, the chapter containing the key to the whole system, headed, "The Vedas?"

But even Welcker is not without his backslidings. In some parts of his work, and particularly in his chapter on Zeus, he admits implicitly the whole argument of comparative mythology. He admits that the first beginnings of Zeus, the God of gods, must be studied in the ancient songs of the Veda, and in the ancient traditions of the chief members of the Aryan family. But afterwards he would like to make his reserves.

He has been studying the Greek gods all his life, and the names and natures of many of them had become clear and intelligible to him without the help of Sanskrit or the Veda. Why should they be handed over to the Aryan crucible? This is a natural feeling. It is the same in Greek etymology. If we can fully explain a Greek word from the resources of the Greek language, why should we go beyond? And yet it cannot be avoided. Some of the most plausible Greek etymologies have had to give way before the most unlikely, and yet irrefragable derivations from Sanskrit.

Many a Greek scholar may very naturally say, why, if we can derive θεός from θέειν, or from τιθέναι, should we go out of our way and derive it from any other root?[1] Any one acquainted with the true principles of etymology will answer this question; and Welcker himself would be the first to admit, that, from whatever source it may be derived, it cannot be derived from θέειν or τιθέναι. But the same argument holds good with regard to the names of the gods. Ζής, the old nominative, of which we have the accusative Ζῆν ("Iliad," viii. 206, formerly Ζῆν'), and Ζήν, of which we have the accusative Ζῆνα, might well have been derived by former Greek etymologists from ζῆν, to live. But Professor Welcker knows that, after etymology has once assumed an historical and scientific character, a derivation, inapplicable to the cognate forms of Ζεύς in Sanskrit, is inapplicable to the word itself in Greek. There are, no doubt, words and mythological names

1 The latest defense of the etymology of θεος as not to be separated from the cluster of words which spring from the root "div," may be seen in Ascoli, *Frammenti Linguistici*, Rendiconti, i. (1864), pp. 185–200.

peculiar to Greece, and framed in Greece after the separation of the Aryan tribes. Κρονίων, for instance, is a Greek word, and a Greek idea, and Professor Welcker was right in explaining it from Greek sources only. But wherever the same mythological name exists in Greek and Sanskrit, no etymology can be admitted which would be applicable to the Greek only, without being applicable to the Sanskrit word. There is no such being as Κρόνος in Sanskrit. Κρόνος did not exist till long after Ζεύς in Greece. Ζεύς was called by the Greeks the son of time. This is a simple and very common form of mythological expression. It meant originally, not that time was the origin or the source of Zeus, but Κρονίων or Κρονίδης was used in the sense of "connected with time, representing time, existing through all time." Derivatives in ιων and ιδης took, in later times, the more exclusive meaning of patronymics, but originally they had a more general qualifying sense, such as we find still in our own, originally Semitic, expressions, "son of pride," "sons of light," "son of Belial." Κρονίων is the most frequent epithet of Ζεύς in Homer; it frequently stands by itself instead of Ζεύς. It was a name fully applicable to the supreme God, the God of time, the eternal God. Who does not think of the Ancient of Days? When this ceased to be understood, particularly as in the current word for time the κ had become aspirated (κρόνος had become χρόνος), people asked themselves the question, why is Ζεύς called Κρονίδης? And the natural and almost inevitable answer was, because he is the son, the offspring of a more ancient god, Κρόνος. This may be a very old myth in Greece; but the misunderstanding which gave rise to it, could have happened in Greece only. We cannot expect, therefore, a god Κρόνος in the Veda. When this myth of Κρόνος had once been started, it would roll on irresistibly. If Ζεύς had once a father called Κρόνος, Κρόνος must have a wife. Yet it should be remembered as a significant fact, that in Homer Ζεύς is not yet called the son of Rhea, and that the name of Κρονίδης belongs originally to Ζεύς only, and not to his later brothers, Poseidon and Hades. Myths of this kind can be analyzed by Greek mythologists, as all the verbs in έω, άω, and όω can be explained by Greek etymologists. But most other names, such as Hermes, Eos, Eros, Erinys require more powerful tests; and Professor Welcker has frequently failed to discover their primitive character, because he was satisfied with a merely Greek etymology. He derives Erinys, or Erinnys, from a verb ἐριννύειν, to be angry, and gives to her the original meaning of Conscience. Others have derived it from the same root as ἔρις, strife; others again from ἐρεείνω, to ask. But Erinys is too old a god for so modern a conception. Erinys is the Vedic Sara*n*yû, the dawn; and even in Greek she is still called ἠεροφοῖτις, hovering in the gloom. There is no word expressive of any abstract quality, which had not originally a material meaning; nor is there in the ancient language of mythology any abstract deity which does not cling with its roots to the soil of nature. Professor Welcker is not the man to whom we need address this remark. He knows the German proverb: —

> "Kein Faden ist so fein gesponnen
> Er kommt doch endlich an der Sonnen."

He also knows how the sun is frequently represented as the avenger of dark crimes. The same idea is expressed by the myth of Erinys. Instead of our lifeless and abstract expression, "a crime is sure to be discovered," the old proverbial and poetical expression was, the Dawn, the Erinys, will bring it to light. Crime itself was called, in the later mythologizing language, the daughter of Night, and her avenger, therefore, could only be the Dawn. Was not the same Dawn called the bloodhound? Could she not find the track of the cattle stolen from the gods? She had a thousand names in ancient language, because she called forth a thousand different feelings in ancient hearts. A few only of these names became current appellatives; others remained as proper names, unintelligible in their etymological meaning and their poetical conception. The Greeks knew as little that Erinys meant the Dawn, as Shakespeare knew the meaning of the Weird Sisters. Weird, however, was originally one of the three Nornes, the German Parcæ. They were called "Vurdh," "Verdhandi," and "Skuld,"—Past, Present, and Future; and the same idea is expressed more graphically by the thread that is spun, the thread passing through the finger, and the thread which is still on the distaff; or by Lachesis singing the past (τὰ γεγονότα), Klotho singing the present (τὰ ὄντα), and Atropos singing the future (τὰ μέλλοντα). The most natural expression for to-morrow was the morn; for the future, the dawn. Thus Sara*n*yû, as one of the names of the dawn, became the name of the future, more especially of the coming avenger, the inevitable light. Homer speaks of the Erinys in the plural, and so do the poets of the Veda. Neither of them, however, know as yet their names and parentage. Hesiod calls them the daughters of the Earth, conceived of the drops of the blood of Ouranos. Sophokles claims the same freedom as Hesiod; he calls them the daughters of Skotos, or Darkness. Thus a mere proverb would supply in time a whole chapter of mythology, and furnish an Æschylus and Plato with subjects for the deepest thought and the most powerful poetry.

Into these, the earliest strata of mythological language and thought, no shaft can reach from the surface of Greece or Italy, and we cannot blame Professor Welcker for having failed in extricating the last roots and fibres of every mythological name. He has done his work; he has opened a mine, and, after bringing to light the treasures he was in search of, he has pointed out the direction in which that mine may be worked with safety. If new light is to be thrown on the most ancient and the most interesting period in the history of the human mind, the period in which names were given and myths were formed, that light must come from the Vedas; and we trust that Professor Welcker's book, by its weak as well as by its strong points, will impress on every classical scholar what Otfried Müller perceived many years ago, "that matters have come to such a point that classical philology must either resign altogether the historical understanding of the growth of language, as well as all etymological researches into the shape of roots and the organism of grammatical forms, or trust itself on these points entirely to the guidance and counsel of comparative philology."

January, 1858.

XVIII.

GREEK LEGENDS.[1]

If the stories of the Greek gods and heroes, as told by Mr. Cox in his "Tales from Greek Mythology," the "Tales of Gods and Heroes," and the "Tales of Thebes and Argos," do not quite possess in the eyes of our children the homely charm of Grimm's "Mährchen" or Dasent's "Norse Tales," we must bear in mind that at heart our children are all Goths or Northmen, not Greeks or Romans; and that, however far we may be removed from the times which gave birth to the stories of Dornröschen, Sneewittchen, and Rumpelstilzchen, there is a chord within us that answers spontaneously to the pathos and humor of those tales, while our sympathy for Hecuba is acquired, and more or less artificial. If the choice were left to children whether they would rather have a story about the Norse trolls read out to them, or the tale of the Trojan War as told by Mr. Cox, we fully believe — in fact we know — that they would all clamor for Dasent or Grimm. But if children are told that they cannot always be treated to trolls and fairies, and that they must learn something about the Greek gods and goddesses, we likewise know that they will rather listen to Mr. Cox's tales from Greek fairyland than to any other book that is used at lessons.

[1] *A Manual of Mythology, in the Form of Question and Answer.* By the Rev. G. W. Cox. London: Longmans & Co. 1867.

The "Manual of Mythology" which Mr. Cox has just published is meant as a lesson-book, more so than any of his former publications. If we add that the whole of Greek and Roman mythology is told in two hundred pages, in the somewhat cumbrous form of question and answer, we need not say that we have only a meagre abstract of classical mythology, a minimum, a stepping-stone, a primer, a skeleton, or whatever unpleasant name we like to apply to it. We wish indeed that Mr. Cox had allowed himself more ample scope, yet we feel bound to acknowledge that, having undertaken to tell what can be told, in two hundred pages, of classical mythology, he has chosen the most important, the most instructive, and the most attractive portions of his subject. Though necessarily leaving large pieces of his canvas mere blanks or covered with the faintest outlines, he has given to some of his sketches more life and expression than can be found in many a lengthy article contributed to cyclopædias and other works of reference.

But while Mr. Cox has thus stinted himself in telling the tales of Greek and Roman mythology, he has made room for what is an entirely new feature in his Manual, namely, the explanations of Greek and Roman myths, supplied by the researches of comparative mythologists. From the earliest philosophers of Greece down to Creuzer, Schelling, and Welcker, everybody who has ever thought or written on mythology has freely admitted that mythology requires an explanation. All are agreed that a myth does not mean what it seems to mean; and this agreement is at all events important, in spite of the divergent explanations which have been proposed by different scholars and philosophers in their endeavors to find sense either in single myths or in the whole system of ancient mythology.

There is also one other point on which of late years a general agreement has been arrived at among most students of mythology, and this is that all mythological explanations must rest on a sound etymological basis. Comparative philology, after working a complete reform in the grammar and etymology of the classical languages, has supplied this new foundation for the proper study of classical mythology, and no explanation of any myth can henceforth be taken into account which is not based on an accurate analysis of the names of the principal actors. If we read in Greek mythology that Helios was the brother of Eos and Selene, this needs no commentary. Helios means the sun, Eos the dawn, Selene the moon; nor does it require any great stretch of poetical imagination to understand how these three heavenly apparitions came to called brothers and sisters.

But if we read that Apollo loved Daphne, that Daphne fled before him and was changed into a laurel-tree, we have here a legend before us which yields no sense till we know the original meaning of Apollo and Daphne. Now Apollo was a solar deity, and although comparative philologists have not yet succeeded in finding the true etymology of Apollo, no doubt can exist as to his original character. The name of Daphne, however, could not have been interpreted without the aid of comparative philology, and it is not till we know that Daphne was originally a name of the dawn, that we begin to understand the meaning of her story. It was by taking myths which were still half intelligible, like those of Apollo and Daphne, Selene and

Endymion, Eos and Tithonos, that the first advance was made towards a right interpretation of Greek and Roman legends. If we read that Pan was wooing Pitys and that Boreas, jealous of Pan, cast Pitys from a rock, and that in her fall she was changed into a pine-tree, we need but walk with our eyes open along the cliffs of Bournemouth in order to see the meaning of that legend. Boreas is the Greek for north wind, Pitys for pine-tree. But what is Pan? Clearly another deity representing the wind in its less destructive character. The same Pan is called the lover of the nymph Echo, and of Syrinx. Why Pan, the wind, should be called the lover of Echo, requires no explanation. As to the nymph Syrinx, — a name which means, in Greek, the shepherd's pipe, — she is further fabled to have thrown herself into the river Ladon in order to escape from Pan, and to have been changed into a reed. Here mythology has simply inverted history; and while, in an account of the invention of musical instruments, we should probably be told that the wind whistling through the river reeds led to the invention of the shepherd's pipe, the poet tells us that Pan, the wind, played with Syrinx, and that Syrinx was changed into a reed. The name of Pan is connected with the Sanskrit name for wind, namely, "pavana." The root from which it is derived means, in Sanskrit, to purify; and as from the root "dyu," to shine, we have in Greek "Zên," "Zênós," corresponding to a supposed Sanskrit derivative, "dyav-an," the bright god, we have from "pû," to purify, the Greek "Pân," "Pânos," the purifying or sweeping wind, strictly corresponding to a possible Sanskrit form "pav-an." If there was anywhere in Greece a seashore covered with pine-forests, like the coast of Dorset, any Greek poet who had ears to hear the sweet and plaintive converse of the wind and the trembling pine-trees, and eyes to see the havoc wrought by a fierce northeaster, would tell his children of the wonders of the forest, and of poor Pitys, the pine-tree wooed by Pan, the gentle wind, and struck down by jealous Boreas, the north wind.

It is thus that mythology arose, and thus that it must be interpreted if it is to be more than a mere conglomerate of meaningless or absurd stories. This has been felt by Mr. Cox; and feeling convinced that, particularly for educational purposes, mythology would be useless — nay, worse than useless — unless it were possible to impart to it some kind of rational meaning, he has endeavored to supply for nearly every important name of the Greek and Roman pantheon an etymological explanation and a rational interpretation. In this manner, as he says in his preface, mythology can be proved to be "simply a collection of the sayings by which men once upon a time described whatever they saw and heard in countries where they lived. These sayings were all perfectly natural, and marvelously beautiful and true. We see the lovely evening twilight die out before the coming night, but when they saw this, they said that the beautiful Eurydike had been stung by the serpent of darkness, and that Orpheus was gone to fetch her back from the land of the dead. We see the light which had vanished in the west reappear in the east; but they said that Eurydike was now returning to the earth. And as this tender light is seen no more when the sun himself is risen, they said that Orpheus had turned round too soon to look at her, and so was parted from the wife whom he loved so dearly." And not only do meaningless legends receive by this process a meaning and a beauty of their own, but some of the most revolting features of classical mythology are removed, and their true purport discovered. Thus Mr. Cox remarks : —

"And as it is with this sad and beautiful tale of Orpheus and Eurydike, so it is with all those which may seem to you coarse, or dull, or ugly. They are so only because the real meaning of the names has been half-forgotten or wholly lost. Œdipus and Perseus, we are told, killed their parents, but it is only because the sun was said to kill the darkness from which it seems to spring. So, again, it was said that the Sun was united in the evening to the light from which he rose in the morning; but in the later story it was said that Œdipus became the husband of his mother Iokaste, and a terrible history was built upon this notion. But none of these fearful stories were ever made on purpose. No one ever sat down to describe gods and great heroes as doing things which all decent men would be ashamed to think of. There can scarcely be a greater mistake than to suppose that whole nations were suddenly seized with a strange madness which drove them to invent all sorts of ridiculous and contemptible tales, and that every nation has at some time or other gone mad in this way."

That the researches of comparative mythologists, so well summed up in Mr. Cox's "Manual of Mythology," are in the main tending in the right direction, is, we believe, admitted by all whose opinion on such matters carries much weight. It has been fully proved that mythology is simply a phase, and an inevitable phase in the growth of language; language being taken in its proper sense, not as the mere outward symbol, but as the only possible embodiment of thought. Everything, while language passes through that peculiar phase, may become mythology. Not only the ideas of men as to the origin of the world, the government of the universe, the phenomena of nature, and the yearnings and misgivings of the heart, are apt to lose their natural and straightforward expression, and to be repeated in a more or less distorted form, but even historical events, the exploits of a powerful man, the destruction of wild animals, the conquest of a new country, the death of a beloved leader, may be spoken of and handed down to later ages in a form decidedly mythological. After the laws that regulate the growth and decay of words have once been clearly established, instead of being any longer surprised at the breaking out of mythological phraseology, we almost wonder how any language could have escaped what may really be called an infantine disease, through which even the healthiest constitution ought to pass sooner or later. The origin of mythological phraseology, whatever outward aspects it may assume, is always the same; it is language forgetting herself. Nor is there anything strange in that self-forgetfulness, if we bear in mind how large a number of names ancient languages possessed for one and the same thing, and how frequently the same word was applied to totally different subjects. If we take the sun, or the dawn, or the moon, or the stars, we find that even in Greek every one of them is still polyonymous, *i. e.* has different names, and is known under various *aliases*. Still more is this the case in Sanskrit, though Sanskrit too is a language which, to judge from its innumerable rings, must have passed through many summers and winters before it grew into that mighty stem which fills us with awe and admiration, even in the earliest relics of its literature. Now, after a time, one out of many names of the same subject necessarily gains a preponderance; it becomes the current and recognized name, while the other names are employed less and less frequently, and at last become obsolete and unintelligible. Yet it frequently happens that, either in proverbs, or in idiomatic phrases, or in popular poetry, some of these obsolete names are kept up, and in that case mythological decay at once sets in. It requires a certain effort to see this quite clearly, because in our modern languages, where everything has its proper name, and where each name is properly defined, a mythological misunderstanding is almost impossible.

But suppose that the exact meaning of the word "gloaming" had been forgotten, and that a proverbial expression, such as "The gloaming sings the sun to sleep," had been preserved, would not the gloaming very soon require an explanation? and would nurses long hesitate to tell their children that the gloaming was a good old woman who came every night to put the sun into his bed, and who would be very angry if she found any little children still awake? The children would soon talk among themselves about Nurse Gloaming, and as they grew up would tell their children again of the same wonderful old nurse. It was in this and in similar ways that in the childhood of the world many a story grew up which, when once repeated and sanctioned by a popular poet, became part and parcel of what we are accustomed to call the mythology of ancient nations.

The mistake most commonly committed is to suppose that mythology has necessarily a religious character, and that it forms a whole or a system, taught in ancient times and believed in as we believe in our Articles, or even as the Roman Catholics believe in the legends of their saints. Religion, no doubt, suffered most from mythological phraseology, but it did not suffer alone. The stories of the Argonauts, or of the Trojan War, or of the Calydonian boar-hunt had very little to do with religion, except that some of the heroes engaged in them were called either the sons or the favorites of some of the so-called gods of Greece. No doubt we call them all gods, Vulcan and Venus, as well as Jupiter and Minerva ; but even the more thoughtful among the Greeks would hardly allow the name of gods to all the inhabitants of Olympus, at least not in that pregnant sense in which Zeus and Apollo and Athene may fairly claim it. If children asked who was the good Nurse Gloaming that sang the sun to sleep, the answer would be easy enough, that she was the daughter of the sky or of the sea, in Greek the daughter of Zeus or of Nereus; but this relationship, though it might give rise to further genealogical complications, would by no means raise the nurse to the rank of a deity. We speak of days and years as perfectly intelligible objects, and we do not hesitate to say that a man has wasted a day or a year, or that he has killed the time. To the ancient world days and nights were still more of a problem; they were strangers that came and went, brothers, or brother and sister, who brought light and darkness, joy and sorrow, who might be called the parents of all living things, or themselves the children of heaven and earth. One poetical image, if poetical it can be called, which occurs very frequently in the ancient language of India, is to represent the days as the herd of the sun, so that the coming and going of each day might be likened to the stepping forth of a cow, leaving its stable in the morning, crossing the heavenly meadows by its appointed path, and returning to its stable in the evening. The number of this solar herd would vary according to the number of days ascribed to each year. In Greek that simple metaphor was no longer present to the mind of Homer; but if we find in Homer that Helios had seven herds of oxen, fifty in each herd, and that their number never grows and never decreases, surely we can easily discover in these 350 oxen the 350 days of the primitive year. And if then we read again, that the foolish companions of Ulysses did not return to their homes because they had killed the oxen of Helios, may we not here too recognize an old proverbial or mythological expression, too literally interpreted even by Homer, and therefore turned into mythology? If the original phrase ran, that while Ulysses, by never-ceasing toil, succeeded in reaching his home, his companions wasted their time, or killed the days, *i. e.* the cattle of Helios, and were therefore punished, nothing would be more natural than that after a time their punishment should have been ascribed to their actually devouring the oxen in the island of Thrinakia; just as St. Patrick, because he converted the Irish and drove out the venomous brood of heresy and heathenism, was soon believed to have destroyed every serpent in that island, or as St. Christopher was represented as actually having carried on his shoulders the infant Christ.

All mythology of this character must yield to that treatment to which Mr. Cox has subjected the whole Greek and Roman pantheon. But there is one point that seems to us to deserve more consideration than it has hitherto received at the hands of comparative mythologists. We see that, for instance, in the very case of St. Patrick, mythological phraseology infected the perfectly historical character of an Irish missionary. The same may have taken place — in fact we need not hesitate to say the same has constantly taken place — in the ancient stories of Greece and Rome, as well as in the legends of the Middle Ages. Those who analyze ancient myths ought, therefore, to be prepared for this historical or irrational element, and ought not to suppose that everything which has a mythical appearance is thoroughly mythical or purely ideal. Mr. Cox has well delineated the general character of the most popular heroes of ancient mythology: —

"In a very large number of legends (he says), the parents, warned that their own offspring will destroy them, expose their children, who are saved by some wild beast and brought up by some herdsman. The children so recovered always grow up beautiful, brave, strong, and generous; but, either unconsciously or against their will, they fulfill the warnings given before their birth, and become the destroyers of their parents. Perseus, Œdipus, Cyrus, Romulus, Paris, are all exposed as infants, are all saved from death, and discovered by the splendor of their countenances and the dignity of their bearing. Either consciously or unconsciously Perseus kills Akrisios, Œdipus kills Laios, Cyrus kills Astyages, Romulus kills Amulius, and Paris brings about the ruin of Priam and the city of Troy."

Mr. Cox supposes that all these names are solar names, and that the mythical history of every one of these heroes is but a disguise of language. Originally there must have existed in ancient languages a large number of names for the sun, and the sky, and the dawn, and the earth. The vernal sun returning with fresh vigor after the deathlike repose of winter had a different name from the sun of summer and autumn; and the setting sun with its fading brilliancy was addressed differently from the "bridegroom coming forth out of his chamber," or "the giant rejoicing to run his course." Certain names, expressions, and phrases sprang up, originally intended to describe the changes of the day and the seasons of the year; after a time these phrases became traditional, idiomatic, proverbial; they ceased to be literally understood, and were misunderstood and misinterpreted into mythical phraseology. At first the phrase "Perseus will kill Akrisios" meant no more than that light will conquer darkness, that the sun will annihilate the night, that the morn is coming. If each day was called the child of the night, it might be truly said that the young child was destined to kill its parents, that Œdipus must kill Laios.[1] And if the violet twilight, Iokaste, was called

[1] Professor Comparetti, in his Essay *Edipo e la Mitologia Comparata* (Pisa, 1867), has endeavored to combat M. Bréal's explanation of the myth of Œdipus. His arguments are most carefully chosen, and supported by much learning and ingenuity which even those, who are not convinced by his able pleading, cannot fail to appreciate. It is not for me to defend the whole theory proposed by M. Bréal in his *Mythe d' Œdipe* (Paris, 1863). But as Professor Comparetti, in controverting the identification of "Laios" with the Sanskrit "dâsa," or "dâsya," denies the possibility of an Aryan *d* appearing in Greek as *l*, I may, in defense of my own identification of "dâsahantâ" with λεωφόντης (Kuhn's *Zeitschrift*, vol. v. p. 152), be allowed to remark that I had supported the change of *d* into *l* in Greek by instances taken from Ahrens, *De Dialecto Dorica*, p. 85, such as λάφνη = δάφνη, 'Ολυσσεύς =

the wife of the nocturnal Laios, the same name of Iokaste, as the violet dawn, might be given to the wife of Œdipus. Hence that strangely entangled skein of mythological sayings which poets and philosophers sought to disentangle as well as they could, and which at last was woven into that extraordinary veil of horrors which covers the sanctuary of Greek religion.

But if this be so — and, strange as it may sound at first, the evidence brought in support of this interpretation of mythology is irresistible — it would seem to follow that Perseus, and Œdipus, and Paris, and Romulus could none of them claim any historical reality. Most historians might be prepared to give up Perseus, Œdipus, and Paris, perhaps even Romulus and Remus; but what about Cyrus? Cyrus, like the other solar heroes, is known to be a fatal child; he is exposed, he is saved, and suckled, and recognized, and restored to his royal dignity, and by slaying Astyages he fulfills the solar prophecy as completely as any one of his compeers. Yet, for all that, Cyrus was a real man, an historical character, whose flesh and bone no sublimating process will destroy. Here then we see that mythology does not always create its own heroes, but that it lays hold of real history, and coils itself round it so

'Οδυσσεύς, and λίσκος = δίσκος. If in any of the local dialects of Greece the dental media could assume the sound of *l*, the admission of the change of a Greek *d* into a Greek *l* was justified for the purpose of explaining the name of one or two among the local heroes of ancient Greece, though I grant that it might be open to objections if admitted in the explanation of ordinary Greek words, such as λαός or μελετάω. If, therefore, Professor Curtius (*Grundzüge der Griechischen Etymologie*, p. 325) calls the transition of *d* into *l* unheard of in Greek, he could only have meant the classical Greek, and not the Greek dialects, which are nevertheless of the greatest importance in the interpretation of the names of local gods and heroes, and in the explanation of local legends.

closely that it is difficult, nay, almost impossible, to separate the ivy from the oak, or the lichen from the granite to which it clings. And here is a lesson which comparative mythologists ought not to neglect. They are naturally bent on explaining everything that can be explained; but they should bear in mind that there may be elements in every mythological riddle which resist etymological analysis, for the simple reason that their origin was not etymological, but historical. The name of "Cyrus" or "Koresh" has been supposed to have some affinity with the Persian name of the sun, "khvar" or "khor"; and, though this is wrong, it can hardly be doubted that the name of "Astyages," the Median king, the enemy of Cyrus, doomed to destruction by a solar prophecy, is but a corruption of the Zend name "Azhi dahâka," the destructive serpent, the offspring of Ahriman, who was chained by Thraêtaona, and is to be killed at the end of days by Keresâspa. Mr. Cox refers several times to this "Azhi dahâka" and his conqueror Thraêtaona, and he mentions the brilliant discovery of Eugène Burnouf, who recognized in the struggle between Thraêtaona and "Azhi dahâka" the more famous struggle celebrated by Firdusi in the "Shahnameh" between Feridun and Zohak.[1] If, then, the Vedic "Ahi," the serpent of darkness destroyed by Trita, Indra, and other solar heroes, is but a mythological name, and if the same applies to "Azhi dahâka," conquered by Thraêtaona, and to the Echidna slain by Phœbus, and to Fafnir slain by Sigurd, what shall we say of Astyages killed by Cyrus? We refer those who take an interest in these questions to a posthumous work of one of the most learned dig-

[1] See *Essay on the Zend-Avesta*, vol. i. p. 97.

nitaries of the Roman Catholic Church, the "Zoroastrische Studien" of F. Windischmann. The historical character of Cyrus can hardly be doubted by any one, but the question whether Astyages was assigned to him as his grandfather merely by the agency of popular songs, or whether Astyages too was a real king, involves very important issues, particularly as, according to Windischmann, there can be no doubt as to the identity of Darius, the Median, of the Book of Daniel, and Astyages. What is called the history of Media before the time of Cyrus is most likely nothing but the echo of ancient mythology repeated by popular ballads. Moses of Khorene distinctly appeals to popular songs which told of "Ajdahak," the serpent,[1] and, with regard to the changes of the name, Modjmil[2] says that the Persians gave to Zohak the name of "Dehak," *i. e.* ten evils, because he introduced ten evils into the world. In Arabic his name is said to have been "Dechak," the laugher, while his other name "Azdehak" is explained as referring to the disease of his shoulders, where two serpents grew up which destroyed men.[3] All this is popular mythology, arising from a misunderstanding of the old name, "Azhi dahâka;" and we should probably not be wrong in supposing that even "Dejoces" was a corruption of "Dehak," another ancestor in that Median dynasty which came to an end in Astyages, the reputed grandfather of Cyrus. We can here only point to the problem as a warning to comparative mythologists, and remind them, in parting, that as many of the old German legends were

[1] Windischmann, *Zoroastrische Studien*, p. 138.
[2] *Journal Asiatique*, vol. xi. p. 156.
[3] Windischmann, l. c. p. 37.

transferred to the Apostles, as some of the ancient heathen prophecies were applied to the emperor Barbarossa, as tricks performed by solar archers were told again of a William Tell, and Robin Hood, and Friar Tuck — nay, as certain ancient legends are now told in Germany of Frederick the Great — it does not always follow that heroes of old who performed what may be called solar feats are therefore nothing but myths. We ought to be prepared, even in the legends of Herakles, or Meleagros, or Theseus, to find some grains of local history on which the sharpest tools of comparative mythology must bend or break.

March 1867.

XIX.

BELLEROPHON.

What was the original intention of the name of "Bellerophon?" That *bellero*, the first part of the word, represents some power of darkness, drought, cold, winter, or of moral evil, is easy to guess. The Greeks say that there was a word τὰ ἔλλερα, which signified anything evil or hateful,[1] and was used in that sense by Kallimachos.[2] Nay, Bellerophon or Bellerophontes is said to have been called also Ellerophontes. That the Greeks in general, however, were no longer conscious of the appellative power of Belleros, is best proved by the fact that, in order to explain the myth of Bellerophon, they invented, very late, it would seem, a legend, according to which Bellerophon had killed a distinguished Corinthian, of the name of Belleros, and had fled to Argos or Tyrins to be purified by Prœtos from the stain of that murder. Nothing, however, is known about this Belleros, and as the ordinary accounts represent Bellerophon as flying to Argos after having killed his brother Deliades, or, as he is also called, Peiren or Alkimenes, there can be little doubt

[1] Preller, *Griechische Mythologie*, vol. ii. p. 55.

[2] Eustath. *ad Il.* p. 635; Naeke, *Opusc.* vol. ii. p. 167.

that the Corinthian nobleman of the name of Belleros owes his origin entirely to a desire of later mythologists, who felt bound to explain the no longer intelligible name of Bellerophon or Bellerophontes.

Such a name, it is quite clear, was not originally without some meaning, and without attempting to unravel the whole tragedy of Hipponoos, who afterwards monopolized the name of Bellerophon, it may be possible to discover by a strict observance of etymological laws, the original form and the original purport of this peculiar name.

With regard to the second half of the name, there can be little doubt that in Bellerophon and Bellerophontes, "phôn" and "phontês" had one and the same meaning. Now "phon-tês" at the end of compounds means the killer, the Sanskrit "han-tâ," killer; and therefore "phôn" can, in our name, hardly mean anything else, and would correspond exactly with the Sanskrit "han," nom. "hâ," killing.

From the reported change in the initial letter of Bellerophon, it is easy to see that it represents a labial liquid, and is in fact the well-known digamma Æolicum. But it is more difficult to determine what letters we ought to look for as corresponding in other languages to the λλ of the Greek word "bellero." In many cases Greek λλ represents a single *l*, followed originally by a sibilant or a liquid.[1] In this manner we can account for the single *l* in πολύς and the double *l* in πολλοί. Πολύς corresponds to the Sanskrit "pulú" (Rv. I. 179, 5), or "purú," gen. "puros," whereas the oblique cases would represent a Sanskrit adjective "pŭrvá," gen. "pŭrvásya." As πολλοί points to a

[1] See Ahrens, *Dial. Dor.* p. 60.

Sanskrit "purvé," ὅλοι points to the Sanskrit "sárve." In Latin, too, a double *l* owes its origin not unfrequently to an original single *l* or *r* followed by *v*.[1] Thus the double *l* in *mellis*, the gen. of *mel*, honey, is explained by the Sanskrit "madhu," raised to "madhv-i," and regularly changed to "madv-i," "malv-i," "mall-i." *Fel*, gen. *fellis*, is explained by "haru" in "haruspex,"[2] raised to "harv-i," "halv-i," "hall-i," "fall-i."[3] *Mollis* corresponds to Sanskrit "m*r*idu," through the intermediate links, "mardv-i," "maldv-i," "malv-i," "mall-i;"[4] nay, if we consider the Vedic word for bee, "*r*idu-pấ" (Rv. VIII. 77, 11), *mel*, *mellis*, too, might be derived from "m*r*idu," and not from "madhu." According to these analogies, then, the Greek βέλλερο would lead us back to a Sanskrit word "varvara." This word actually occurs in the Sanskrit language, and means hairy, woolly, shaggy, rough. It is applied to the negro-like aboriginal inhabitants of India who were conquered and driven back by Aryan conquerors, and it has been identified with the Greek βάρβαρος. Sandal-wood, for instance, which grows chiefly on the Malabar coast, is called in Sanskrit "barbarottha," sprung up among Barbaras, because that coast was always held by Tamulian or non-Aryan people. Professor Kuhn, identifying *barbara* and βάρβαρος, refers the meaning of both words, not to the shaggy or woolly hair, but to the confused speech (*balbutire*) of non-Aryan tribes. It will be difficult to prove with what intent the Greeks and the Hindus first applied βάρβα-

1 Corssen, *Kritische Beiträge*, p. 385.

2 Aufrecht, in Kuhn's *Zeitschrift*, vol. iii. p. 198.

3 As to the interchange of *h* and *f* in Latin, see Corssen, *Kritische Beiträge*, p. 208; as to the etymology of "fel," Ib. p. 318

4 Corssen, *Kritische Beiträge*, p. 323.

ρος and *barbara* to tribes differing from themselves both in speech and aspect. It is true that in Greek the word occurs for the first time in Homer with a special reference to language ("Iliad," ii. 876, Κᾶρες βαρβαρόφωνοι); and in Sanskrit also the earliest passage in which "barbara" is found refers to speech (Rig-veda Prâtisâkhya, Sûtra 784; XIV. 6). But the "barbaratâ" there mentioned as a fault of pronunciation, is explained by the same word ("asaukumâryam") which in Sûtra 778 serves as an explanation of "lomasya;" and this "lomasya," meaning shagginess, is, like the Greek δασύτης, clearly transferred from the shagginess of hair ("loman," hair) to the shagginess of pronunciation, so that after all, in Sanskrit at least, the original conception of the adjective "barbara" seems to have been shaggy.

However that may be, it is clear that many words for wool are derived from the same root "var" which yielded "varvara" or "barbara." This root means originally to cover, and it yielded in Sanskrit "ura" in ura-bhra," ram, i. e. *laniger;* in Greek εἶρος and ἔρ-ιον. In the Veda we have likewise the feminine "ûrâ," sheep (Rv. VIII. 34, 3), —

"úrâm nâ dhûnute vrikah,"

"(the stone tears the Soma plant) as the wolf tears the sheep." The wolf is called "urâmathi" (Rv. VIII. 66, 8), literally the sheep-shaker, or sheep-lifter.

From the same root are formed, by means of the suffix *na*, the Sanskrit "ûr*n*â," wool, particularly of sheep; afterwards "ûr*n*âyu," a goat, and a spider; the one from wearing, growing, or supplying wool; the other from, as it were, spinning or weaving it. Thus the spider is also called in Sanskrit "ûr*n*a-nâbhi" and "ûr*n*a-vâbhi," literally the wool-weaver; and one of the enemies killed by Indra is "Aur*n*avâbha," which seems to mean a ram rather, a wool-provider, than a spider. This "ûr*n*â," as Bopp has shown, appears again in Russian as "vòlna," in Gothic as "vulla," *r* having been changed to *l*, and *ln* into *ll*. The same assimilation is found in Latin *villus*, gen. *villi*, and *vellus*, gen. *velleris*. It might be difficult to convince a classical scholar that *vellus* was not derived from the Latin *vellere*, particularly as Varro himself gives that etymology; but it would be equally difficult to establish such an etymology by any analogies. It is curious, however, to remark, for reasons to be explained hereafter, that *vellera* in Latin signifies light, fleecy clouds. (Virg. "Georg." 1, 397; Luc. iv. 124.)

"Ura," therefore, from a root "var," to cover, meant originally cover, then skin, fleece, wool. In its derivatives, too, these various meanings of the root "var" appear again and again, Thus "úra*nah*" means ram, "ura*n*î," sheep; but "urâ*n*á*h*," quite a different formation, means protector. For instance, with the genitive: —

Rv. I. 173, 7. "samátsu tvâ *s*ûra satấm urâ*n*ám pra-pathíntamam,"
"Thee, O hero, in battles the protector of the brave, the best guide!'
Rv. VII. 73, 3. "áhema ya*g*ñám pathấm urâ*n*ấ*h*,"
"Let us speed the sacrifice, as keepers of the (old) ways!"

With the accusative: —

Rv. III. 19, 2. "(Agni*h*) devá-tâtim urâ*n*á*h*,"
"Agni, who protects the gods."
Rv. IX. 109, 9. "índu*h* punâná*h* pra*g*ấm urâ*n*á*h*,"
"The purified Soma, protecting the people."

Without any case: —

Rv. IV. 6, 4. "(Agni*h*) pra-díva*h* urâ*n*á*h*,"
"Agni, the old guardian." See also Rv. IV. 7, 3; VI. 63, 4.

Now if "ur*n*â," wool, meant originally a covering,

"var-*n*a" also, which now means color, would seem to have started from the same conception. Color might naturally be conceived as the covering, the outside, as χρώς and χρῶμα in Greek combine the meanings of skin and color. From "var*n*a," color (brightness), we have in Sanskrit "var*n*i," gold, as from "rûpa," form (beauty), we have "rûpya," silver, from which "Rupee;" for we cannot well derive the name of silver, the metal, from the figure ("rûpa") that was stamped on a silver coin.

In the Veda "var*n*a" appears in the sense of color, of bright color or light, and of race.

In the sense of color in general, "var*n*a" occurs, —

Rv. I. 73, 7. "k*r*ish*n*ám *k*a vár*n*am aru*n*ám *k*a sám dhu*h*,"
"They placed together the dark and the bright color (of night and day)."

Rv. I. 113, 2. "dyắvâ vár*n*am *k*aratha*h* â-minâné,"
"Day and night move on destroying their color."

Frequently "var*n*a" is used in the Veda as implying bright color or light: —

Rv. II. 34, 13. "ni-méghamânâ*h* átyena pắ*g*asâ su-*sk*andrám vâr*n*am dadhire su-pé*s*asam,"
"They (the Rudras) strongly showering down on their horse, made shining, beautiful light." (On "pắ*g*as" and its supposed connection with Pegasos, see Kuhn, in his "Zeitschrift," vol. i. p. 461; and Sonne, Ib. vol. x. p. 174, seq.)

Rv. II. 1, 12. "táva spârhé vár*n*e,"
"In thy sparkling light, O Agni!"

Rv. III. 34, 5. "prá imám vár*n*am atirat *s*ukrám âsâm,"
"He, Indra, spread out the bright light of the dawn."

In the ninth Ma*n*dala the color ("var*n*a") of the Soma juice is frequently mentioned, as "hári," "rú*s*at," "*s*ú*k*i," also as "asúrya": —

Rv. X. 3, 3. "Agní*h* vi-tísh*th*an rú*s*adbhi*h* vár*n*ai*h*,"
"Agni far-striding with shining colors."

Even without determining adjectives, "vár*n*a" has occasionally the sense of light: —

Rv. I. 92, 10. "samânám várnam abhí sumbhamânâ,"
"The old Dawn that clothes herself in the same light."
Rv. X. 124, 7. "tâh asya várnam súkayah bharibhrati,"
"They (the dawns), the bright ones, carry always the light of the sun." See also Rv. II. 4, 5; II. 5, 5; IV. 15, 3.

Hence we may take "varna" in the same sense in another passage, where the commentator explains it as Indra, the protector: —

Rv. I. 104, 2. "devâsah manyúm dâsasya skamnan
té nah â vakshan suvitâya várnam,"
"The gods broke the pride of Dâsa (the enemy); may they bring to us light for the sacrifice."

Lastly, "varna" means color, or tribe, or caste, the difference in color being undoubtedly one of the principal causes of that feeling of strangeness and heterogeneousness which found expression in the name of tribe, and, in India, of caste.[1] The commentators generally take "varna" in the technical sense of caste, and refer it to the three highest castes ("traivarnika") in opposition to the fourth, the *S*ûdras.

Rv. III. 34, 9. "hatvî dásyûn prâ âryam várnam âvah,"
"Indra, killing the Dasyus (the enemies), has protected the Aryan color."
Rv. II. 12, 4. "yáh dâsam várnam ádharam gúhâ âkar,"
"Indra who brought the color of the Dâsas low in secret."
Rv. II. 3, 5. "várnam punânâh yasásam su-vîram,"
"(The heavenly gates) which illuminate the glorious color (race), rich in heroes."

But to return to "varvara," to which on etymological grounds we should assign the meaning of shaggy, hairy, *villosus*, it need hardly be said that such a word, though it supplies an intelligible meaning of the Greek myth of Belleros, as slain by Bellerophon, does not occur in the Veda among the numerous names of the demons slain by Indra, Agni, and other bright gods.

[1] See my letter to Chevalier Bunsen, *On the Turanian Languages*, p. 84.

The same happens very frequently, namely, that Sanskrit supplies us with the etymological meaning of a term used in Greek mythology, although the corresponding word does not occur in the actual or mythological language of India. Thus the Greek "Hêrâ" is easily explained by "Svârâ," or, according to Sonne (Kuhn, "Zeitschrift," vol. x. p. 366, vol. ix. p. 202), by "Vasrâ;" but neither of these words occurs in the mythological phraseology of the Veda. There remains, however, a question which has still to be answered, namely, Do we find among the demons slain by solar deities, one to whom the name of "varvara,"[1] in the sense of shaggy, would be applicable? and this question we may answer with a decided Yes.

One of the principal enemies or "dâsas" conquered by Indra is the black cloud. This black cloud contains the rain or the fertilizing waters which Indra is asked to send down upon the earth, and this he can only do by slaying the black demon that keeps them in prison. This black cloud itself is sometimes spoken of in the Veda as the black skin: —

> Rv. IX. 41, 1. "ghnántah krishnâm ápa tvákam,"
> "Pushing away the black skin, *i. e.* cloud."

In other places the cloud is called the rain-giving and fertilizing skin: —

> Rv. I. 129, 3. "dasmáh hí sma vríshanam pínvasi tvákam,"
> "For thou, the strong one, fillest the rainy skin."

[1] Βέλλερος may either be simply identified with "varvara," in the sense of shaggy, or by taking Ϝελλος as representing the Latin *villus*, an adjective Ϝελλερος might have been formed, like φθονε-ρός from φθόνος. The transition into λλ appears also in μάλλος, sheep's-wool, where the μ represents the labial liquid. See Lobeck, *De Prothesi et Aphæresi*, p. 111 seq.; and Curtius, in Kuhn's *Zeitschrift*, vol. iii. p. 410: μαρπ = vrik; μέλδων = Ϝέλδων, μάτην = vrithâ.

While thus the cloud itself is spoken of as a black skin, the demon of the cloud, or the cloud personified, appears in the Veda as a ram, *i. e.* as a shaggy, hairy animal, in fact, as a Βέλλερος.

Thus Ura*n*a, which, as we saw before, meant ram or *laniger*, is a name of a demon, slain by Indra: —

Rv. II. 14. "Ye priests, bring hither Soma for Indra, pour from the bowls the delicious food! The hero truly always loves to drink of it; sacrifice to the strong, for he desires it!

"Ye priests, he who struck down V*r*itra, when he had hid the waters, as a tree is struck by lightning, — to him who desires this Soma, offer it; for that Indra desires to drink it!

"Ye priests, he who slew D*r*ibhîka, who drove out the cows, for he had opened the stable, to him offer this Soma! Cover him with Somas as the wind in the sky, as an old woman covers herself with clothes!

"Ye priests, he who slew Ura*n*a, who had shown his ninety-nine arms, — he who slew down to the ground Arbuda, that Indra call hither to the offering of Soma!"

Here Ura*n*a is no doubt a proper name, but the idea which it suggested originally could only have been that of "ura*n*a," meaning ram or some other shaggy animal. And the same applies to the Greek Βέλλερος. Though in Greek it has become a mere proper name, its original meaning was clearly that of the shaggy ram as the symbol of the shaggy cloud, a *monstrum villosum*, this being the very adjective which Roman poets like to apply to monsters of the same kith and kin, such as Gorgo or Cacus; *e. g.* Ov. "Met." x. 21: —

"Nec uti villosa colubris
Terna Medusæi vincirem guttura monstri."

"Æn." viii. 266 (of Cacus): —

"Terribiles oculos, vultum, villosaque setis
Pectora semiferi" . . . .

We cannot therefore claim the name of Belleros or

Bellerophon for that period of mythology which preceded the Aryan separation, a period during which such names as Dyaus = Ζεύς, Varu*n*a = Οὐρανός, Ushas = Ἠώς, Sara*n*yû = Ἐρινύς, Ahanâ = Δάφνη and Ἀθήνη, *R*ibhu = Ὀρφεύς, Haritas = Χάριτες were current among the ancient worshippers of the Devas or bright gods. But we can see at least this, that Bellerophontes had an intelligible meaning, and a meaning analogous to that of other names of solar heroes, the enemies of the dark powers of nature, whether in the shape of night, or dark clouds, or winter. In the Veda one of the principal representatives of that class of demons is V*r*itra, literally the coverer, the hider, whether of light or rain. Indra, the great solar deity of the Veda, is emphatically called "V*r*itrahan," the killer of V*r*itra. It is well known that the name of Indra, as the supreme deity of the Vedic pantheon, is a name of Indian growth. Derived from the same root as "indu," drop, it represents the Jupiter *pluvius*, whose supremacy among the gods of India is fully accounted for by the climatic character of that country. Dyaus, *i. e.* Ζεύς, the god of the bright sky, the original supreme deity of the undivided Aryans, was replaced in India by Indra, who is sometimes called the son of Dyaus, so that in India the prophecy of Prometheus may be said to have been fulfilled, even before it was uttered under a Greek sky.

But though we must not look in Greek mythology for traces of a name like Indra, which did not spring into existence before the separation of the Aryans, it is not impossible that some of the names of Indra's enemies may have been preserved in other countries. These enemies were the enemies of Dyaus and other gods as well as of Indra; and as they belong to an earlier period, the appearance of their names in the new homes of the Aryan emigrants could have nothing to surprise us.

One of the names belonging to this class of beings, hostile to men and the bright gods, and common to India and Greece, I observed many years ago, and having communicated my observation to several of my friends, it was mentioned by them even before I found an opportunity of laying it before the public, and supporting it by sufficient proof. My excellent friend, Professor Trithen, whose early death has deprived Sanskrit scholarship of a man of real genius and high promise, mentioned my identification of Kerberos with the Sanskrit "*s*arvara" in a Paper read in April, 1848, and published in the "Transactions of the Philological Society;" and another learned friend of mine referred to it with approval a few years later, though neither of them represented correctly the steps by which I had arrived at my conclusion. My first point was that, as "*s*ârvarî" in the Veda means the night, "*s*arvara" must have had the original sense of dark or pale: —

Rv. V. 52, 3. "té syandrâso ná ukshá*n*a*h* áti skandanti *s*árvarî*h*,"
"These (the Storm-gods), like powerful bulls, rise over the dark nights (or the dark clouds?)."

My second point was that the *r* in "*s*arvara" may be dropt, and this I proved by comparing "*s*arvaríka," a low, vile man, with "*s*avara," a barbarian; or "*s*ârvara,"[1] mischievous, nocturnal, with "*s*âvara," low, vile. I thus arrived at "*s*avara," as a modified form

[1] Durga, in his *Commentary on the Nirukta* (MS. E. I. H. 357, p. 223), says of the Dawn: "*s*ârvare*n*a tamasâ digdhâni sarvadravyâ*n*i prakâ*s*odakena dhautânîva karoti."

of "*sarvara*," in the sense of dark, pale, or nocturnal. Lastly, by admitting the frequent change of *r* into *l*, I connected "*sabála*," the Vedic epithet of the dog of Yama, the son of Saramâ, with Kérberos, though I drew attention to the difference in the accent as a point that still required explanation. Kerberos, therefore, in Greek, would have meant originally the dark one, the dog of night, watching the path to the lower world. In the Veda we find two such dogs, but they have not yet received any proper names, and are without that individuality which was imparted to them by later legends. All we learn of them from the Veda is that they have four eyes and broad snouts, that their color is dark or tawny, that they guard the road to the abode of Yama, the king of the departed, and that the dead must pass by them before they can come to Yama and the Fathers. They are also said to move about among men, as the messengers of Yama, to feast on the life of men, so that Yama is implored to protect men from their fury, while, in other places, they themselves are invoked, like Yama and M*r*ityu, to grant a long life to man. As the offspring of Saramâ, they are called Sârameya; but they have, as yet, no real proper names. The same applies to Kerberos. His proper name does not occur in Homer, but the dog of Hades in Erebos is mentioned by him without further particulars. Hesiod is the first who mentions the name and genealogy of Kerberos, and with him he is already fifty-headed, brazen-voiced, and furious. Later poets speak of him as three-headed, with serpents for his tail and mane; and at last he becomes hundred-headed. This Kerberos, as we know, is seized by Herakles and brought up to the daylight, though thrown back again into Hades.

But, besides Kerberos, there is another dog conquered by Herakles, and as he, like Kerberos, is born of Typhaon and Echidna, we may well look upon him as the brother or ditto of Kerberos. He is the dog of Geryones, sometimes called Kerberos himself (" Palæph." 40); and as Herakles, before conquering Kerberos, has first to struggle with Menœtios, the cowherd, we find that in his eighth labor, too, Herakles has to struggle with the cowherd Eurytion and his dog; nay, according to some authorities, Menœtios himself takes part again in this struggle. This second dog is known by the name of " Orthros," the exact copy, I believe, of the Vedic V*r*itra. That the Vedic V*r*itra should appear in Greece in the shape of a dog, need not surprise us, particularly as there are traces to show that in Greek mythology also he was originally a monster of a less definite character. We find him, in Hesiod's " Theogony," v. 308 seq., among the children of Echidna and Typhaon: —

ἡ δ' ὑποκυσαμένη τέκετο κρατερόφρονα τέκνα,
"Ορθρον μὲν πρῶτον κύνα γείνατο Γηρυονῆϊ.
δεύτερον αὖτις ἔτικτεν ἀμήχανον, οὔτι φατειόν
Κέρβερον, ὠμηστήν, 'Αΐδεω κύνα χαλκεόφωνον,
πεντηκοντακάρηνον, ἀναιδέα τε κρατερόν τε.

Soon after, "Ορθρος, for this is, no doubt, the right reading, instead of "Ορθος, is called the parent of the Nemæan lion. And what indicates still more the original meaning of "Ορθρος as a representative of darkness struggling with light, is the idiomatic use of ὄρθρος as signifying the time before sunrise. Thus we read in Hesiod, " O. D." 575, ὄρθρου ἀνιστάμενος, rising early, *i. e.* while the darkness still reigns, and while the last portion of the night is not yet driven away by the dawn (*entre chien et loup*). The swallow, too, is called ὀρθρόγοη (568), literally "the early wailing;" the cock ὀρθροβόας, the earlier caller. Thus we read in Hom. "Hymn. Merc." 98, —

> ὀρφναίη δ' ἐπίκουρος ἐπαύετο δαιμονίη νύξ,
> ἡ πλείων, τάχα δ' ὄρθρος ἐγίγνετο δημιοεργος,

where ὄρθρος might simply be translated by V*r*itra, if we consider how, in Vedic phraseology, V*r*itra is the thief who keeps the cows or the rays of the morning shut up in his stable, and how the first peep of day is expressed by Saramâ discovering the dark stables of V*r*itra and the Pa*n*is. Of Hermês (the Sârameya) it is said (v. 145) that he comes ὄρθριος, *i. e.* with V*r*itra, at the time of the final discomfiture of V*r*itra,[1] and that he comes silently, so that not even the dogs bark at him, οὔτε κύνες λελάκοντο.

Thus we discover in Herakles, the victor of Orthros, a real V*r*itrahan, what might have been in Greek an Ὀρθροφῶν or Ὀρθροφόντης; and, though the names may differ, we now see in Βελλεροφῶν or Βελλεροφόντης, who killed, if not a he-goat (Ura*n*a), at least a she-goat, *i. e.* Χίμαιρα, a mere variation of the same solar hero, and a reflection of the Vedic Indra V*r*itrahan. Chimæra, like Orthros and Kerberos, is a being with three heads or three bodies (τρισώματος and τρικέφαλος); nay, like Orthros and Kerberos, Chimæra, too, is the offspring of Typhaon and Echidna.

Nay, further, although the name of Ὀρθροφῶν or Ὀρθροφόντης has not been preserved in Greek mythology, it is possible, I think, to discover in Greek traces of another name, having the same import in Sanskrit,

[1] The same place where V*r*itra lies (i. 52, 6, "rá*g*asa*h* budhnám") is also called the birthplace of Indra, iv. 1, 11.

and frequently used as a synonym of "vritrahan." This is "dasyuhan," the killer of Dasyu. "Dasyu" or "dâsa" is in the Veda the general name of the enemies of the bright gods, as well as of their worshippers, the Aryan settlers of India. "Dasyuhantâ" or "dâsa-hantâ" would in Greek assume the form of δεωφόντης, or, as in some places of ancient Greece δ was pronounced like λ,[1] this might assume the form of λεωφόντης. Now this Leophontes occurs in Greek mythology as another name of Bellerophon, and it is clear that the meaning of that name could not have been lion-killer, for that would have been Leontophontes, but that it could only signify killer of whatever is expressed by λεω or δεω.

It is perfectly true that the change of *d* into *l* is in Greek restricted to certain dialects, and that it cannot

[1] That *d* and *l* are interchangeable letters is perfectly true, but this general rule is liable to many limitations as applied to different languages. An original *l*, for instance, is hardly ever changed to *d*, and hence the derivation of *lingua* from *lih*, to lick, is very doubtful; for *dingua*, which is mentioned as the older form of *lingua*, could well have been changed to *lingua*, but not vice versa. On the same ground I doubt whether in *adeps* the *d* represents an original Aryan *l*, although the Greek ἄλειφα, ointment, λίπα, fat, and Sanskrit "lip," to anoint, would seem to support this view. My former identification of μελετάω and *meditor* is equally untenable. All we can say for certain is that an original or Aryan *d* may become *l* in Latin: *e. g.* Sansk. "devara," Greek δάηρ = Lat. *levir*; Sansk. "dih," Goth. "deiga" = Lat. *pol-lingo*; Greek δάκρυ, Goth. "tagr" = Lat. *lacru-ma*; Greek θώραξ = Lat. *lorica*; Greek Ὀδυσσεύς = Lat. *Ulyxes*. In Latin itself an original *d* changes dialectically with *l*, as in *odor* and *olfacit*; *impedimenta* and *impelimenta*; *dedicare* and *delicare*; *cassida* and *cassila*; *sedere* and *solium*; *præsidium* and *præsilium*, and *sul* in *præsul*, etc.; *dautia* and *lautia*; *dingua* ("tuggô" Goth.) and *lingua*; *Medicæ* and *Melicæ*; *redivia* and *relurium*, if from *reduo*, like *induviæ*, and not from *luo*, as proposed by Festus; *Diumpais* (Osc.) and *lymphis*; *Akudunnia* (Osk.) and *Aquilonia*, of unknown origin, but with original *d*, as proved even by the modern name "Lacedogna." In Greek the same dialectic change is recorded in λάφνη = δάφνη, λίσκος = δίσκος, Ὀλυσσεύς = Ὀδυσσεύς.

be admitted as a general rule, unless there be some new evidence to that effect. Were it not so, one might feel inclined to trace even the common Greek word for people λαός, back to the same source as the Sanskrit, "dâsa." For "dasyu," meaning originally enemies, *hostes*, assumed in Zend "da*n*hu" and "daqyu, the sense of province, — a transition of meaning which is rendered intelligible by the use of "dahyu" in the cuneiform inscriptions, where Darius calls himself king of Persia and king of the Dahyus, *i. e.* of the conquered people or provinces.[1] The same transition of meaning must be admitted in Greek, if, as Professor Pott suggests, the Greek δεσ-πότης and δέσ-ποινα correspond to Sanskrit "dâsa-pati" and "dâsá-patnî," in the sense of lord of subjects. The only difficulty here, would be the retention of the *s* of dâsá," which, according to general practice, would have been dropt between two vowels. The true form of "dâsá" in Greek would be δαός or δεώς. Δᾶός is well known as a name of slaves, but it admits of a different explanation.[2] The adjective δάϊος, however, or δήϊος, hostile, is clearly derived from the same source, the root being "das," to perish; though it is true that in its frequent application to fire, the adjective δάϊος might also be referred to the root "du," to burn.[3] After we have once discovered on Greek soil the traces of "dâsa" in the sense of enemy, we see clearly that Leophontes, as the name of Bellerophon, could not have meant originally the killer of the people, but only

[1] Lassen, *Zeitschrift für die Kunde des Morgenlandes*, vol. vi. p. 12.

[2] See Niebuhr, *Kleinere Schriften*, vol. i. p. 377.

[3] See Aufrecht, in Kuhn's *Zeitschrift*, vol. vii. p. 312; Pott, Ib. vol. viii. p. 428.

the killer of enemies. And if Leophontes meant the killer of enemies or fiends, it can only be explained as corresponding to the Sanskrit "dâsahantâ," the destroyer of enemies, these enemies being the very "Dâsas" or demons of the Veda, such as V*r*itra (Ὄρθρος), Namu*k*i (Ἀμυκός),[1] *S*ambara,[2] and others.

November, 1855.[3]

[1] A. Fick, in Benfey's *Orient und Occident*, vol. iii. p. 126.

[2] *S*ambara, a very common name of a demon slain by Indra, invites comparison with "*s*abara" and "*s*arbara," the Sanskrit original of Kerberos. In the Zend-Avesta, too, "*s*rvara" occurs as the name of a serpent ("azhi").

[3] Some critical remarks on the subject of this article may be seen in Professor Pott's *Etymologische Forschungen*, second edition, vol. ii. p. 744.

XX.

THE NORSEMEN IN ICELAND.[1]

THERE is, after Anglo-Saxon, no language, no literature, no mythology so full of interest for the elucidation of the earliest history of the race which now inhabits these British Isles as the Icelandic. Nay, in one respect, Icelandic beats every other dialect of the great Teutonic family of speech, not excepting Anglo-Saxon and Old High-German and Gothic. It is in Icelandic alone that we find complete remains of genuine Teutonic heathendom. Gothic, as a language, is more ancient than Icelandic; but the only literary work which we possess in Gothic is a translation of the Bible. The Anglo-Saxon literature, with the exception of the "Beowulf," is Christian. The old heroes of the "Nibelunge," such as we find them represented in the Suabian epic, have been converted into church-going knights; whereas, in the ballads of the elder "Edda," Sigurd and Brynhild appear before us in their full pagan grandeur, holding nothing sacred but their love, and defying all laws, human and divine, in the name of that one almighty passion. The Icelandic contains the key to many a riddle in the English lan

[1] *The Norsemen in Iceland.* By Dr. G. W. Dasent. *Oxford Essays,* 1858.

guage, and to many a mystery in the English character. Though the Old Norse is but a dialect of the same language which the Angles and Saxons brought to Britain, though the Norman blood is the same blood that floods and ebbs in every German heart, yet there is an accent of defiance in that rugged Northern speech, and a spring of daring madness in that throbbing Northern heart, which marks the Northman wherever he appears, whether in Iceland or in Sicily, whether on the Seine or on the Thames. At the beginning of the ninth century, when the great Northern exodus began, Europe, as Dr. Dasent remarks, "was in danger of becoming too comfortable. The two nations destined to run neck-and-neck in the great race of civilization, Frank and Anglo-Saxon, had a tendency to become dull and lazy, and neither could arrive at perfection till it had been chastised by the Norsemen, and finally forced to admit an infusion of Northern blood into its sluggish veins. The vigor of the various branches of the Teutonic stock may be measured by the proportion of Norman blood which they received; and the national character of England owes more to the descendants of Hrolf Ganger than to the followers of Hengist and Horsa."

But what is known of the early history of the Norsemen? Theirs was the life of reckless freebooters, and they had no time to dream and ponder on the past, which they had left behind in Norway. Where they settled as colonists or as rulers, their own traditions, their very language, were soon forgotten. Their language has nowhere struck root on foreign ground, even where, as in Normandy, they became earls of Rouen, or, as in these isles, kings of England. There is but one exception — Iceland. Iceland was discovered, peopled, and civilized by Norsemen in the ninth century; and in the nineteenth century, the language spoken there is still the dialect of Harold Fairhair, and the stories told there are still the stories of the "Edda," or the Venerable Grandmother. Dr. Dasent gives us a rapid sketch of the first landings of the Norwegian refugees on the fells and forths of Iceland. He describes how love of freedom drove the subjects of Harold Fairhair forth from their home; how the Teutonic tribes, though they loved their kings, the sons of Odin, and sovereigns by the grace of God, detested the dictatorship of Harold. "He was a mighty warrior," so says the ancient Saga, "and laid Norway under him, and put out of the way some of those who held districts, and some of them he drove out of the land; and, besides, many men escaped out of Norway because of the overbearing of Harold Fairhair, for they would not stay to be subject to him." These early emigrants were Pagans, and it was not till the end of the tenth century that Christianity reached the Ultima Thule of Europe. The missionaries, however, who converted the freemen of Iceland were freemen themselves. They did not come with the pomp and the pretensions of the Church of Rome. They preached Christ rather than the Pope; they taught religion rather than theology. Nor were they afraid of the old heathen gods, or angry with every custom that was not of Christian growth. Sometimes this tolerance may have been carried too far, for we read of kings, like Helgi, "mixed in their faith, who trusted in Christ, but at the same time invoked Thor's aid whenever they went to sea, or got into any difficulty."

But on the whole, the kindly feeling of the Icelandic priesthood toward the national traditions and customs and prejudices of their converts must have been beneficial. Sons and daughters were not forced to call the gods whom their fathers and mothers had worshipped, devils; and they were allowed to use the name of "Allfadir," whom they had invoked in the prayers of their childhood when praying to Him who is "Our Father in Heaven."

The Icelandic missionaries had peculiar advantages in their relation to the system of paganism which they came to combat. Nowhere else, perhaps, in the whole history of Christianity, has the missionary been brought face to face with a race of gods who were believed by their own worshippers to be doomed to death. The missionaries had only to proclaim that Balder was dead, that the mighty Odin and Thor were dead. The people knew that these gods were to die, and the message of the One Ever-living God must have touched their ears and their hearts with comfort and joy. Thus, while in Germany the priests were occupied for a long time in destroying every trace of heathenism, in condemning every ancient lay as the work of the devil, in felling sacred trees and abolishing national customs, the missionaries of Iceland were able to take a more charitable view of the past, and they became the keepers of those very poems, and laws, and proverbs, and Runic inscriptions, which on the Continent had to be put down with inquisitorial cruelty. The men to whom the collection of the ancient pagan poetry of Iceland is commonly ascribed, were men of Christian learning: the one, the founder of a public school; the other, famous as the author of a history of the North, the "Heimskringla." It is owing to their labors that we know anything of the ancient religion, the traditions, the maxims, the habits of the Norsemen, and it is from these sources that Dr. Dasent has drawn his stores of information, and composed his vigorous and living sketch of primitive Northern life. It is but a sketch, but a sketch that will bear addition and completion. Dr. Dasent dwells most fully on the religious system of Iceland, which is the same, at least in its general outline, as that believed in by all the members of the Teutonic family, and may truly be called one of the various dialects of the primitive religious and mythological language of the Aryan race. There is nothing more interesting than religion in the whole history of man. By its side, poetry and art, science and law, sink into comparative insignificance. Dr. Dasent, however, has not confined his essay to the religious life of Iceland. He has added some minute descriptions of the domestic habits, the dress, the armor, the diet, the laws, and the customs of the race, and he has proved himself well at home in the Icelandic homestead. One thing only we miss, — an account of their epic poetry; and this, we believe, would on several points have furnished a truer picture of the very early and purely pagan life of the Norsemen than the extracts from their histories and law books, which are more or less, if not under the influence of Christianity, at least touched by the spirit of a more advanced civilization. The old poems, in their alliterating metre, were proof against later modifications. We probably possess what we do possess of them, in its original form. As they were composed in Norway in the sixth century after Christ, they were carried to

Iceland in the ninth, and written down in the eleventh century. The prose portions of the "Old Edda," and still more of the "Young Edda," may be of later origin. They betray in many instances the hand of a Christian writer. And the same applies to the later Sagas and law books. Here much is still to be done by the critic, and we look forward with great interest to a fuller inquiry into the age of the various parts of Icelandic literature, the history of the MSS., the genuineness of their titles, and similar questions. Such subjects are hardly fit for popular treatment, and we do not blame Dr. Dasent for having passed them over in his essay. But the translator of the younger "Edda" ought to tell us hereafter what is the history of this, and of the older collection of Icelandic poetry. How do we know, for instance, that Sæmund (1056–1133) collected the Old, Snorro Sturlason (1178–1241) the Young "Edda?" How do we know that the MSS. which we now possess, have a right to the title of "Edda?" All this rests, as far as we know, on the authority of Bishop Brynjulf Swendsen, who discovered the "Codex regius" in 1643, and wrote on the copy of it, with his own hand, the title of "Edda Sæmundar hinns froda." None of the MSS. of the second, or prose "Edda," bear that title in any well-authenticated form; still less is it known whether Snorro composed either part or the whole of it. All these questions ought to be answered, as far as they can be answered, before we can hope to see the life of the ancient Norsemen drawn with truthfulness and accuracy. The greater part of the poems, however, bear an expression of genuineness which cannot be challenged; and a comparison of the mythology of the "Edda" with that of the Teutonic tribes, and again, in a more general manner, with that of the other Indo-Germanic races, is best calculated to convince the skeptic that the names and the legends of the Eddic gods are not of late invention. There are passages in the "Edda" which sound like verses from the Veda. Dr. Dasent quotes the following lines from the elder "Edda:" —

> "'Twas the morning of time,
> When yet naught was,
> Nor sand nor sea were there,
> Nor cooling streams;
> Earth was not formed,
> Nor heaven above;
> A yawning gap there was,
> And grass nowhere."

A hymn of the Veda begins in a very similar way: —

> "Nor Aught nor Naught existed; yon bright sky
> Was not, nor heaven's broad woof outstretched above.
> What covered all? what sheltered? what concealed?
> Was it the waters fathomless abyss?" etc.

There are several mythological expressions common to the "Edda" and Homer. In the "Edda," man is said to have been created out of an ash-tree. In Hesiod, Zeus creates the third race of men out of ash-trees; and that this tradition was not unknown to Homer, we learn from Penelope's address to Ulysses: "Tell me thy family, from whence thou art; for thou art not sprung from the olden tree, or from the rock."

There are, however, other passages in the "Edda," particularly in the prose "Edda," which ought to be carefully examined before they are admitted as evidence on the primitive paganism of the Norsemen. The prose "Edda" was written by a man who mixed classical learning and Christian ideas with Northern traditions. This is clearly seen in the preface. But traces of the same influence may be discovered in other parts, as, for instance, in the dialogue called "Gylfi's Mocking." The ideas which it contains are meant to be pagan, but are they really pagan in their origin? Dr. Dasent gives the following extract:—

"Who is first and eldest of all gods? He is called "Allfadir" (the Father of All, the Great Father) in our tongue. He lives from all ages, and rules over his realm, and sways all things, great and small. He made heaven and earth, and the sky, and all that belongs to them; and he made man, and gave him a soul that shall live and never perish, though the body rot to mould or burn to ashes. All men that are right-minded shall live and be with him in the place called "Vingolf:" but wicked ones fare to Hell, and thence into Niflhell, that is, beneath in the ninth world."

We ask Dr. Dasent, Is this pure, genuine, unsophisticated paganism? Is it language that Sigurd and Brynhild would have understood? Is that "Allfadir" really nothing more than Odin, who himself must perish, and whom at the day of doom the wolf, the Fenris-wolf, was to swallow at one gulp? We can only ask the question here, but we doubt not that in his next work on the antiquities of the Northern races, Dr. Dasent will give us a full and complete answer, and thus satisfy the curiosity which he has raised by his valuable contribution to the "Oxford Essays."

***July*, 1858**

XXI.

FOLK-LORE.[1]

As the science of language has supplied a new basis for the science of mythology, the science of mythology bids fair, in its turn, to open the way to a new and scientific study of the folk-lore of the Aryan nations. Not only have the radical and formal elements of language been proved to be the same in India, Greece, Italy, among the Celtic, Teutonic, and Slavonic nations; not only have the names of many of their gods, the forms of their worship, and the mainsprings of their religious sentiment been traced back to one common Aryan source; but a further advance has been made. A myth, it was argued, dwindles down to a legend, a legend to the tale; and if the myths were originally identical in India, Greece, Italy, and Germany, why should not the tales also of these countries show some similarity even in the songs of the Indian ayah and the English nurse? There is some truth in this line of argument, but there is likewise great danger of error. Granted that words and myths were originally identical among all the members of the Aryan family; granted likewise that they all went through the same vicissi-

[1] *Curiosities of Indo-European Tradition and Folk-Lore.* By W. K. Kelly. London: Chapman & Hall. 1863.

tudes; would it not follow that, as no sound scholar thinks of comparing Hindustani and English, or Italian and Russian, no attempt at comparing the modern tales of Europe to the modern tales of India could ever lead to any satisfactory results? The tales, or "Mährchen," are the modern *patois* of mythology, and if they are to become the subject of scientific treatment, the first task that has to be accomplished is to trace back each modern tale to some earlier legend, and each legend to some primitive myth. And here it is very important to remark that, although originally our popular tales were reproductions of more ancient legends, yet after a time a general taste was created for marvelous stories, and new ones were invented, in large numbers whenever they were required, by every grandmother and every nurse. Even in these purely imaginative tales, analogies may no doubt be discovered with more genuine tales, because they were made after original patterns, and in many cases, were mere variations of an ancient air. But if we tried to analyze them by the same tests as the genuine tales, if we attempted to recognize in them the features of ancient legends, or to discover in these fanciful strains the key-notes of sacred mythology, we should certainly share the fate of those valiant knights who were led through an enchanted forest by the voices of fairies till they found themselves landed in a bottomless quagmire. Jacob Grimm, as Mr. Kelly tells us in his work on "Indo-European Tradition and Folk-Lore," was the first scholar who pointed out the importance of collecting all that could be saved of popular stories, customs, sayings, superstitions, and beliefs. His "German Mythology" is a store-house of such curiosities, and, together with his collection of "Mährchen," it shows how much there is still floating about of the most ancient language, thought, fancy, and belief, that might be, and ought to be collected in every part of the world. The Norse Tales lately published by Dr. Dasent are another instance that shows how much there is to reward the labors of a careful collector and a thoughtful interpreter. Sufficient material has been collected to enable scholars to see that these tales and translations are not arbitrary inventions or modern fictions, but that their fibres cling in many instances to the very germs of ancient language and ancient thought. Among those who, in Germany, have followed in the track of Grimm, and endeavored to trace the modern folk-lore back to its most primitive sources, the names of Kuhn, Schwartz, Mannhardt, and Wolf held a prominent place; and it has been the object of Mr. Kelly to make known to us in his book the most remarkable discoveries which have been achieved by the successors and countrymen of Jacob Grimm in this field of antiquarian research.

Mr. Kelly deserves great credit for the pains he has taken in mastering this difficult subject, but we regret the form in which he has thought fit to communicate to an English public the results of his labors. He tells us that a work by Dr. Kuhn, "On the Descent of Fire and the Drink of the Gods," is his chief authority; but he adds: —

"Although the very different nature of my work has seldom allowed me to translate two or three consecutive sentences from Dr. Kuhn's elaborate treatise, yet I wish it to be fully understood that, but for the latter, the former could not have been written. I am the more bound to state this once for all, as emphatically as I can, because the very extent of my indebtedness has hindered me from acknowledging my obligations to Dr. Kuhn, in the text or in foot-notes, as constantly as I have done in most other cases."

We cannot help considering this an unsatisfactory arrangement. If Mr. Kelly had given a translation of Dr. Kuhn's essay, English readers would have known whom to hold responsible for the statements, many of them very startling, as to the coincidences in the tales and traditions of the Aryan nations. Or, again, if Mr. Kelly had written a book of his own, we should have had the same advantage; for he would, no doubt, have considered himself bound to substantiate every fact quoted from the "Edda" or from the Veda by a suitable reference. As it is, the reader's curiosity is certainly excited to the highest degree, but his incredulity is in no way relieved. Mr. Kelly does not tell us that he is a Sanskrit or an Icelandic scholar, and hence we naturally infer that his assertions about the gods of the Indian and Northern pantheons are borrowed from Dr. Kuhn and other German writers. But, if so, it would have been far preferable to give the *ipsissima verba* of these scholars, because, in descriptions of ancient forms of belief or superstition, the slightest change of expression is apt to change the whole bearing of a sentence. Many of Dr. Kuhn's opinions have been challenged and controverted by his own countrymen, — by Welcker, Bunsen, Pott, and others; some he has successfully supported by new evidence, others he may be supposed to have surrendered. All this could not be otherwise in a subject so new and necessarily so full of guess-work as the study of folk-lore, and it detracts in no way from the value of the excellent essays in which Dr. Kuhn and others have analyzed various myths of the Aryan nations. All we insist on is this, that before we can accept any conclusions as to the Vedic character of Greek gods, or the deep meaning of so whimsical a custom as divination with the sieve and shears, we must have chapter and verse from the Veda, and well authenticated descriptions of the customs referred to. People do not object to general assertions about the Bible, or Homer, or Virgil, or Shakespeare, because here they can judge for themselves, and would not mind the trouble of checking statements which seem at all startling. But if they are asked to believe that the Veda contains the true theogony of Greece, that Orpheus is "*R*ibhu," or the wind, that the Charites are the Vedic "Haritas," or horses, the Erinnys "Sara*n*yû," or the lightning, they will naturally insist on evidence such as should enable them to judge for themselves, before assenting to even the most plausible theories. What authority is there for saying (p. 14) that, —

"The Sanskrit tongue in which the Vedas are written, is the sacred language of India, that is to say, the oldest language, the one which was spoken, as the Hindus believe, by the gods themselves, when gods and men were in frequent fellowship with each other, from the time when Yama descended from heaven to become the first of mortals."

The Hindus, as far as we know, never say that the gods spoke Vedic as opposed to ordinary Sanskrit; they never held that during the Vedic period the gods lived in more frequent fellowship with men; they never speak of Yama as descending from heaven to become the first of mortals. These are three mistakes, or at least three entirely un-Indian ideas, in one sentence. Again, when we are told (p. 19) that, "in the Vedas, Yama is the first lightning-born mortal," we imagine that this is a simple statement from the Veda, whereas it is a merely hypothetical and, we believe, erroneous view of the nature of Yama, drawn from the interpretation of the names of some Vedic deities. If given as a guess, with all its pros and cons, it would be valuable; if given, as here, as a simple fact, it is utterly deceptive.

In page 18 we are told:—

"On the whole, it is manifest that all these divine tribes, Maruts, *R*ibhus, Bh*r*igus, and Angiras, are beings identical in nature, distinguished from each other only by their elemental functions, and not essentially different from the Pit*r*is or fathers. The latter are simply the souls of the pious dead."

Now these are strong and startling assertions, but again given dogmatically, and without any proof. The Pit*r*is are, no doubt, the fathers, and they might be called the souls of the pious dead; but, if so, they have no elementary origin, like the gods of the storms, the days, and the seasons; nor can they have any elementary functions. To say that the Pit*r*is or Manes shone as stars to mortal eyes (p. 20) is another assertion that requires considerable limitation, and is apt to convey as false an idea of the primitive faith of the Vedic Rishis, as when (p. 21) we read that the "Âpas" (waters) are cloud-maidens, brides of the gods, or navigators of the celestial sea ("nâvya*h*"), and that the "Apsaras" are damsels destined to delight the souls of heroes — the houris, in fact, of the

Vedic paradise. The germs of some of these ideas may, perhaps, be discovered in the hymns of the Veda, but to speak thus broadly of a Vedic paradise, of houris, and cloud-maidens, is to convey, as far as we can judge from texts and translations hitherto published, an utterly false idea of the simple religion of the Vedic poets.

One other instance must suffice. At the end of the sixth chapter, in order to explain why a healing virtue is ascribed in German folk-lore to the mistletoe and the ash, Mr. Kelly makes the following statement: "This healing virtue, which the mistletoe shares with the ash, is a long-descended tradition, for the Kush*th*a, the embodiment of the Soma, a healing plant of the highest renown among the Southern Aryans, was one that grew beneath the heavenly A*s*vattha." We tried in vain to understand the exact power of the *for* in this sentence. Great stress is laid in Northern Mythology on the fact that the mistletoe grows upon a tree, and does not, like all other plants, spring from the earth. But the Kush*th*a is never said to grow upon the heavenly A*s*vattha, which Mr. Kelly translates by religious fig, but beneath it. In fact, it is the A*s*vattha, or Pippal, which, if found growing on another tree, the *S*ami (*Acacia suma*), is considered by the Brahmans as peculiarly fitted for sacrificial purposes. The *for*, therefore, must refer to something else as forming the *tertium comparationis* between the mistletoe and the Kush*th*a. Is it their healing power? Hardly; for, in the case of the mistletoe, the healing power is a popular superstition; in the case of the Kush*th*a, the *Costus speciosus*, it is, we believe, a medicinal fact. We suppose, therefore, that Mr. Kelly perceived the similarity between the German and the Indian plants to consist in this, that the Kush*th*a was really an embodiment of Soma, for in another passage he says : —

"Besides the earthly Soma, the Hindus recognize a heavenly Soma or Am*r*ita (*ambrosia*), that drops from the imperishable A*s*vattha or Peepul (*Ficus religiosa*), out of which the immortals shaped the heaven and the earth. Beneath this mighty tree, which spreads its branches over the third heaven, dwell Yama and the Pit*r*is, and quaff the drink of immortality with the gods. At its foot grow plants of all healing virtue, incorporations of the Soma."

Mr. Kelly then proceeds to remark that "the parallelism between the Indian and the Iranian world-tree on the one hand, and the ash Yggdrasil on the other, is very striking." We shall pass by the Iranian world-tree, the fact being that the Zend-Avesta does not recognize one, but always speaks of two trees.[1] But fixing our attention on Mr. Kelly's comparison of what he calls the Indian world-tree and the ash Yggdrasil, the case would stand thus: The Hindus believe in the existence of a Pippal-tree (*Ficus religiosa*) that drops Soma (*Asclepias acida*), at the foot of which grows the Kush*th*a (*Costus speciosus*), a medicinal plant, the incorporation of the Soma dropping from the Pippal. As there is a similarity between the ash Yggdrasil and the Pippal, both representing originally, as is maintained, the clouds of heaven, therefore a healing virtue was ascribed to the ash and the mistletoe by the Aryans that came to settle in Europe. We will not deny that if the facts, as here stated, were quite cor-

1 See vol. i. p. 154.

rect, some similarity of conception might be discovered in the German Yggdrasil and the Indian Pippal. But did the Brahmans ever believe in a Pippal dropping Soma, and in that Soma becoming embodied in a Ços-tus? Mr. Kelly here, for once, gives a reference to Rig-veda II. 164, which, as we find from the original work of Dr. Kuhn, is intended for Rig-veda II. 164, 19–22. In that hymn the word Kush*th*a never occurs. A tree is indeed mentioned there, but it is not called A*s*vattha, nor is it said to drop Soma, nor is there any allusion to the fact that heaven and earth were made of that tree. All that can be gathered from the extremely obscure language of that hymn is that the fruit of the tree there described is called Pippala; that birds settle on it eating that fruit; that they sing praises in honor of a share of immortality, and that these birds are called eaters of sweet things. That the word used for "immortality" may mean Soma, that the word meaning "sweet" may stand for the same beverage, is perfectly true; but, even if that conjectural rendering should be adopted, it would still leave the general meaning of the verses far too obscure to justify us in making them the basis of any mythological comparisons. As to the Kush*th*a — the *Costus speciosus*, which is said to be called in the Rig-veda an incorporation of Soma, we doubt whether such a word ever occurs in the Rig-veda. It is mentioned in the mystical formulas of the Atharva-veda, but there again it is called, indeed, the friend of Soma (Ath.-veda, V. 4, 7), but not its embodiment; nor is there any statement that under the A*s*vattha-tree there mentioned, the gods drink Soma, but simply that Yama drinks there with the gods.

It is impossible to be too careful in these matters, otherwise everything becomes everything. Although Mr. Kelly takes it for granted that the poets of the Veda knew a tree similar to the tree Yggdrasil, — a world-tree, or a cloud-tree, or whatever else it may be called, — there is not a single passage that has been brought forward in support by Mr. Kelly or by Dr. Kuhn himself, which could stand a more severe criticism. When the poets exclaim, "What wood, what tree was it, of which they made heaven and earth?" — this means no more in the ancient language of religious poetry than, Out of what material were heaven and earth formed? As to the tree Ilpa — or more correctly, Ilya — nothing is known of it beyond its name in one of the latest works of Vedic literature, the Upanishads, and the remarks of so modern a commentator as *S*ankara. There is no proof whatever of anything like the conception of the Yggdrasil having entered the thoughts of the Vedic poets; and to ascribe the healing virtue of ash or mistletoe to any reminiscence of a plant, Kush*th*a, that might have grown under a Vedic fig-tree, or Soma-tree, or Yggdrasil, is to attempt to lay hold of the shadow of a dream.

There is but one way in which a comparative study of the popular traditions of the Aryan nations can lead to any satisfactory result. Let each tale be traced back to its most original form, let that form be analyzed and interpreted in strict accordance with the rules of comparative philology, and after the kernel, or the simple and original conception of the myth, has been found, let us see how the same conception and the same myth have gradually expanded and become diversified under the bright sky of India and in the forests of Germany. Before the Northern Yggdrasil is compared to a supposed Indian world-tree it is absolutely necessary to gain a clear insight into the nature of the myth of Yggdrasil. That myth seems to be of a decidedly cosmogonic and philosophical character. The tree seems to express the Universe. It is said to have three roots: one in Niflheim, near the well called "Hvergelmir;" a second in Jötunheim, near the well of the wise Mimir; and a third in heaven, near the well of Vurdh. Its branches embrace the whole world. In heaven the gods hold their meetings under the shadow of this tree, near the well of Vurdh. The place is guarded by the three Nornas (Vurdh, Verdhandi, and Skuld, — Past, Present, and Future), who water the roots of the tree with the water of Vurdh. In the crown of the tree sits an eagle, and in the well of Hvergelmir lies the serpent Nidhöggr, and gnaws its roots. In none of these conceptions are there any clear traces of clouds or thunder-storms; but if there were, this would be the very reason why the Yggdrasil could not be compared to the Indian Asvattha, in which no ingenuity will ever discover either a bank of clouds or a thunder-storm.

December, 1863.

XXII.

ZULU NURSERY TALES.[1]

WE should before now have brought the Rev. Dr. Callaway's collection of the Nursery Tales, Traditions, and Histories of the Zulus to the notice of our readers, if we had not been waiting for a new instalment of his interesting work. Dr. Callaway calls what he has published the first part of the first volume, and as this part contained only about three or four sheets, we looked forward to a speedy continuation. The fact is that one cannot well form an opinion of the real character of nursery tales and popular stories without seeing a good many of them. Each story by itself may seem rather meaningless or absurd, but if certain features occur again and again, they become important in spite of their childishness, and enable us to discover some method in their absurdity. If we knew of only three or four of the stories of Jupiter or Herakles, we should hardly give much thought to them; but having before us the immense quantity of fables about Greek gods and goddesses, heroes and heroines, we naturally look upon them, with all their strangeness and extravagance, as a problem in the history of the Greek nation,

1 *Izinganekwane nensumansumane nezindaba zabantu.* "Nursery Tales, Traditions, and Histories of the Zulus." By the Rev. Henry Callaway, M. D. Vol. i. part i. Natal, 1866.

and we try to discover in them certain characteristics which throw light on the origin of these abnormal creations of the human mind. It was the same with the German nursery tales. Their existence in every country where German races had settled was perfectly well known, but they did not become the subject of historical and psychological inquiry till the brothers Grimm published their large collection, and thus enabled scholars to generalize on these popular fictions. By this time the study of popular tales has become a recognized branch of the study of mankind. It is known that such tales are not the invention of individual writers, but that, in Germany as well as everywhere else, they are the last remnants — the *detritus*, if we may say so — of an ancient mythology; that some of the principal heroes bear the nicknames of old heathen gods; and that in spite of the powerful dilution produced by the admixture of Christian ideas, the old leaven of heathendom can still be discovered in many of the stories now innocently told by German nurses of saints, apostles, and the Virgin Mary.

From this point of view, the mere fact that the Zulus possess nursery tales is curious, because nursery tales, at least such as treat of ghosts and fairies and giants, generally point back to a distant civilization, or at least to a long-continued national growth. Like the anomalies of a language, they show by their very strangeness that time enough has elapsed for the consolidation of purely traditional formations, and that a time must have been when what is now meaningless or irregular was formed with a purpose, and according to rule. But before it is possible to analyze these Zulu tales, two things are necessary. First, we must have a much larger collection of them than we now possess; and, secondly, more collections must be made among tribes of the same large race to which the Zulus belong. The Zulus are a Kafir race, and recent researches have made it very clear that the Kafir races occupy the whole east coast of Africa from the South to several degrees beyond the Equator. They migrated from North to South, and in the South they are bounded by the Hottentots, who belong to a different race. The Hottentots, too, are now believed to have migrated from the North of Africa, and their language is supposed to be akin to the dialects spoken in the countries south of Egypt. If the ethnological outlines of the continent of Africa are once firmly established, the study of the sacred and profane traditions of the several African tribes will acquire a new interest; and it is highly creditable to Dr. Callaway, Dr. Bleek, and others, to have made a beginning in a field of research which at first sight is not very attractive or promising. Many people, no doubt, will treat these stories with contempt, and will declare that they are not worth the paper on which they are printed. The same thing was said of Grimm's "Mährchen;" nay, it was said by Sir William Jones of the Zend-Avesta, and, by less distinguished scholars, of the Veda. But fifty years hence the collection of these stories may become as valuable as the few remaining bones of the dodo. Stories become extinct like dodos and megatheria, and they die out so rapidly that in Germany, for instance, it would be impossible at present to discover traces of many of the stories which the brothers Grimm and their friends caught up from the mouth of an old granny or a village doctor half a century ago.

Nor it it an easy matter to catch popular stories. The people who know them are willing enough to tell them to their children, but they do not like to repeat them to grown up people, least of all to strangers, who are supposed to laugh at them. Thus Dr. Callaways says: —

"Like most other people, the Zulus have their nursery tales. They have not hitherto, as far as I know, been collected. Indeed, it is probable that their existence even is suspected but by a few, for the women are the depositaries of these tales; and it is not common to meet with a man who is well acquainted with them, or who is willing to speak of them in any other way than as something which he has some dim recollection of having heard his grandmother relate. It has been no easy matter to drag out the following tales; and it is evident that many of them are but fragments of some more perfect narration."

Waiting, then, for a larger instalment of Zulu stories before we venture to pronounce an opinion of their value for ethnological purposes, we proceed to point out a few of their most curious features, which may serve as a lesson and as a warning to the student of the folk-lore of European and Indo-European nations. If we admit for the present, in the absence of any evidence to the contrary, that the Zulus were free from the influence of German missionaries or Dutch settlers in the formation of their popular stories, it is certainly surprising to see so many points of similarity between the heroes of their kraals and of our own nurseries. The introduction of animals, speaking and acting the parts of human beings, was long considered as an original thought of the Greek and the Teutonic tribes. We now find exactly the same kind of "animal fables" among the Zulus, and Dr. Bleek has actually discovered among the Hottentots traces of the stories of Renard the Fox.[1] The idea that among animals cunning is more successful than brute force,— an idea which pervades the stories of "Reinecke Fuchs," and of many other fables,—predominates likewise in the fables of the Zulus. In the Basuto legend of the "Little Hare," the hare has entered into an alliance with the lion, but, having been ill-treated by the latter, determines to be avenged. "My father," said he to the lion, "we are exposed to the rain and hail; let us build a hut." The lion, too lazy to work, left it to the hare to do, and "the wily runner" took the lion's tail, and interwove it so cleverly into the stakes and reeds of the hut that it remained there confined forever, and the hare had the pleasure of seeing his rival die of hunger and thirst. The trick is not quite so clever as that of Reinecke, when he persuades the bear to go out fishing on the ice; but then the hare compasses the death of the lion, while Reinecke by his stratagem only deprives the bear of his ornamental tail.

As in the German tales the character of Renard the Fox is repeated in a humanized shape as Till Eulenspiegel, so among the Zulus one of the most favorite characters is the young rogue, the boy U*h*lakanyana,

[1] *Reynard the Fox in South Africa.* By W. H. I. Bleek. London, 1864. "Whether these fables are indeed the real offspring of the desert, and can be considered as truly indigenous native literature, or whether they have been either purloined from the superior white race or at least brought into existence by the stimulus which contact with the latter gave to the native mind (like that resulting in the invention of the Tshiroki and Vei alphabets) may be matters of dispute for some time to come, and it may require as much research as was expended upon the solving of the riddle of the originality of the Ossianic poems" (p. xiii.).

who at first is despised and laughed at, but who always succeeds in the end in having the laugh on his side. This U*h*lakanyana performs, for instance, the same trick on a cannibal by which the hare entrapped the lion. The two have struck up a friendship, and are going to thatch their house before they sit down to devour two cows. U*h*lakanyana is bent on having the fat cow, but is afraid the cannibal will assign to him the lean cow. So he says to the cannibal, "Let the house be thatched now; then we can eat our meat. You see the sky, that we shall get wet." The cannibal said, "You are right, child of my sister." U*h*lakanyana said, "Do you do it then; I will go inside and push the thatching-needle for you." The cannibal went up. His hair was very, very long. U*h*lakanyana went inside and pushed the needle for him. He thatched in the hair of the cannibal, tying it very tightly; he knotted it into the thatch constantly, taking it by separate locks and fastening it firmly. He saw the hair was fast enough, and that the cannibal could not get down. When he was outside, U*h*lakanyana went to the fire, where the udder of the cow was boiled. He took it out and filled his mouth. The cannibal said, "What are you about, child of my sister? Let us just finish the house; afterwards we can do that; we can do it together." U*h*lakanyana replied, "Come down, then." The cannibal assented. When he was going to quit the house, he was unable to quit it. He cried out, "Child of my sister, how have you managed your thatching? U*h*lakanyana said, "See to it yourself. I have thatched well, for I shall not have any dispute. Now I am about to eat in peace; I no longer dispute with anybody, for I am alone with my cow." It hailed and rained. The cannibal cried on the top of the house; he was struck with the hailstones, and died there on the house. It cleared. U*h*lakanyana went out, and said, "Uncle, just come down. It has become clear. It no longer rains, and there is no longer hail, neither is there any more lightning. Why are you silent?" So U*h*lakanyana eat his cow alone, and then went his way.

Dr. Callaway compares the history of the travels and adventures of U*h*lakanyana to those of Tom Thumb and Jack the Giant-killer, and it is curious, indeed, to observe how many of the tricks which we admired as children in English or German story-books are here repeated with but trifling modifications. The feat performed by U*h*lakanyana of speaking before he was born exceeds indeed the achievements even of the most precocious of German imps, and can only be matched, as Dr. Callaway points out, by St. Benedict, who, according to Mabillon, sang eucharistic hymns in the same state in which U*h*lakanyana was clamoring for meat. But the stratagem by which this Zulu "Boots," after being delivered to the cannibal's mother to be boiled, manages to boil the old woman herself, can easily be matched by Peggy or Grethel who bakes the cannibal witch in her own oven, or by the Shifty Highland Lad, or by Maol a Chliobain who puts the giant's mother in the sack in which she had been suspended. U*h*lakanyana had been caught by cannibals, and was to be boiled by their mother; so, while the cannibals are away, U*h*lakanyana persuades the old mother to play with him at boiling each other. The game was to begin with him, a proposal to which the old dame readily assented. But he took care to prevent the water from boiling, and after having been in the pot for some time, he insisted on the old mother fulfilling her part of the bargain. He put her in, and put on the lid. She cried out, "Take me out, I am scalded to death." He said, "No, indeed, you are not. If you were scalded to death, you could not say so." So she was boiled, and said no more.

There is a story of a cook which we remember reading not long ago in a collection of German anecdotes. His master gives him a brace of partridges to roast, and being very hungry, the cook eats one of them. When his master returns, he eats one partridge, and then asks for the other. "But this was the other," says the cook, and nothing can persuade him that it wasn't. The same witticism, such as it is, reappears in the story of U*h*lakanyana teaching the leopard how to suckle her cubs. The leopard wants to have both her cubs together, but he insists that only one ought to be suckled at a time, the fact being that he had eaten one of the cubs. He then gives her the one that is still alive, and after it has been suckled, he gives it back to her as the second cub.

Those of our readers who still recollect the fearful sensations occasioned by the "Fee fo fum, I smell the blood of an Englishmun," will meet with several equally harrowing situations in the stories of the Zulus, and of other races, too, to whom the eating of an Englishman is a much less startling event than it seemed to us. Usikulmui, a young Zulu hero, goes to court two daughters of Uzembeni, who had devoured all the men of the country in which she lived. The two girls dug a hole in the house to conceal their sweetheart, but towards sunset Uzembeni, the mother, returned. She had a large toe; her toe came first, she came after it; and as soon as she came, she laughed and rolled herself on the ground, saying, "Eh, eh! in my house here to-day there is a delicious odor; my children, what is there here in the house?" The girls said, "Away! Don't bother us; we do not know where we could get anything; we will not get up." Thus Usikulumi escapes, and after many more adventures and fights with his mother-in-law, carries off her two girls.

It is impossible of course to determine the age of these stories, so as to show that foreign influences are entirely out of the question. Yet nursery tales are generally the last things to be adopted by one nation from another, and even in the few stories which we possess we should probably have been able to discover more palpable traces of foreign influences, if such influences had really existed. Nay, there is one feature in these stories which to a certain extent attests their antiquity. Several of the customs to which they allude are no longer in existence among the Zulus. It is not, for instance, any longer the custom among the natives of South Africa to bake meat by means of heated stones, the recognized mode of cookery among the Polynesians. Yet when Usikulumi orders a calf to be roasted, he calls upon the boys of his kraal to collect large stones, and to heat them. There are several other peculiarities which the Zulus seem to share in common with the Polynesians. The avoiding of certain words which form part of the names of deceased kings or chieftains is a distinguishing feature of the Zulu and Polynesian languages, being called Ukuhlonipa in the one, and Tepi in the other. If a person who has disappeared for some time, and is supposed to be dead, returns unexpectedly to his people, it is the custom both among the Zulus and Polynesians to salute him first by making a funeral lamentation. There are other coincidences in the stories of both races which make it more than probable that at some distant period they lived either together or in close neighborhood; and if we find that some of the customs represented as actually existing in the Zulu stories, have long become extinct on the African continent, while they continue to be observed by the Polynesian islanders, we might indeed venture to conclude, though only as a guess at truth, that the origin of the Zulu stories must be referred to a time preceding the complete separation of these two races. While some customs that have become obsolete at present are represented as still in force among the Zulus of the nursery tales, as, for instance, the use of the U*h*lakula or wooden weeding-stick which is now generally replaced by an iron pick; other things, such as the use of medicines, so much talked of now among the natives, and which they imagine can produce the most marvelous results, are never alluded to. All this would be so much *primâ facie* evidence of the genuineness and antiquity of these Zulu tales, and would seem to exclude the idea of European influences. The only allusion to foreigners occurs in a story where one of the heroes, in order to be taken for a stranger, commits a number of grammatical blunders by leaving out the prefixes that form so essential a feature in all Kafir dialects. But this would not necessarily point to Europeans, as other strangers too, such as Hottentots, for instance, would naturally neglect these grammatical niceties.

We hope that Dr. Callaway will soon be able to continue his interesting publication. Apart from other points of interest, his book, as it contains the Zulu text and an English translation on opposite columns, will be of great use to the student of that language. The system of writing the Zulu words with Roman letters, adopted by Dr. Callaway, seems both rational and practical. Like many others, he has tried Dr. Lepsius' standard alphabet, and found it wanting. "The practical difficulties," he writes, "in the way of using the alphabet of Lepsius are insuperable, even if we were prepared to admit the soundness of all the principles on which it is founded."

March, 1867.

XXIII.

POPULAR TALES FROM THE NORSE.[1]

We had thought that the Popular Tales, the "Kinder und Hausmärchen" which the brothers Grimm collected from the mouths of old women in the spinning-rooms of German villages, could never be matched. But here we have a collection from the Norse as like those German tales as "Dapplegrim was to Dapplegrim," "there wasn't a hair on one which wasn't on the other as well." These Scandinavian "Folkeeventyr" were collected by MM. Asbjörnsen and Moe during the last fifteen years, and they have now been translated into English by Dr. Dasent, the translator of the "Icelandic Edda," and the writer of an excellent article in the last "Oxford Essays," "On the Norsemen in Iceland." The translation shows in every line that it has been a work of love and unflagging enjoyment; and we doubt not that, even transplanted on a foreign soil, these fragrant flowers will strike root and live, and be the delight of children — young and old — for many generations to come.

Who can tell what gives to these childish stories their irresistible charm? There is no plot in them to

1 *Popular Tales from the Norse.* By George Webbe Dasent, D. C. L. With an Introductory Essay on the Origin and Diffusion of Popular Tales Edinburgh: Edmonston & Douglas, 1859.

excite our curiosity. No gorgeous description of scenery, *à la* Kingsley, dazzles our eyes; no anatomy of human passion, *à la* Thackeray, rivets our attention. No, it is all about kings and queens, about princes and princesses, about starving beggars and kind fairies, about doughty boys and clumsy trolls, about old hags that bawl and screech, and about young maidens as white as snow and as red as blood. The Devil, too, is a very important personage on this primitive stage. The tales are short and quaint, full of downright absurdities and sorry jokes. We know from the beginning how it will all end. Poor Boots will marry the Princess and get half the kingdom. The stepmother will be torn to pieces, and Cinderella will be a great queen. The troll will burst as soon as the sun shines on him; and the Devil himself will be squeezed and cheated till he is glad to go to his own abode. And yet we sit and read, we almost cry, and we certainly chuckle, and we are very sorry when —

"Snip, snap, snout,
This tale's told out."

There is witchery in these simple old stories yet! But it seems useless to try to define in what it consists. We sometimes see a landscape with nothing particular in it. There is only a river, and a bridge, and a red-brick house, and a few dark trees, and yet we gaze and gaze till our eyes grow dim. Why we are charmed we cannot tell. Perhaps there is something in that simple scenery which reminds us of our home, or of some place which once we saw in a happy dream. Or we watch the gray sky and the heavy clouds on a dreary day. There is nothing in that picture that would strike an artist's eye. We have seen it all hundreds of times before; and yet we gaze and gaze, till the clouds, with their fantastic outlines, settle round the sun, and vanish beyond the horizon. They were only clouds on a gray afternoon, and yet they have left a shadow on our mind that will never vanish. Is it the same, perhaps, with these simple stories? Do they remind us of a distant home, of a happy childhood? Do they recall fantastic dreams, long vanished from our horizon, hopes that have set, never to rise again? Is there some childhood left in us, that is called out by these childish tales? If there is — and there is with most of us — we have only to open our book, and we shall fly away into Dream-land, like "the lassie who rode on the north wind's back to the castle that lies east o' the sun and west o' the moon." Nor is it Dream-land altogether. There is a kind of real life in these tales — life, such as a child believes in — a life, where good is always rewarded, wrong always punished; where every one, not excepting the Devil, gets his due; where all is possible that we truly want, and nothing seems so wonderful that it might not happen to-morrow. We may smile at those dreams of inexhaustible possibilities; but, in one sense, that child's world is a real world too, and those children's stories are not mere pantomimes. What can be truer than Dr. Dasent's happy description of the character of Boots, as it runs through the whole cycle of these tales?

"There he sits idle whilst all work; there he lies with that deep irony of conscious power which knows its time must one day come, and meantime can afford to wait. When that time comes he girds himself to the feat, amidst the scoffs and scorn of his flesh and blood; but even then, after he has done some great deed, he conceals it, returns to his ashes, and again sits idly by the kitchen fire, dirty, lazy, despised, until the time for final recognition comes; and then his dirt and rags fall off — he stands out in all the majesty of his royal robes, and is acknowledged once for all a King."

And then we see, —

"The proud, haughty Princess, subdued and tamed by natural affection into a faithful, loving wife. We begin by being angry at her pride; we are glad at the retribution which overtakes her, but we are gradually melted at her sufferings and hardships when she gives up all for the Beggar and follows him; we feel for her when she exclaims, 'O, the Beggar, and the babe, and the cabin!' and we rejoice with her when the Prince says, 'Here is the Beggar, and there is the babe, and so let the cabin be burnt away.'"

There is genuine fun in the old woman who does not know whether she is herself. She has been dipped into a tar-barrel, and then rolled on a heap of feathers; and when she sees herself feathered all over, she wants to find out whether it is her or not. And how well she reasons! "O! I know," she says, "how I shall be able to tell whether it is me; if the calves come and lick me, and our dog Tray doesn't bark at me when I get home, then it must be me, and no one else." It is, however, quite superfluous to say anything in praise of these tales. They will make their way in the world and win everybody's heart, as sure as Boots made the Princess say, "That is a story!"

But we have not done with Dr. Dasent's book yet. There is one part of it, the Introduction, which in reality tells the most wonderful of all wonderful stories — the migration of these tales from Asia to the North of Europe. It might seem strange, indeed, that so great a scholar as Grimm should have spent so much of his precious time in collecting his "Mährchen," if these "Mährchen" had only been intended for the amusement of children. When we see a Lyell or Owen pick up pretty shells and stones, we may be sure that, however much little girls may admire these pretty things, this was not the object which these wise collectors had in view. Like the blue and green and rosy sands which children play with in the Isle of Wight, these tales of the people, which Grimm was the first to discover and collect, are the *detritus* of many an ancient stratum of thought and language, buried deep in the past. They have a scientific interest. The results of the science of language are by this time known to every educated man, and boys learn at school — what fifty years ago would have been scouted as absurd — that English, together with all the Teutonic dialects of the Continent, belongs to that large family of speech which comprises, besides the Teutonic, Latin, Greek, Slavonic, and Celtic, the oriental languages of Persia and India. Previously to the dispersion of these languages, there was, of course, one common language, spoken by the common ancestors of our own race, and of the Greeks, the Romans, the Hindus, and Persians, a language which was neither Greek, nor Latin, nor Persian, nor Sanskrit, but stood to all of them in a relation similar to that in which Latin stands to French, Italian, and Spanish; or Sanskrit to Bengali, Hindustani, and Marathi. It has also been proved that the various tribes who started from this central home to discover Europe in the North and India in the South carried away with them, not only a common language, but a common faith and a common mythology, These are facts which may be ignored but cannot be disputed, and the two sciences of Comparative Grammar and Comparative Mythology, though but of recent origin, rest on a foundation as sound and safe as that of any of the inductive sciences: —

"The affinity," says Dr. Dasent, "which exists in a mythological and philological point of view between the Aryan or Indo-European languages is now the first article of a literary creed; and the man who denies it puts himself as much beyond the pale of argument as he who, in a religious discussion, should meet a grave divine of the Church of England with the strict contradictory of her first article, and loudly declare his conviction that there was no God."

And again: —

"We all came, Greek, Latin, Celt, Teuton, Slavonian, from the East, as kith and kin, leaving kith and kin behind us, and after thousands of years, the language and traditions of those who went East and those who went West bear such an affinity to each other as to have established, beyond discussion or dispute, the fact of their descent from a common stock."

But now we go beyond this. Not only do we find the same words and the same terminations in Sanskrit and Gothic; not only do we find the same names for Zeus and many other deities in Sanskrit, Latin, and German; not only is the abstract name for God the same in India, Greece, and Italy; but these very stories, these "Mährchen," which nurses still tell, with almost the same words, in the Thuringian forest and in the Norwegian villages, and to which crowds of children listen under the Pippal-trees of India, these stories, too, belonged to the common heir-loom of the Indo-European race, and their origin carries us back to the same distant past, when no Greek had set foot in Europe, no Hindu had bathed in the sacred waters of the Ganges. No doubt this sounds strange, and it requires a certain limitation. We do not mean to say that the old nurse who rocked on her mighty knees the two ancestors of the Indian and the German races, told each of them the story of Snow-white and Rosy-red, exactly as we read it in the "Tales from the Norse," and that these told it to their children, and thus it was handed down to our own times. It is true indeed — and a comparison of our "Norwegian Tales" with the "Mährchen" collected by the Grimms in Germany shows it most clearly — that the memory of a nation clings to its popular stories with a marvelous tenacity. For more than a thousand years the Scandinavian inhabitants of Norway have been separated in language from their Teutonic brethren on the Continent, and yet both have not only preserved the same stock of popular stories, but they tell them in several instances in almost the same words. It is a much more startling supposition — or, we should say, a much more startling fact — that those Aryan boys, the ancestors of the Hindus, Romans, Greeks, and Germans, should have preserved the ancient words from "one" to "ten," and that these dry words should have been handed down to our own school-boy days, in several instances, without the change of a single letter. Thus 2 in English is still "two," in Hindustani "do," in Persian "du," in French "deux;" 3 is still "three" in English, and "trys" in Lithuanian; 9 is still "nine" in English, and "nuh" in Persian. Surely it was not less difficult to remember these and thousands of other words than to remember the pretty stories of Snow-white and Rosy-red. For the present, however, all we want to prove is that the elements of the seeds of these fairy tales belong to the period that preceded the dispersion of the Aryan race; that the same people who, in their migrations to the North and the South carried along with them the names of the Sun and the Dawn, and their belief in the bright gods of Heaven, possessed in their very language, in their mythological and proverbial phraseology, the more or less developed germs that were sure to grow up into the same or very similar plants on every soil and under every sky.

This is a subject which requires the most delicate handling, and the most careful analysis. Before we attempt to compare the popular stories, as they are found in India and Europe at the present day, and to trace them to a common source, we have to answer one very important question, — Was there no other channel through which some of them could have flowed from India to Europe, or from Europe to India, at a later time? We have to take the same precaution in comparative philology with regard to words. Besides the words which Greek and Latin share in common because they are both derived from one common, source, there is a class of words which Latin took over from Greek ready made. These are called foreign words, and they form a considerable element, particularly in modern languages. The question is whether the same does not apply to some of our common Indo-

European stories. How is it that some of Lafontaine's fables should be identically the same as those which we find in two collections of fables in Sanskrit, the "Pan*k*atantra" and the "Hitopade*s*a?" This is a question, which, many years ago, has been most fully treated in one of the most learned and most brilliant essays of Sylvestre de Sacy. He there proves that, about 570 after Christ, a Sanskrit work which contained these very fables was brought to the court of the Persian king, Khosru Nushirvan, and translated into ancient Persian, or Pehlevi. The kings of Persia preserved this book as a treasure till their kingdom was conquered by the Arabs. A hundred years later, the book was discovered and translated into Arabic by Almokaffa, about 770 after Christ. It then passed through the hands of several Arabic poets, and was afterwards retranslated into Persian, first into verse, by Rudaki, in the tenth century, then into prose, by Nasrallah, in the twelfth. The most famous version, however, appeared towards the end of the fifteeth century, under the name of "Anvari Suhaili," by Husain Vaiz. Now, as early as the eleventh century the Arabic work of Almokaffa, called "Kalila Dimna," was translated into Greek by Simeon. The Greek text and a Latin version have been published, under the title of "Sapientia Indorum Veterum," by Starkius, Berlin, 1697. This work passed into Italian. Again the Arabic text was translated into Hebrew by Rabbi Joel; and this Hebrew translation became the principal source of the European books of fables. Before the end of the fifteenth century, John of Capua had published his famous Latin translation, "Directorium humanæ vitæ, alias, parabolæ antiquorum sapientium."

In his preface, he states that this book was called "Belile et Dimne;" that it was originally in the language of India, then translated into Persian, afterwards into Arabic, then into Hebrew, and lastly by himself into Latin. This work, to judge from the numerous German, Italian, Spanish, and French translations, must have been extremely popular all over Europe in the sixteenth century. In the seventeenth century a new stream of oriental fables reached the literary world of Europe, through a translation of the "Anvari Suhaili" (the Persian "Kalila Dimna") into French, by David Sahid d'Ispahan. This work was called "Le Livre des Lumières, ou la conduite des rois, composé par le sage Bilpay, Indien." It afterwards went by the name of "Les Fables de Pilpay." This was the book from which Lafontaine borrowed the subjects of his later fables. An excellent English translation, we may here state, of the "Anvari Suhaili" has lately been published by Professor Eastwick.

This migration of fables from India to Europe is a matter of history, and has to be taken into account, before we refer the coincidences between the popular stories of India and Norway to that much earlier intercourse of the ancestors of the Indo-European races of which we have spoken before. Dr. Dasent is so great an admirer of Grimm, that he has hardly done justice to the researches of Sylvestre de Sacy. He says: —

"That all the thousand shades of resemblance and affinity which gleam and flicker through the whole body of popular tradition in the Aryan race, as the Aurora plays and flashes in countless rays athwart the

Northern heavens, should be the result of mere servile copying of one tribe's traditions by another, is a supposition as absurd as that of those good country-folk, who, when they see an Aurora, fancy it must be a great fire, the work of some incendiary, and send off the parish engine to put it out. No! when we find in such a story as the 'Master Thief' traits which are to be found in the Sanskrit 'Hitopadesa,' and which are also to be found in the story of Rampsinitus in Herodotos, which are also to be found in German, Italian, and Flemish popular tales, but told in all with such variations of character and detail, and such adaptation to time and place, as evidently show the original working of the national consciousness upon a stock of tradition common to all the race, but belonging to no tribe of that race in particular, and when we find this occurring not in one tale, but in twenty, we are forced to abandon the theory of such universal copying, for fear lest we should fall into a greater difficulty than that for which we were striving to account."

The instance which Dr. Dasent has here chosen to illustrate his theory does seem to us inconclusive. The story of the "Master Thief" is told in the "Hitopadesa." A Brahman, who had vowed a sacrifice, went to the market to buy a goat. Three thieves saw him, and wanted to get hold of the goat. They stationed themselves at intervals on the high road. When the Brahman, who carried the goat on his back, approached the first thief, the thief said, "Brahman, why do you carry a dog on your back?" The Brahman replied: "It is not a dog, it is a goat." A little while after, he was accosted by the second thief, who said, "Brahman, why do you carry a dog on your back?"

The Brahman felt perplexed, put the goat down, examined it, and walked on. Soon after he was stopped by the third thief, who said, "Brahman, why do you carry a dog on your back?" Then the Brahman was frightened, threw down the goat, and walked home to perform his ablutions for having touched an unclean animal. The thieves took the goat and ate it. The gist of the story is that a man will believe almost anything if he is told the same by three different people. The Indian story, with slight variations, is told in the Arabic translation, the "Kalila and Dimna." It was known through the Greek translation at Constantinople, at least at the beginning of the Crusades, and was spread all over Europe, in the Latin of the "Directorium humanæ vitæ." The Norwegian story of the "Master Thief" is not a translation, such as we find in the "Filosofia morale," nor an adaptation, such as a similar story in the "Facétieuses Nuits de Straparole." But the key-note of the story is nevertheless the same.

That key-note might have been caught up by any Norman sailor, or any Northern traveller or student, of whom there were many in the Middle Ages, who visited the principal seats of learning in Europe. And, that key-note given, nothing was easier than to invent the three variations which we find in the Norse "Master Thief." If the same story, as Dr. Dasent says, occurred in Herodotos the case would be different. At the time of Herodotos the translations of the "Hitopadesa" had not yet reached Europe, and we should be obliged to include the "Master Thief" within the most primitive stock of Aryan lore. But there is nothing in the story of the two sons of the architect who robbed the treasury of Rampsinitus which turns on the trick of the "Master Thief." There were thieves, more or less clever, in Egypt as well as in India, and some of their stratagems were possibly the same at all times. But there is a keen and well-defined humor in the story of the Brahman and his deference to public opinion. Of this there is no trace in the anecdote told by Herodotos. That anecdote deals with mere matters of fact, whether imaginary or historical. The story of Rampsinitus did enter into the popular literature of Europe, but through a different channel. We find it in the "Gesta Romanorum," where Octavianus has taken the place of Rampsinitus, and we can hardly doubt that there it came originally from Herodotos. There are other stories in the "Gesta Romanorum" which are borrowed directly from the "Hitopadesa" and its translations. We need only mention that of Prince Llewellyn and his hound Gellert, which Dr. Dasent would likewise refer to the period previous to the dispersion of the Aryan race, but which, as can be proved, reached Europe by a much shorter route.

But if in these special instances we differ from Dr. Dasent, we fully agree with him in the main. There are stories, common to the different branches of the Aryan stock, which could not have travelled from India to Europe at so late a time as that of Nushirvan. They are ancient Aryan stories, older than the "Pañ*k*atantra," older than the "Odyssey," older than the dispersion of the Aryan race. We can only mention one or two instances.

In the "Pañ*k*atantra," there is the story of the King who asked his pet monkey to watch over him while he was asleep. A bee settled on the King's head, the monkey could not drive her away, so he took his sword, killed the bee, and in killing her killed the King. A very similar parable is put into the mouth by Buddha. A bald carpenter was attacked by a mosquito. He called his son to drive it away. The son took the axe, aimed a blow at the insect, but split his father's head in two, and killed him. This fable reached Lafontaine through the "Anvari Suhaili," and appears in the French as the "Bear and the Gardener." But the same fable had reached Europe at a much earlier time, and though the moral has been altered, it can hardly be doubted that the fable in Phædros of the bald man who in trying to kill a gnat gives himself a severe blow in the face, came originally from the East. There may have been some direct communication, and Æsop of old may have done very much the same as Khosru Nushirvan did at a later time. But it is more likely that there was some old Aryan proverb, some homely saw, such as "Protect us from our friends," or "Think of the king and the bee." Such a saying would call for explanation, and stories would readily be told to explain it. There is in our Norwegian Tales a passage very much to the same effect:—

"A man saw a goody hard at work banging her husband across the head with a beetle, and over his head she had drawn a shirt without any slit for the neck.

"'Why, Goody!' he asked, 'will you beat your husband to death?'

"'No," she said, 'I only must have a hole in this shirt for his neck to come through.'"

The story of the Donkey in the Lion's skin was

known as a proverb to Plato. It exists as a fable in the "Hitopadesa," "The Donkey in the Tiger's skin." Many of the most striking traits of animal life which are familiar to us from Phædros, are used for similar purposes in the "Hitopadesa." The mouse delivering her friends by gnawing the net, the turtle flying and dying, the tiger or fox as pious hermits, the serpent as king, or friend of the frogs, all these are elements common to the early fabulists of Greece and India. One of the earliest Roman apologues, "the dispute between the belly and the other members of the body," was told in India long before it was told by Menenius Agrippa at Rome. Several collections of fables have just been discovered in Chinese by M. Stanislas Julien, and will soon be published in a French translation.

With regard to the ancient Aryan fables, which are common to all the members of the Aryan family, it has been said that there is something so natural in most of them, that they might well have been invented more than once. This is a sneaking argument, but nevertheless it has a certain weight. It does not apply, however, to our fairy tales. They surely cannot be called natural. They are full of the most unnatural conceptions — of monsters such as no human eye has ever seen. Of many of them we know for certain that they were not invented at all, but that they are the *detritus* of ancient mythology, half-forgotten, misunderstood, and reconstructed. Dr. Dasent has traced the gradual transition of myth into story in the case of the Wild Huntsman, who was originally the German god Odin. He might have traced the last fibres of "Odin, the hunter," back to Indra, the god of

Storms, in the Veda; and lower even than the "Grand Veneur" in the Forest of Fontainebleau, he might have dodged the Hellequin of France to the very Harlequin of our Christmas Pantomimes. William Tell, the good archer, whose mythological character Dr. Dasent has established beyond contradiction, is the last reflection of the Sun-god, whether we call him Indra, or Apollo, or Ulysses. Their darts are unerring. They hit the apple, or any other point; and they destroy their enemies with the same bow with which they have hit the mark. The countless stories of all the princesses and snow-white ladies who were kept in dark prisons, and were invariably delivered by a young bright hero, can all be traced back to mythological traditions about the Spring being released from the bonds of Winter, the Sun being rescued from the darkness of the Night, the Dawn being brought back from the far West, the Waters being set free from the prison of the clouds. In the songs of the Veda, where the powers of nature have hardly assumed as yet their fixed divine personality, we read over and over again of the treasures which the God of light recovers from the dark clouds. These treasures are the Waters conquered after a fierce thunder-storm. Sometimes these Waters are called the cows, which the robbers had hidden in caves — sometimes, the wives of the gods (Devapatnî), who had become the wives of the fiend (Dâsapatnî or Deianeira=" dâsa-narî). Their imprisonment is called a curse; and when they are delivered from it, Indra is praised for having destroyed "the seven castles of the autumn." In the Veda the thief or the fiend is called the serpent with seven heads.

Every one of these expressions may be traced in

the German "Mährchen." The loves and feuds of the powers of nature, after they had been told, first of gods, then of heroes, appear in the tales of the people as the flirting and teasing of fairies and imps. Christianity had destroyed the old gods of the Teutonic tribes, and supplied new heroes in the saints and martyrs of the Church. The gods were dead, and the heroes, the sons of the gods, forgotten. But the stories told of them would not die, and in spite of the excommunications of the priests they were welcomed wherever they appeared in their strange disguises. Kind-hearted grannies would tell the pretty stories of old, if it was only to keep their little folk quiet. They did not tell them of the gods; for those gods were dead, or, worse than that, had been changed into devils. They told them of nobody; ay, sometimes they would tell them of the very saints and martyrs, and the apostles themselves have had to wear some of the old rags that belonged by right to Odin and other heathen gods. The oddest figure of all is that of the Devil in his half-Christian and half-heathen garb. The Aryan nations had no Devil. Pluto, though of a sombre character, was a very respectable personage; and Loki, though a mischievous person, was not a fiend. The German goddess, Hell, too — like Proserpina — had once seen better days. Thus, when the Germans were indoctrinated with the idea of a real Devil, the Semitic Satan or Diabolus, they treated him in the most good-humored manner. They ascribed to him all the mischievous tricks of their most mischievous gods. But while the old Northern story-tellers delighted in the success of cunning, the new generation felt in duty bound to represent the Devil in the end as always defeated. He was outwitted in all the tricks which had formerly proved successful, and thus quite a new character was produced — the poor or stupid Devil, who appears not unfrequently in the German and in Norwegian tales.

All this Dr. Dasent has described very tersely and graphically in his Introduction, and we recommend the readers of his tales not to treat that Introduction as most introductions are treated. We should particularly recommend to the attention of those who have leisure to devote to such subjects, what Dr. Dasent says at the close of his Essay: —

"Enough has been said, at least, to prove that even nursery tales may have a science of their own, and to show how the old Nornir and divine spinners can revenge themselves if their old wives' tales are insulted and attacked. The inquiry itself might be almost indefinitely prolonged, for this is a journey where each turn of the road brings out a new point of view, and the longer we linger on our path the longer we find something fresh to see. Popular mythology is a virgin mine, and its ore, so far from being exhausted or worked out, has here, in England at least, been scarcely touched. It may, indeed, be dreaded lest the time for collecting such English traditions is not past and gone; whether the steam-engine and printing-press have not played their great part of enlightenment too well; and whether the popular tales, of which, no doubt, the land was once full, have not faded away before these great inventions, as the race of giants waned before the might of Odin and the Æsir. Still the example of this very Norway, which at one time was thought, even by her own sons, to have few tales of her own, and now has been found to have them so fresh and full, may serve as a warning not to abandon a search, which, indeed, can scarcely be said to have been ever begun; and to suggest a doubt whether the ill success which may have attended this or that particular attempt, may not have been from the fault rather of the seekers after traditions, than from the want of the traditions themselves. In point of fact, it is a matter of the utmost difficulty to gather such tales in any country, as those who have collected them most successfully will be the first to confess. It is hard to make old and feeble women, who generally are the depositaries of these national treasures, believe that the inquirer can have any real interest in the matter. They fear that the question is only put to turn them into ridicule; for the popular mind is a sensitive plant; it becomes coy, and closes its leaves at the first rude touch; and when once shut, it is hard to make these aged lips reveal the secrets of the memory. There they remain, however, forming part of an under-current of tradition, of which the educated classes, through whose minds flows the bright upper-current of faith, are apt to forget the very existence. Things out of sight, and therefore out of mind. Now and then a wave of chance tosses them to the surface from those hidden depths, and all her Majesty's inspectors of schools are shocked at the wild shapes which still haunt the minds of the great mass of the community. It cannot be said that the English are not a superstitious people. Here we have gone on for more than a hundred years proclaiming our opinion that the belief in witches, and wizards, and ghosts, and fetches was extinct throughout the land. Ministers of all denominations have preached them down, and philosophers convinced all the world of the absurdity of such vain superstitions ; and yet it has been reserved for another learned profession, the Law, to produce in one trial at the Staffordshire Assizes, a year or two ago, such a host of witnesses who firmly believed in witchcraft, and swore to their belief in spectre dogs and wizards, as to show that, in the Midland Counties at least, such traditions are anything but extinct. If so much of the bad has been spared by steam, by natural philosophy, and by the Church, let us hope that some of the good may still linger along with it, and that an English Grimm may yet arise who may carry out what Mr. Chambers has so well begun in Scotland, and discover in the mouth of an Anglo-Saxon Gammer Grethel some, at least, of those popular tales which England once had in common with all the Aryan race."

***January*, 1859.**

XXIV.

TALES OF THE WEST HIGHLANDS.[1]

WHEN reviewing, some time ago, Dr. Dasent's "Popular Tales from the Norse," we expressed a hope that something might still be done for recovering at least a few fragments here and there of similar tales once current in England. Ever since the brothers Grimm surprised the world by their "Kinder und Hausmärchen," which they had picked up in various parts of Germany — in beer-houses, in spinning-rooms, or in the warm kitchen of an old goody — an active search has been set on foot in every corner of Germany, in Denmark, Sweden, Norway, nay, even in Finland and Lapland, for everything in the shape of popular sayings, proverbs, riddles, or tales. The result has been more than could have been expected. A considerable literature has been brought together, and we have gained an insight into the natural growth of popular lore, more instructive than anything that could be gathered from chronicles or historians. Our hope that Dr. Dasent's work would give a powerful impulse to similar researches in this country has not been disappointed. Good books seem to beget good

1 *Popular Tales of the West Highlands.* Orally collected, with a translation by J. F. Campbell. Edinburgh: Edmonston & Douglas, 1860.

books, and in Mr. Campbell's "Popular Tales of the West Highlands," orally collected, with a translation, we are glad to welcome the first response to the appeal made by the translator of the Norse Tales. It might be feared, indeed, as Dr. Dasent said in his learned and eloquent Introduction, whether the time for collecting such English traditions was not past and gone; whether the steam-engine and printing-press had not played their great work of enlightenment too well; and whether the popular tales, of which, no doubt, the land was once full, had not faded away before these great inventions, as the race of giants waned before the might of Odin and the Æsir. But not so. Of course such stories were not to be found in London or its immediate neighborhood. People who went out story-fishing to Richmond or Gravesend would find but poor sport among white-tied waiters or barmaids in silk. However, even in St. James' Street, a practiced hand may get a rise, as witness the following passage from Mr. Campbell's preface: —

"I met two tinkers in St. James' Street, in February, with black faces and a pan of burning coals each. They were followed by a wife, and preceded by a mangy terrier with a stiff tail. I joined the party, and one told me a version of 'the man who travelled to learn what shivering meant,' while we walked together through the Park to Westminster."

But though a stray story may thus be bagged in the West-end of London, Mr. Campbell knew full well that his best chance would lie as far away from the centre of civilization as railways could carry him, and as far away from railways as his legs could take him. So he went to his own native country, the Western

Islands and Highlands of Scotland. There he knew he would meet with people who could neither read nor write, who hardly knew a word of English, and from whom he remembered as a child to have heard stories exactly like those which Dr. Dasent had lately imported from Norway. We must copy at least one description of the haunts explored by Mr. Campbell: —

"Let me describe one of these old story-men as a type of his kind. I trust he will not be offended, for he was very polite to me. His name is MacPhie; he lives at the north end of South Uist, where the road ends at a sound, which has to be forded at the ebb to go to Benbecula. The house is built of a double wall of loose boulders, with a layer of peat three feet thick between the walls. The ends are round, and the roof rests on the inner wall, leaving room for a crop of yellow gowans. A man might walk round the roof on the top of the wall. There is but one room, with two low doors, one on each side of the house. The fire is on the floor; the chimney is a hole above it; and the rafters are hung with pendants and festoons of shining black peat reek. They are of birch of the main-land, American drift-wood, or broken wreck. They support a covering of turf and straw, and stones and heather ropes, which keep out the rain well enough.

"The house stands on a green bank, with gray rocks protruding through the turf; and the whole neighborhood is pervaded by cockle shells, which indicate the food of the people and their fishing pursuits. In a neighboring kiln there were many cart-loads about to be burned, to make that lime which is so durable in the old castles. The owner of the house, whom I visited twice, is seventy-nine. He told me nine stories, and, like all the others, declared that there was no man in the island who knew them so well. 'He could not say how many he knew;' he seemed to know versions of nearly everything I had got; and he told me plainly that my versions were good for nothing. 'Huch! thou hast not got them right at all.' 'They came into his mind,' he said, 'sometimes at night when he could not sleep — old tales that he had not heard for threescore years.'

"He had the manner of a practiced narrator, and it is quite evident that he is one; he chuckled at the interesting parts, and laid his withered finger on my knee as he gave out the terrible bits with due solemnity. A small boy in a kilt, with large, round, glittering eyes, was standing mute at his knee, gazing at his wrinkled face, and devouring every word. The boy's mother first boiled and then mashed potatoes; and his father, a well grown man in tartan breeks, ate them. Ducks and ducklings, a cat and a kitten, some hens, and a baby, all tumbled about on the clay floor together, and expressed their delight at the savory prospect, each in his own fashion; and then wayfarers dropped in and listened for a spell, and passed their remarks, till the ford was shallow. The light came streaming down the chimney, and through a single pane of glass, lighting up a track in the blue mist of the peat smoke; and fell on the white hair and brown, withered face of the old man, as he sat on a low stool, with his feet to the fire; and the rest of the dwelling, with all its plenishing of boxes and box-beds, dishes and dresser, and gear of all sorts, faded away, through shades of deepening brown, to the black darkness of the smoked roof and the 'peat corner.' There we sat, and smoked and talked for hours till the tide ebbed; and then I crossed the ford by wading up to the waist, and dried my clothes in the wind in Benbecula."

Mr. Campbell, we see, can describe well, and the small sketches which he inserts in his preface — bits of scenery from Scotland or Lapland, from Spain or Algiers — are evidently the work of a man who can handle brush and pen with equal skill. If he had simply given a description of his travels in the Western Highlands, interspersed with some stories gathered from the mouths of the people, he would have given us a most charming Christmas-book. But Mr. Campbell had a higher aim. He had learned from Dr. Dasent's preface, that popular stories may be made to tell a story of their own, and that they may yield most valuable materials for the palæontology of the human race. The nations who are comprehended under the common appellation of Aryan or Indo-European — the Hindus, the Persians, the Celts, Germans, Romans, Greeks, and Slaves — do not only share the same words and the same grammar slightly modified in each country, but they seem to have likewise preserved a mass of popular tradition which had grown up before they had left their common home. That this is true with regard to mythological traditions has been fully proved, and comparative mythology has by this time taken its place as a recognized science, side by side with comparative philology. But it is equally known that the gods of ancient mythology were changed into the demi-gods and heroes of ancient epic poetry, and that these demigods again became, at a later age, the principal characters of our nursery tales. If, therefore, the Saxons,

Celts, Romans, Greeks, Slaves, Persians, and Hindus once spoke the same language, if they worshipped the same gods and believed in the same myths and legends, we need not be surprised that even at the present day there is still a palpable similarity between the stories told by MacPhie of South Uist and those for which we are indebted to the old grannies in every village of Germany — nay, that the general features of their tales should be discovered in the stories of Vish*n*u-sarman and Somadeva in India.

The discovery of such similarities is no doubt highly interesting, but at the same time the subject requires the most delicate handling. Such has been the later literary intercourse between the nations of the East and the West, that many channels, besides that of the one common primitive language, were open for the spreading of popular stories. The researches of De Sacy and Benfey have laid open several of these channels through which stories, ready made, were carried through successive translations from India to Persia and Greece and the rest of Europe. This took place during the Middle Ages; whereas the original seeds of Indo-European legends must have been brought to Europe by the first Aryans who settled in Greece, Italy, Germany, and Gaul. These two classes of legends must, therefore, be carefully kept apart, though their separation is often a work of great difficulty. The first class of legends — those which were known to the primeval Aryan race, before it broke up into Hindus, Greeks, Romans, Germans, and Celts — may be called primitive, or organic. The second — those which were imported in later times from one literature into another — may be called secondary, or inorganic. The former represent one common ancient stratum of language and thought, reaching from India to Europe; the latter consist of boulders of various strata carried along by natural and artificial means from one country to another. As we distinguish in each Aryan language between common and foreign words,— the former constituting the ancient heir-loom of the Aryan race, the latter being borrowed by Romans from Greeks, by Germans from Romans, by Celts from Germans, — so we ought to distinguish between common aboriginal Aryan legends and legends borrowed and transplanted at later times. The rules which apply to the treatment of words apply with equal force to the comparative analysis of legends. If we find words in Sanskrit exactly the same as in Greek, we know that they cannot be the same words. The phonetic system of Greek is different from that of Sanskrit; and words, in order to prove their original identity, must be shown to have suffered the modifying influences of the phonetic system peculiar to each language. "Ekatara" in Sanskrit cannot be the same word as ἑκάτερος in Greek; "better" in English cannot be the same as "behter" in Persian. "Ei" in German cannot be the same as English "eye." If they were the same words, they would necessarily have diverged more widely through the same influence which made Greek different from Sanskrit, Persian different from English, and English different from German. This of course does not apply to foreign words. When the Romans adopted the word "philosophos" from Greek, they hardly changed it at all; whereas the root "sap" had, by a perfectly natural process, produced *sapiens* in Latin, and "sophos" in Greek.

Another rule of the science of language which ought to be carefully observed in the comparative study of legends is this, that no comparison should be made before each word is traced back to its most primitive form and meaning. We cannot compare English and Hindustani, but we can trace an English word back to Anglo-Saxon and Gothic, and a Hindustani word back to Hindu and Sanskrit; and then from Gothic and Sanskrit we can measure and discover the central point from whence the original Aryan word proceeded. We thus discover not only its original form, but at the same time its etymological meaning. Applying this rule to the comparison of popular tales, we maintain that before any comparison can be instituted between nursery tales of Germany, England, and India, each tale must be traced back to a legend or myth from whence it arose, and in which it had a natural meaning: otherwise we cannot hope to arrive at any satisfactory results. One instance must suffice to illustrate the application of these rules. In Mr. Campbell's West Highland Tales we meet with the story of a frog who wishes to marry the daughter of a queen, and who, when the youngest daughter of the queen consents to become his wife, is freed from a spell and changed into a handsome man. This story can be traced back to the year 1548. In Germany it is well known as the story of the "Froschkönig." Mr. Campbell thinks it is of Gaelic origin, because the speech of the frog in Gaelic is an imitation of the gurgling and quacking of spring frogs. However, the first question to answer is this, How came such a story ever to be invented? Human beings, we may hope, were at all times sufficiently enlightened to know that a marriage between a frog and the daughter of a queen was absurd. No poet could ever have sat down to invent sheer nonsense like this. We may ascribe to our ancestors any amount of childlike simplicity, but we must take care not to degrade them to the rank of mere idiots. There must have been something rational in the early stories and myths; and until we find a reason for each, we must just leave them alone as we leave a curious petrifaction which has not yet been traced back to any living type. Now, in our case it can be shown that frog was used as a name of the sun. In the ancient floating speech of the Aryan family the sun had hundreds of names. Each poet thought he had a right to call the sun by his own name; and he would even call it by a different name at sunrise and at sunset, in spring and in winter, in war or in peace. Their ancient language was throughout poetical and metaphorical. The sun might be called the nourisher, the awakener, the giver of life, the messenger of death, the brilliant eye of heaven, the golden swan, the dog, the wolf, the lion. Now at sunrise and sunset, when the sun seemed squatting on the water, it was called the frog. This may have been at first the expression of one individual poet, or the slang name once used by a fisherman watching the sun as it slowly emerged from the clouds in winter. But the name possessed vitality; it remained current for a time; it was amplified into short proverbial sayings; and at last, when the original metaphor was lost sight of, when people no longer knew that the frog spoken of in their saws and proverbs was meant for the sun, these saws and proverbs became changed into myths and legends. In Sanskrit the name of the frog is "Bheka," and from it a feminine was formed, "Bhekî." This feminine, "Bhekî," must have been at one time used as a name of the sun, for the sun was under certain circumstances feminine in India as well as in Germany. After a time, when this name had become obsolete, stories were told of "Bhekî" which had a natural sense only when told of the sun, and which are the same in character as other stories told of heroes or heroines whose original solar character cannot be doubted. Thus we find in Sanskrit the story that "Bhekî," the frog, was a beautiful girl; and that one day, when sitting near a well, she was discovered by a king, who asked her to be his wife. She consented, on condition that he should never show her a drop of water. One day, being tired, she asked the king for water, the king forgot his promise, brought water, and "Bhekî" disappeared. This story was known at the time when Kapila wrote his philosophical aphorisms in India, for it is there quoted as an illustration. But long before Kapila the story of "Bhekî" must have grown up gradually, beginning with a short saying about the sun, — such as that "Bhekî," the sun, will die at the sight of water, as we should say that the sun will set when it approaches the water from which it rose in the morning. Thus, viewed as a woman, the sun-frog might be changed into a woman and married to a king; viewed as a man he might be married to a princess. In either case stories would naturally arise to explain more or less fully all that seemed strange in these marriages between frog and man, and the change from sun to frog, and from frog to man, which was at first due to the mere spell of language, would, in our nursery tales, be ascribed to miraculous charms more familiar to a later age.

It is in this way alone that a comparison of tales, legends, and myths can lead to truly scientific results. Mere similarity between stories discovered in distant parts of the world is no more than similarity of sound between words. Words may be identical in sound, and yet totally distinct in origin. In all branches of science we want to know the origin of things, and to watch their growth and decay. If "Storiology," as Mr. Campbell calls it, is to be a scientific study, it must follow the same course. Mr. Campbell has brought together in his introduction and his notes much that is valuable and curious. The coincidences which he has pointed out between the stories of the Western Highlands and other parts of the Aryan world, are striking in themselves, and will be useful for further researches. But the most valuable parts of his work are the stories themselves. For these he will receive the thanks of all who are interested in the study of language and popular literature, and we hope that he will feel encouraged to go on with his work, and that his example will be followed by others, in other parts of England, Scotland, and Ireland.

February, 1861.

XXV.

ON MANNERS AND CUSTOMS.[1]

THE study of mankind is making rapid progress in our days. The early history of the human race, which in former centuries was written chiefly by poets or philosophers, has now been taken up in good earnest by men who care for facts, and for facts only, and who, if they cannot reveal to us the very beginnings of human life and human thought, have succeeded, at least, in opening broad views into a distant past, hitherto impenetrable, and have brought together fragments of language, religion, mythology, legends, laws, and customs which give us a real and living idea of the early ancestors of our race.

The first impulse to these researches was given by the science of language. By a mere classification of languages and by a careful analysis of words, that science has shed a dazzling light on the darkest ages in the history of man. Where all was guess-work before, we have now a well-established pedigree of languages and races, which still stands the test of the most uncompromising skepticism. Who in the last century could have dreamt of a genealogical relation-

[1] *Researches into the Early History of Mankind, and the Development of Civilization.* By Edward Burnet Tylor, author of *Mexico and the Mexicans.* London: John Murray, 1865.

ship between the languages of the Greeks and Romans and that of the ancient Hindus, or the Persians of Zoroaster and Darius. Who would have ventured to maintain that the Teutonic, Celtic, and Slavonic nations were in reality of the same kith and kin as the Greeks and Romans, who looked down upon them as mere barbarians? The change from the Ptolemaic system to that which placed the sun in the centre of our planetary world was hardly more startling than the discovery of an Indo-European or Aryan family of speech, which unites by a common bond nations so distant as the inhabitants of Ceylon and Iceland. And by how close a bond! Let us consider but one instance. "I know" in modern German is "ich weiss;" "we know," in the plural, "wir wissen." Why this change of vowel in the singular and plural? Modern German can give us no answer, nor ancient German, not even the most ancient German of the fourth century, the Gothic of Ulphilas. Here, too, we find "vait," I know, with the diphthong in the singular, but "vitum," we know, with the simple vowel. A similar change meets us in the ancient language of England, and King Alfred would have said "wât," I know, but "witon," we know. If, then, we turn to Greek we see here, too, the same anomalous transition from "(v)oida," I know, to "(v)ismen," we know; but we look in vain for any intelligible explanation of so capricious a change. At last we turn to Sanskrit, and there not only do we meet with the change from "veda," I know, to "vidma," we know, but we also discover the key to it. In Sanskrit the accent of the perfect falls throughout on the first syllable in the singular, in the plural on the last; and it was this change of accent which produced the analogous change in the length of the radical vowel. So small and apparently insignificant a fact as this, the change of *i* into *ė* (ai) whenever the accent falls on it, teaches us lessons more important than all the traditions put together which the inhabitants of India, Greece, and Germany have preserved of their earliest migrations and of the foundations of their empires, ascribed to their gods, or to the sons of their gods and heroines. This one fact proves that before the Hindus migrated to the southern peninsula of Asia, and before the Greeks and Germans had trodden the soil of Europe, the common ancestors of these three races spoke one and the same language, a language so well regulated and so firmly settled that we can discover the same definite outlines in the grammar of the ancient songs of the Veda, the poems of Homer, and the Gothic Bible of Ulphilas. What does it mean, then, that in each of these three languages, "I know" is expressed by a perfect, originally meaning "I have perceived?" It means that this fashion or idiom had become permanent before the Greeks separated from the Hindus, before the Hindus became unintelligible to the Germans. And what is the import of the shortening of the vowel in the plural, or rather of its strengthening in the singular? Its import is that, at an early period in the growth of the most ancient Aryan language, the terminations of the first, second, and third persons singular had ceased to be felt as independent personal pronouns; that hence they had lost the accent, which fell back on the radical vowel; while in the plural the terminations, continuing to be felt as modificatory pronominal suffixes, retained the accent and left the radical vowel unchanged. This rule continued to be observed in Sanskrit long after the reason of it had ceased to be perceived. The change of accent and the change of vowel remained in harmony. In Greek, on the contrary, the accentuation was gradually changed. The accent in the perfect remained in the plural on the same vowel as in the singular; yet, although thus the efficient cause for the change in the vowel had disappeared, we find the Greek continuing to strengthen the vowel in the singular "(v)oida," and to shorten it in the plural "(v)ismen," instead of "(v)idmen," just as their forefathers had done before their common language had been broken up into so many national dialects — the Sanskrit, the Greek, the German. The facts of language, however small, are historical facts, and require an historical explanation; and no explanation of the fact just mentioned, which is one out of thousands, has yet been started, except that long before the earliest literary documents of Sanskrit, which go back to 1500 B. C., long before Homer, long before the first appearance of Latin, Celtic, German, and Slavonic speech, there must have been an earlier and more primitive language, the fountain-head of all, just as Latin was the fountain-head of Italian, French, and Spanish. How much time was required for this gradual change and separation, — how long it took before the Hindus and Greeks, starting from the same centre, became so different in their language as the Sanskrit of the Veda is from the Greek of Homer, — is a question which no honest scholar would venture to answer in definite chronological language. It must have taken several generations; it may have taken hundreds or thousands of years. We have no adequate measures for such changes, and analogies derived from the time required for modern changes are as deceptive in language as in geology. The facts established once for all by the science of language are important enough in themselves, even though the ancient periods in the growth of human thought which have thus unexpectedly been opened before our eyes should resist all attempts at chronological measurement. There is a perspective order of facts which to those acquainted with the facts is more instructive than mere chronological perspective; and he who, after examining the grammars of Greek and Sanskrit, simply wonders how long it must have taken before two branches of speech, once united, could diverge so far, has a far more real and useful impression of the long process that led to such results than he who should assert that a thousand years is the minimum to account for such changes.

What it is important to know, and more important than any dates, is this, that if we search for monuments of the earliest history of our race, we have but to look around us. "Si monumentum quæris, circumspice." Our language, the dialects spoken at the present moment in every town and village of these islands, not excluding the Celtic vernaculars of Wales, Ireland, and Scotland; the languages again of Germany, Sweden, Denmark, of Italy, France, Spain, of Russia and her dependencies, of Persia and of India; these are the most ancient monuments, these are the ancient mounds through which we may run our trenches if we wish to discover beneath their surface the very palaces which were the homes of our forefathers, the very temples in which they prayed and worshipped. Languages, it is true, are constantly changing, but never in the history of man has there been a new language. What does that mean? Neither more nor less than that in speaking as we do, we are using the same materials, however broken up, crushed, and put together anew, which were handled by the first speaker, *i. e.* the first real ancestor of our race. Call that ancestor Adam, and the world is still speaking the language of Adam. Call those ancestors Shem, Ham, and Japhet, and the races of mankind are still speaking the languages of Shem, Ham, and Japhet. Or if we use the terminology of the science of language, we say again that all Aryan nations are still speaking the language of the founders and fathers of the Aryan family, in the same sense in which Dante speaks the language of Virgil, or Guizot the language of Cicero; that all Semitic nations speak but varieties of the original speech of their first ancestors, and that the languages of the Turanian or Allophylic tribes are so many rivers and rivulets diverging from distant centres, changing so rapidly as almost to lose their own identity, yet in their first beginnings as ancient as any of the Aryan or Semitic branches of speech. The very words, which we are here using have their first beginning nowhere within the recollection of history. We hear of the invention of new tools and weapons, we never hear of the invention of new languages or even of new words. New words are old words; old in their material elements, though new, and constantly renewed, in their form. If we analyze any word, its last radical elements, those elements which resist further analysis, are prehistoric, primordial, older than anything human in the realm of nature or the realm of thought. In these words, if carefully analyzed, is to be read the history of the human mind, the gradual progress from simple to mixed modes of thought, from material to abstract conceptions, from clear to obscure metaphors. Let us take one instance. Do we want to know what was uppermost in the minds of those who formed the word for punishment, the Latin *pœna*, or *punio*, to punish; the root "pû" in Sanskrit, which means to cleanse, to purify, tells us that the Latin derivative was originally formed, not to express mere striking or torturing, but cleansing, correcting, delivering from the stain of sin. In Sanskrit many a god is implored to cleanse away ("punîhi") the sins of men, and the substantive "pâvana," though it did not come to mean punishment,—this in Sanskrit is called by the most appropriate name "da*nd*a," stick,—took in later times the sense of purification and penance. Now, it is clear that the train of thought which leads from purification to penance or from purification to punishment reveals a moral and even a religious sentiment in the conception and naming of *pœna;* and it shows us that in the very infancy of criminal justice punishment was looked upon, not simply as a retribution or revenge, but as a correction, as a removal of guilt. We do not feel the presence of these early thoughts when we speak of corporal punishment or castigation; yet "castigation," too, was originally "chastening," from *castus*, pure; and *incestum* was impurity or sin, which, according to Roman law, the priests had to make good, or to punish, by a *supplicium*, a supplication or prostration before the gods. The power of punishment, originally belonging to the father, as part of his *patria potestas*, was gradually transferred to the king; and if we want to know the original conception of kingship among the Aryan nations, we have again only to analyze etymologically some of their names for king. These names tell us nothing of divinely given prerogative, nor of the possession of supereminent strength, courage, and wisdom. "*G*anaka," one of the words for king in Sanskrit, means originally parent, father, then king, thus showing the natural transition from father to king, from *patria* to *regia potestas*. It was an important remark of one of the most thoughtful etymologists, Jacob Grimm, that the Old Norse word for king, "Konungr," or "Kôngr," cannot, as was commonly supposed, be derived from the Old Norse "kyn," race, nor the Anglo Saxon "cyning," from "cyn," kin, family. King is an old word common to the three branches of the Teutonic races, not coined afresh in Sweden, England, and Germany, nay, not even coined out of purely German ore. It did not mean originally a man of family, a man of noble birth, but it is, as we said, in reality the same word, both in form and meaning, as the Sanskrit "*g*anaka," formed previously to the separation of Sanskrit, from German, and meaning originally father, secondly, king.

And here we perceive the difference between etymology and definition, which has so often been overlooked. The etymology of a word can never give us its definition; it can only supply us with historical evidence that at the time when a word was formed, its predicative power represented one out of many characteristic features of the object to which it was applied. We are not justified in saying that because *punire* meant originally to purify, therefore the Roman conception of punishment was exclusively that of purification. All we can say is that one aspect of punishment, which struck the earliest framers of the language of Italy, was that of *expiation*. Other views of punishment, however, were by no means overlooked, but found manifold expression in synonymous words. Thus the transition of meaning from father to king shows that as in each family the eldest male parent was supreme, so when families grew into clans, tribes, and nations, a similar supremacy over these larger communities was allowed to one of the fathers or elders. It shows us one phase in the origin of patriarchal kingship, one so well brought out by Mr. Maine in his "Ancient Law;" but it neither proves that kingly government among the Aryan nations was always paternal, nor that there were no other steps to sovereign power. Words such as *rex*, from *regere*, to steer; *dux*, from *ducere*, to lead, or *imperator*, a general, tell us of different ways in which ancient dynasties were founded.

By this process of comparing and analyzing words, particularly words common to many or all of the Aryan nations, it has been possible to recover some of the thoughts that filled the hearts and minds of our own most distant ancestors, of a race of men who lived we know not where and when, but to whose intellectual labors we owe not only the precious ore, but much of the ready money which still forms the intellectual currency of the Aryan world. Our dictionaries are but new editions of their dictionary; our grammars but abstracts of their grammar. If we are what we are, not only by flesh and blood, but by thought and language, then our true kith and kin are to be found among the nations of Greece and Italy, of India and Persia; our true ancestors lie buried in that central Aryan home from which, at a time long before the fifteenth century B. C., migrated those who brought to India the language of the Vedas, and to the shores of the Ægean Sea the language of the Homeric songs.

Here, however, the science of language does not stop. Not satisfied with having proved the original identity of the grammatical structure of Sanskrit, Persian, Greek, Latin, the Teutonic, Slavonic, and Celtic dialects, and thus having brought to light the original meaning of their words, it proceeded to establish another fact of equal importance, and to open a new field of research of even greater interest. It showed that the broad outlines of the ancient relgiions of those races were likewise the same; that originally they all worshipped the same gods, and that their earliest communities were not broken up before such pregnant conceptions as "God," "evil spirit," "heaven," "sacred," "to worship," "to believe," had found expression. The comparison of the different forms of Aryan religion and mythology in India, Persia, Greece, Italy, and Germany, has followed closely in the wake of comparative philology, and its results cannot fail to modify largely the views commonly entertained of the origin of the religions of mankind.

Nor was this all. It was soon perceived that in each of these nations there was a tendency to change the original conception of divine powers, to misunderstand the many names given to these powers, and to misinterpret the praises addressed to them. In this manner some of the divine names were changed into half-divine, half-human heroes; and at last the myths which were true and intelligible as told originally of the sun, or the dawn, or the storms, were turned into legends or fables too marvelous to be believed of common mortals, yet too profane to be believed any longer of gods like those who were worshipped by the contemporaries of Thales or Herakleitos. This process can be watched in India, in Greece, in Germany. The same story, or nearly the same, is told of gods, of heroes, and of men. The divine myth becomes an heroic legend, and the heroic legend fades away into a nursery tale. Our nursery tales have well been called the modern *patois* of the ancient sacred mythology of the Aryan race, and as there are similarities between Hindustani and French (such similarities as we may expect between distant cousins), we may well understand how it came to pass that in many of the Norse tales or in Grimm's "Mährchen" the burden of the story is the same as in the Eastern fairy tales and in Grecian fables. Here, too, the ground-plan of a new science has been sketched out, and broken relics of the ancient folk-lore of the Aryan family have been picked up in the cottages of Scotland, the spinning-rooms of Germany, the bazaars of Herat, and the monasteries of Ceylon.

Thus we have finished our survey of the various inquiries into the ancient "works and days" of mankind which have been set on foot by the students of the science of language, and we have reached at last that point where we may properly appreciate the object and character of Mr. Tylor's book, "Researches into the Early History of Mankind and the Development of Civilization." The question had often been asked, — if everything in language which seems modern is really so very old, if an unbroken chain unites our thoughts with the first stammerings of our Aryan forefathers, if the Robin Hood of our nursery tales is only a disguise of the Northern god Wodan or Odin, and our Harlequin a mollified representative of the Hellequin of the Franks, why should not the same apply to many of our manners and customs? It is true we are no longer shepherds and hunters, like our earlier forefathers. We wash, and comb, and dress, and shave, while they had no names for soap or razors, for combs or kilts. They were uncivilized Pagans — we are civilized Christians. Yet, in spite of all these differences, it was thought to be a question of interest whether some of our modern customs might not be traced back to earlier sources, and be shown to have prevailed not only on Teutonic soil, but among several, or all, of the races which together form the Aryan family. Jacob Grimm wrote a most interesting paper on the different forms of burial, and he came to the conclusion that both burning and burying were recognized forms of sepulture among the Aryan nations from the earliest times, but that burning was originally preferred by nomadic, burying by agricultural tribes. He likewise showed that the burning of widows was by no means a custom confined to India, but that it existed in earlier times among Thracians, Getæ, and Scythians, and that the self-immolation of Brynhild on the pile of Sigurd was by no means an isolated instance in the mythology of the Teutonic race. Curious coincidences have likewise been pointed out in the marriage ceremonies of the Hindus, Greeks, Romans, and Germans, and not a few of the laws and customs of the Teutonic tribes have been traced back by Grimm, with a more or less success, to corresponding laws and customs in India, Greece, and Italy.

It is, no doubt, desirable in researches of this kind to keep at first within the bounds laid down by the science of language, and to compare the customs of those nations only whose languages are known to be of the same origin. A comparative study of Aryan customs, of Semitic customs, of Turanian customs, would yield more satisfactory results than a promiscuous intercomparison of the customs of all mankind. In a book recently published by Mr. McLennan "On Primitive Marriage," in which he proves that among many nations wives were originally captured, and that the form of capture remained as a symbol in the marriage ceremonies of later ages, the want of some systematic treatment of this kind is felt very much, and while we find evidence from all quarters of the globe in support of his theory, we miss a due consideration of what is nearer home; for instance, the Old Norse word "quân-fang," "wife-catching," and the German "brût-loufti," "bride-racing," both used in the sense of marriage.

At the same time, a more comprehensive study of customs is necessary as a corrective for more special inquiries. If we find the same custom in India and in Greece, we are apt to suppose that it must have sprung from a common source, and we are inclined to ascribe its origin to the times preceding the Aryan separation. But if we find exactly the same custom in America or Australia, we are warned at once against too hasty conclusions. In this respect Mr. McLennan's book is very useful. We learn, for instance, that bride-racing, even as a merely symbolic ceremony, was by no means confined to the Aryan nations. Among the wild tribes of the Malay peninsula the bride and bridegroom are led by one of the old men of the tribe towards a circle. The girl runs round first, and the young man pursues a short distance behind; if he succeed in reaching and retaining her, she becomes his wife; if not, he loses all claim to her. As in a comparative study of laws we must learn to distinguish the surface of conventional statutes from the lower and far more widely extending substratum of morality, so in a comparative study of customs, it is necessary to separate what is conventional, individual, local, or national from what is natural, general, universal, and simply human. If, for instance, we found metrical and rhythmical poetry in Greece, Rome, and India only, we might look upon it as an invention peculiar to the Aryan race; but if we find the same among Semitic and Turanian races, we see at once that metre and rhythm are forms which human language naturally assumes, and which may be brought to more or less perfection under circumstances more or less favorable. Lolling out the tongue as a sign of contempt is certainly an ancient Aryan custom, for the verb "lal" is found in Sanskrit with the same meaning as in English. Yet this gesture is not restricted to Aryan nations. Rubbing of noses, by way of salutation, might seem peculiar to the New Zealander; but it exists in China, and Linnæus found the same habit in the Lapland Alps. Here we perceive the principal difficulty in what may be called *ethological* as distinguished from *ethnological* researches; and we see why it is necessary that in a comparative study of manners special studies should always be checked by more general observations.

In the volume before us, which we hope is only the first of a long series, Mr. Tylor has brought together the most valuable evidence as to the similarity of customs, not only among races linguistically related to each other, but likewise among races whose languages are totally distinct. He has been a most patient and accurate collector of facts, and, considering how few predecessors he has had in this branch of study, he deserves great credit for his industry in collecting and his good sense in arranging his evidence. He expresses himself indebted to Dr. Gustav Clemm, of Dresden, and Dr. Bastian, whose works on the history of civilization are frequently quoted. But Mr. Tylor has supplied that which was wanting in those works, by giving life and purpose to facts, and making them instructive, instead of being simply oppressive. Some articles by Professor Lazarus, too, are quoted from a German periodical specially devoted to what is called "Völkerpsychologie," or ethnic psychology; but they are the works of a philosopher rather than of a collector of facts. They are full of deep metaphysical speculations, and we do not wonder at Mr. Tylor's remarks, who, when quoting a particularly lucid and eloquent passage on the relation of speech to thought, observes, "Transcendental as it is, it is put in such clear terms that we may almost think we understand it."

Mr. Tylor is particularly free from foregone conclusions; nay, he has been blamed for not attempting to bring his researches more to a point, and drawing general conclusions from the statements which he has grouped so well together. We have no doubt that his book would have been read with keener interest, if it had been written in support of any popular or unpopular theory, or if certain conclusions to which his researches seem to lead had been laid down as indubitable facts. But what thus detracts from the ephemeral interest will increase the permanent value of his work.

"The ethnologist," says Mr. Tylor (p. 273), "must have derived from observation of many cases a general notion of what man does and does not do before he can say of any particular custom which he finds in two distant places either that it is likely that a similar state of things may have produced it more than once, or that it is unlikely — that it is even so unlikely as to approach the limit of impossibility — that such a thing should have grown up independently in the two, or three, or twenty places where he finds it. In the first case, it is worth little or nothing to him as evidence bearing on the early history of mankind, but in the latter it goes with more or less force to prove that the people who possess it are allied by blood, or have been in contact, or have been influenced indirectly one from the other, or both from a common source, or that some combination of these things has happened; in a word, that there has been historical connection between them."

Thus, Mr. Tylor argues very correctly that a belief in immortality, which is found in many parts of the world, is no proof of any historical contact between the nations that hold it. The ancient Hindus believed in immortality, and in personal immortality; and we find them in the Veda praying to their gods that they might see their fathers and mothers again in the bright world to come. We can hardly imagine such a prayer from the lips of a Greek or a Roman, though it would not surprise us in the sacred groves of ancient Germany. What a deeply interesting work might be written on this one subject — on the different forms which a belief in immortality has assumed among the different races of mankind! We shall here only mention a few of its lowest forms.

The Greenlander believes that when a man dies his soul travels to Torngarsuk, the land where reigns perpetual summer, all sunshine, and no night; where there is good water, and birds, fish, seals, and reindeer without end, that are to be caught without trouble, or are found cooking alive in a huge kettle. But the journey to this land is difficult; the souls have to slide five days or more down a precipice all stained with the blood of those who have gone down before. And it is especially grievous for the poor souls, when the journey must be made in winter or in tempest, for then a soul may come to harm, or suffer the other death, as they call it, when it perishes utterly, and nothing is left. The bridge Es-Sirat, which stretches over the midst of the Moslem hell, finer than a hair, and sharper than the edge of a sword, conveys a similar conception; and the Jews, too, when they came to believe in immortality, imagined a bridge of hell, at least for unbelievers to pass. Mr. Tylor traces this idea of a bridge in Java, in North America, in South America, and he shows how, in Polynesia, the bridge is replaced by canoes in which the souls had to pass the great gulf.

The native tribes of the lower end of South America believe in two great powers of good and evil, but likewise in a number of inferior deities. These are supposed to have been the creators and ancestors of different families, and hence when an Indian dies his soul goes to live with the deity who presides over his particular family. These deities have each their separate habitations in vast caverns under the earth, and thither the departed repair to enjoy the happiness of being eternally drunk.

Messrs. Lewis and Clarke give the following account of the belief in a future state entertained by another American tribe, the Mandans: —

"Their belief in a future state is connected with this tradition of their origin: The whole nation resided in one large village underground near a subterraneous lake. A grape-vine extended its roots down to their habitation and gave them a view of the light. Some of the most adventurous climbed up the vine, and were delighted with the sight of the earth, which they found covered with buffalo, and rich with every kind of fruit. Returning with the grapes they had gathered, their countrymen were so pleased with the taste of them that the whole nation resolved to leave their dull residence for the charms of the upper region. Men, women, and children ascended by means of the vine, but when about half the nation had reached the surface of the earth, a corpulent woman who was clambering up the vine broke it with her weight, and closed upon herself and the rest of the nation the light of the sun. Those who were left on earth made a village below where we saw the vine villages; and when the Mandans die they expect to return to the original seats of their forefathers, the good reaching the ancient village by means of the lake, which the burden of the sins of the wicked will not enable them to cross."

Mr. Tylor aptly compares the fable of the vine and the fat woman with the story of "Jack and the Bean-stalk," and he brings other stories from Malay and Polynesian districts embodying the same idea. Among the different ways by which it was thought possible to ascend from earth to heaven, Mr. Tylor mentions the rank spear-grass, a rope or thong, a spider's web, a ladder of iron or gold, a column of smoke, or the rainbow. In the Mongolic tales of Gesser Chan the hero lets himself down from heaven and ascends again by means of a chain.

The Polynesians imagine that the sky descends at the horizon and incloses the earth. Hence they call foreigners "papalangi," or "heaven-bursters," as having broken in from another world outside. According to their views, we live upon the ground-floor of a great house, with upper stories rising one over another above us and cellars down below. There are holes in the ceiling to let the rain through, and as men are supposed to visit the dwellers above, the dwellers from below are believed to come sometimes up to the surface, and likewise to receive visits from men in return.

Catlin's account of the Choctaw belief in a future state is equally curious. They hold that the spirit lives after death, and that it has a great distance to travel towards the west; that it has to cross a dreadful, deep, and rapid stream, over which, from hill to hill, there lies a long, slippery pine log, with the bark peeled off. Over this the dead have to pass before they reach the delightful hunting-grounds. The good walk on safely, though six people from the other side throw stones at them; but the wicked, trying to dodge the stones, slip off the log, and fall thousands of feet into the water which is dashing over the rocks.

The New Hollanders, according to Mr. Oldfield, believe that all who are good men and have been properly buried, enter heaven after death. Heaven, which is the abode of the two good divinities, is represented as a delightful place, where there is abundance of game and food, never any excess of heat or cold, rain or drought, no malign spirits, no sickness or death; but plenty of rioting, singing, and dancing for evermore. They also believe in an evil spirit who dwells in the nethermost regions, and, strange to say, they represent him with horns and a tail, though one would think that prior to the introduction of cattle into New Holland, the natives could not have been aware of the existence of horned beasts.

Now, with regard to all these forms of belief in a future state, Mr. Tylor would hold that they had arisen independently among different races, and that they supply no argument in favor of any historical connection between these races. But let us now take a different instance. When we find in Africa the same beast fables with which we are familiar from "Reynard the Fox," then the coincidence is such that, according to Mr. Tylor, it cannot be ascribed to natural causes.

"Dr. Dasent," he writes, "in his Introduction to the Norse Tales, has shown that popular stories found in the west and south of Africa must have come from the same source with old myths current in distant regions of Europe. Still later, Dr. Bleek has published a collection of Hottentot Fables, 'Reynard the Fox in South Africa,' which shows that other mythic episodes, long familiar in remote countries, have established themselves among these rude people as household tales. As it happens, we know from other sources enough to explain the appearance in South Africa of stories from Reynard by referring them to European, and more particularly to Dutch influences. But, even without such knowledge, the tales themselves prove an historical connection, near or remote, between Europe and the Cape of Good Hope."

Where coincidences occur in the customs and traditions of nations who, as far as history tells us, have never had any intercourse together, Mr. Tylor simply registers the fact, without drawing further conclusions. He has, indeed, endeavored in one instance to establish an historical connection between the mythology of America and that of Asia and the rest of the world, on the strength of a certain similarity of legends; but we doubt whether his evidence, however striking, is strong enough to support so bold an arch. There is in the popular traditions of Central America the story of two brothers who, starting on their dangerous journey to the land of Xibalba, where their father had perished, plant each a cane in the middle of their grandmother's house that she may know by its flourishing or withering whether they are alive or dead. Exactly the same conception occurs in Grimm's "Mährchen." When the two gold-children wish to see the world and to leave their father, and when their father is sad and asks them how he shall have news of them, they tell him, "We leave you the two golden lilies; from these you can see how we fare. If they are fresh, we are well; if they fade, we are ill; if they fall, we are dead." Grimm traces the same idea in Indian stories. Now this idea is strange enough, and its occurrence in India, Germany, and Central America is stranger still. If it occurred in Indian and German tales only, we might consider it as ancient Aryan property, but when we find it again in Central America, nothing remains but either to admit a later communication between

European settlers and native American story-tellers — an admission which, though difficult, is not quite impossible; or to inquire whether there is not some intelligible and truly human element in this supposed sympathy between the life of flowers and the life of man. Mr. Tylor himself has brought together analogous cases in his chapter of images and names. Thus, when a Maori war-party is to start, the priests set up sticks in the ground to represent the warriors, and he whose stick is blown down, is to fall in the battle. In British Guiana, when young children are betrothed, trees are planted by the respective parties in witness of the contract, and if either tree should happen to wither, the child it belongs to is sure to die. And surely this is a feeling in which many can share even in this enlightened age. Perhaps we should only call it unlucky if a tree planted by an absent child were suddenly to wither, or if a distant friend's portrait were to fall from the wall, or if a wedding-ring were to roll off the finger; yet the fact that we call such things unlucky shows that there must be something human in the sentiment which prompted the story of the gold-children, and of the brothers who went to Xibalba, and that we need not on that account admit an historical intercourse between the aborigines of Guatemala and the Aryans of India and Germany.

It is likewise a curious coincidence that the Mexicans represent an eclipse of the moon as the moon being devoured by a dragon, and that the Hindus do just the same; nay, both nations continued to use this expression long after they had discovered the true cause of an eclipse. Yet here again the original conception is natural and intelligible, and its occurrence in India and Mexico need not be the result of any historical intercourse. We know that such an intercourse was suspected by Alexander von Humboldt, and we are far from considering it impossible. But the evidence on the American side requires more careful sifting than it has yet received; and we must remind Mr. Tylor that even the MS. of the "Popul Vuh," to which he refers for ancient American traditions, has never been traced beyond the end of the seventeenth century, and that even had it been written towards the end of the sixteenth century, it would not have been quite safe from European influences.

That there was in very early days a migration from the northeast of Asia to the northwest of America is, as yet, a postulate only. There are scattered indications in the languages and traditions, as well as in the fauna and flora of the two opposite continents, which seem to require the admission of a primeval bridge of islands across Behring's Straits. Yet the evidence has never been carefully sifted and properly summed up, and till that is done a verdict cannot be given. As a contribution, apparently small, yet by no means insignificant, towards a solution of this important problem, we shall mention only one of Mr. Tylor's observations. Joannes de Plano Carpini, describing in 1246 the manners and customs of the Tartars, says that one of their superstitious traditions concerns sticking a knife into the fire, or in any way touching the fire with a knife, or even taking meat out of a kettle with a knife, or cutting near the fire with an axe, for they believe that so the head of the fire would be cut off. In the far northeast of Asia, it may be found, in the remarkable catalogue of ceremonial sins of the Kamchadals, among whom it is a sin to take up a burning ember with the knife-point, and light tobacco; but it must be taken hold of with the bare hands. How is it possible to separate from these the following statement taken out of a list of superstitions of the Sioux Indians of North America? "They must not stick an awl or needle into . . . . a stick of wood on the fire. No person must chop on it with an axe or knife, or stick an awl into it; neither are they allowed to take a coal from the fire with a knife, or any other sharp instrument."

These, no doubt, are striking coincidences; but do they not at once lose much of their force by the fact, mentioned by Mr. Tylor himself, that among the ancient Pythagorean maxims we find, *πῦρ μαχαίρᾳ μὴ σκαλεύειν*, "not to stir the fire with a sword."

Mr. Tylor seems almost to despair of the existence of any custom anywhere which cannot be matched somewhere else. "Indeed," he says (p. 175), "any one who claims a particular place as the source of even the smallest art, from the mere fact of finding it there, must feel that he may be using his own ignorance as evidence, as though it were knowledge. An ingenious little drilling instrument which I and other observers had set down as peculiar to the South Sea Islanders, in or near the Samoan group, I found kept one day in stock in the London tool-shops."

It is impossible to be too cautious in a comparative study of manners before admitting an historical connection on the strength of ethological coincidences, however startling. Let those who are inclined to blame Mr. Tylor for not having dogmatized more broadly on these problems, consider but one case, that of the Couvade, so well described in his book. Who could believe that there was one single tribe, however silly in other respects, which should carry its silliness so far as to demand that on the birth of a child the father should take to his bed, while the mother attends to all the duties of the household? Yet there are few customs more widely spread than this, and better attested by historical evidence during nearly 2,000 years. The Chinese, whose usages are quaint enough, have long been credited with this custom, but, as it would seem, without good reason, Marco Polo, passing through China in the thirteenth century, observed this custom in the Chinese province of West Yunnan, and the widow's remark to Sir Hudibras owes its origin most probably to Marco Polo's travels: —

> "For though Chineses go to bed,
> And lie-in in their ladies' stead."

The people, however, among whom the Venetian traveller observed this custom were not properly Chinese, but the aboriginal tribes of the land. Among these tribes, commonly called Miau-tze, soil-children, the custom remarked by Marco Polo in the thirteenth century exists to the present day. The father of a new-born child, as soon as its mother has become strong enough to leave her couch, gets into bed himself, and there receives the congratulations of his acquaintances. But the custom is more ancient than the thirteenth century. About the beginning of the Christian era one of the most trustworthy geographers, Strabo,[1] mentions that among the Iberians of the north of Spain

[1] Strabo, III. 4, 17. Κοινὰ δὲ καὶ ταῦτα πρὸς τὰ Κελτικὰ ἔθνη καὶ τὰ Θρᾴκια καὶ Σκυθικά, κοινὰ δὲ καὶ τὰ πρὸς ἀνδρείαν τήν τε τῶν ἀνδρῶν καὶ τὴν τῶν γυναικῶν. γεωργοῦσι αὗται, τεκοῦσαί τε διακονοῦσι τοῖς ἀνδράσιν, ἐκείνους ἀνθ' ἑαυτῶν κατακλίνασαι.

the women, after the birth of a child, tend their husbands, putting them to bed, instead of going themselves. In the same locality, and among the modern Basques, the descendants of the Iberians, M. F. Michel found the same custom in existence but a few years ago. "In Biscay," he says, "the women rise immediately after childbirth, and attend to the duties of the household, while the husband goes to bed, taking the baby with him, and thus receives the neighbors' compliments." From the Basques in the Pyrenees this absurd custom seems to have spread to France, where it received the name of *faire la couvade.*

"It has been found in Navarre," Mr. Tylor writes, "and on the French side of the Pyrenees. Legrand d'Aussy mentions that in an old French fabliau, the king of Torelore is *au lit et en couche*, when Aucassin arrives and takes a stick to him and makes him promise to abolish the custom in his realm. And the same author goes on to say that the practice is said still to exist in some cantons of Béarn." Nor is this all. We have the respectable authority of Diodorus Siculus that among the natives of Corsica the wife was neglected and the husband put to bed and treated as the patient. And, if we may trust Apollonius Rhodius,[1] the same

[1] Apollonius, *Argonautica*, II. 1009–1014: —

> Τοὺς δὲ μέτ' αὐτίκ' ἔπειτα Γενηταίου Διὸς ἄκρην
> γνάμψαντες, σώοντο παρὲξ Τιβαρηνίδα γαῖαν.
> Ἔνθ' ἐπεὶ ἄρ κε τέκωνται ὑπ' ἀνδράσι τέκνα γυναῖκες,
> αὐτοὶ μὲν στενάχουσιν ἐνὶ λεχέεσσι πεσόντες,
> κράατα δησάμενοι· ταὶ δ' εὖ κομέουσι ἐδωδῇ
> ἀνέρας, ἠδὲ λοετρὰ λεχώϊα τοῖσι πένονται.

See also Valerius Flaccus, *Argon.* V. 148: —

> "Inde Genetæi rupem Jovis, hinc Tibarenûm
> Dant virides post terga lacus, ubi deside mitra
> Feta ligat, partuque virum fovet ipsa soluto."

almost incredible custom prevailed at the south of the Black Sea, among a people called Tibareni, where, when the child was born, the father lay groaning in bed with his head tied up, while the mother tended him with food and prepared his baths.

Thus, a custom which ought to be peculiar to Bedlam has been traced during more than 1,800 years in the most distant parts of the world — in Western China, near the Black Sea, in Corsica, in Spain, and among tribes who, as far as we know, had no historical intercourse with each other, and whose languages certainly show no traces of relationship. Is it, then, a natural custom? Is there anything rational or intelligible in it to which there might be some response from every human heart? Mr. Tylor thinks that he has discovered such an element. "The Couvade," he says, "implicitly denies that physical separation of individuals which a civilized man would probably set down as a first principle. It shows us a number of distinct and distant tribes deliberately holding the opinion that the connection between father and child is not only, as we think, a mere relation of parentage, affection, and duty, but that their very bodies are joined by a physical bond; so that what is done to the one acts directly upon the other!" Mr. Tylor fixes on what he calls a "fusion of objective and subjective relations in the mind" as the source of this and other superstitions; and though allowing that it is difficult to place ourselves at the same angle of thought, he traces the effects of a similar confusion in many of the customs and ceremonies of earlier ages.

Without denying the existence of this mental confusion, nay, readily allowing to it some influence on the latter modifications of the Couvade, we are inclined to take a different view of the origin of that extraordinary custom. Customs, however extraordinary, after a lapse of time, have generally very simple beginnings. Now, without exaggerating the treatment which a husband receives among ourselves at the time of his wife's confinement, not only from mothers-in-law, sisters-in-law, and other female relatives, but from nurses, from every consequential maid-servant in the house, it cannot be denied that while his wife is suffering, his immunity from pain is generally remarked upon, and if anything goes wrong for which it is possible to blame him, he is sure to hear of it. If his boots are creaking, if his dog is barking, if the straw has not been properly laid down, does he not catch it? And would it not be best for him to take to his bed at once, and not to get up till all is well over? If something of this kind exists in our highly civilized age, let us try to imagine what it must have been among nomadic races; or, rather, let us hear evidence. Among the land Dayaks of Borneo the husband, before the birth of his child, may do no work with a sharp instrument except what is necessary for the farm; nor may he fire guns, nor strike animals, nor do any violent work, lest bad influences should affect the child; and after it is born, the father is kept in seclusion in-doors for several days and dieted on rice and salt, to prevent not his own but his child's stomach from swelling. In Kamschatka the husband must not do such things as bend sledge-staves across his knee before his child is born. In Greenland he must for some weeks before his wife's confinement do no work except what is necessary to procure food, and this, it is believed, in order that the child may not die. Among the Arawaks of Surinam for some time after the birth of his child the father must fell no tree, fire no gun, hunt no large game; he may stay near home, shoot little birds with a bow and arrow, and angle for little fish, but, his time hanging heavy on his head, the most comfortable thing he can do is to lounge in his hammock.

In all these arrangements the original intention is very clear. The husband was to keep quiet before as well as after the birth of his child, and he was told by the goodies of the house that if he went out hunting or came home drunk, it would injure the child. If the child happened to die he would never hear the last of his carelessness and want of consideration. Now, if this train of ideas was once started, the rest would follow. If a timid and kind-hearted husband had once been frightened into the belief that it was his eating too much or his coming home drunk from the Club that killed the child, need we wonder if the next time he tried to be on his good behavior, and even took to fasting in order to benefit his child, *i. e* in reality, to save his servants the trouble of preparing dinner for him? Other husbands would then be told with significant looks what a pattern of a husband he had been, and how his children never died, and thus the belief would soon spread that if a child died it was the husband who killed it by some neglect or other. Fasting before or after the birth of a child would become meritorious, and would soon be followed by other kinds of mortification which the natural spitefulness of the female population against the unfortunate husband would tend to multiply and increase *ad infinitum.* Now, let us see whether in the peculiar formalities of the Couvade we can still discover motives of this kind. The following account is given by Du Tertre of the Carib Couvade in the West Indies: —

"When a child is born the mother goes presently to her work, but the father begins to complain and takes to his hammock, and there he is visited as though he were sick, and undergoes a course of dieting which would cure of the gout the most replete of Frenchmen. How they can fast so much, and not die of it (continues the narrator) is amazing to me. When the forty days are up, they invite their relations, who, being arrived, before they set to eating hack the skin of this poor wretch with agouti teeth, and draw blood from all parts of his body, in such sort that from being sick by pure imagination they often make a real patient of him. This is, however, so to speak, only the fish, for now comes the sauce they prepare for him; they take sixty or eighty large grains of pimento, or Indian pepper, the strongest they can get, and after well washing it in water, they wash with this peppery infusion the wounds and scars of the poor fellow, who, I believe, suffers no less than if he were burnt alive; however, he must not utter a single word if he will not pass for a coward and a wretch.[1] This ceremony ended, they bring him back to his bed, where he remains some days more, and the rest go and make good cheer in the house at his expense. Nor is this all. Through the

[1] Among the Koriaks, who inhabit the northern half of the peninsula of Kamtschatka, the bridegroom, when he receives his bride, is beaten with sticks by his future parents and neighbors. If he endures this manfully, he proves his ability "to bear up against the ills of life," and is then conducted without further ceremony to the apartment of his betrothed. See A. S. Bickmore, "The Ainos or Hairy Men," *American Journal of Science*, May, 1868, p. 12.

space of six whole months he eats neither birds nor fish, firmly believing that this would injure the child's stomach, and that it would participate in the natural faults of the animals on which its father had fed; for example, if the father ate turtle — poor alderman! — the child would be deaf and have no brains like this animal!"

The Jesuit missionary Dobrizhofer gives the following account of the Abipones in South America: —

"No sooner do you hear that the wife has borne a child than you will see the Abipone husband lying in bed huddled up with mats and skins, lest some ruder breath of air should touch him, fasting, kept in private, and for a number of days abstaining religiously from certain viands; you would aver it was he who had had the child. And in truth they observe this ancestral custom, troublesome as it is, the more willingly and diligently, from their being altogether persuaded that the sobriety and quiet of the father is effectual for the well-being of the new-born offspring, and is even necessary. They believe that the father's carelessness influences the new-born offspring, from a natural bond and sympathy of both. Hence if the child comes to a premature end, its death is attributed by the women to the father's intemperance, this or that cause being assigned: he did not abstain from mead; he had loaded his stomach with water-hog; he had swam across the river when the air was chilly; he had neglected to shave off his long eyebrows; he had devoured underground honey, stamping on the bees with his feet; he had ridden till he was tired and sweated. With raving like this the crowd of women accuse the father with impunity of causing the child's death, and are accustomed to pour curses on the unoffending husband."

These statements, such as they are, given by unprejudiced observers, seem to support very strongly the natural explanation which we proposed of the Couvade. It is clear that the poor husband was at first tyrannized over by his female relations, and afterwards frightened into superstition. He then began to make a martyr of himself till he made himself really ill or took to his bed in self-defense. Strange and absurd as the Couvade appears at first sight, there is something in it with which, we believe, most mothers-in-law can sympathize; and if we consider that it has been proved to exist in Spain, Corsica, Pontus, Africa, the Eastern Archipelago, the West Indies, North and South America, we shall be inclined to admit that it arose from some secret spring in human nature, the effects of which may be modified by civilization, but are, perhaps, never entirely obliterated.

It is one of the principal charms in the study of customs to watch their growth and their extraordinary tenacity. It is true we are no longer savages; we do not thrust rings and bones and feathers through the cartilage of our noses, nor pull our ears in long nooses down to the shoulders by heavy weights. Still less do we put wooden plugs as big as table spoons through slits in the under lip, or stick the teeth of animals point outwards through holes in the cheeks. Yet the ears of female children are still mutilated even in Europe, and ladies are not ashamed to hang jewels in them.

What is the meaning of the wedding-ring which the wife has to wear? There is no authority for it either in the Old or New Testament. It is simply a heathen custom, whether Roman or Teutonic we shall not attempt to decide, but originally expressive of the fetter by which the wife was tied to her husband. In England it is the wife only who wears the golden fetter, while all over Germany the tie is mutual; both husband and wife wearing the badge of the loss of their liberty. We thought, indeed, we had discovered among the wild tribes in the interior of the Malay peninsula an independent instance of the use of wedding-rings. But although every trace of Christianity seems extinct among the Mantras, there can be no doubt, from the description given by Father Bourien ("Transactions of Ethnological Society," vol. iii. p. 82) that Christian missionaries had reached these people, though it may be, before the time when they migrated to their present seats.

We should not venture to call our levees and drawing-rooms the remnants of barbarism and savagery. Yet they must clearly be traced back to the Middle Ages, when homage was done by each subject by putting his hands joined between the hands of the king. This, again, was originally a mere symbol, an imitation of the act by which a vanquished enemy surrendered himself to his despoiler. We know from the sculptures of Nineveh and from other sources that it was the custom of the conqueror to put his foot on the neck of his enemy. This, too, has been abbreviated; and as in Europe gentlemen now only kiss the king's hand, we find that in the Tonga Islands, when a subject approaches to do homage, the chief has to hold up his foot behind, as a horse does, and the subject touches the sole with his fingers, thus placing himself, as it were, under the sole of his lord's foot. Every one seems to have the right of doing reverence in this way when he pleases; and chiefs get so tired of holding up their feet to be touched that they make their escape at the very sight of a loyal subject.

Who has not wondered sometimes at the fumbling efforts of gentlemen in removing their gloves before shaking hands with a lady, the only object being, it would seem, to substitute a warm hand for a cool glove? Yet in the ages of chivalry there was a good reason for it. A knight's glove was a steel gauntlet, and a squeeze with that would have been painful.

Another extraordinary feature in the history of manners is the utter disability of people to judge of the manners of other nations or of former ages with anything like fairness or common sense. An English lady travelling in the East turns away her face with disgust when she sees oriental women passing by with bare feet and bare legs; while the Eastern ladies are horrified at the idea of women in Europe walking about barefaced. Admirers of Goethe may get over the idea that this great poet certainly ate fish with a knife; but when we are told that Beatrice never used a fork, and that Dante never changed his linen for weeks, some of our illusions are rudely disturbed. We mourn in black, and think that nothing can be more natural; the aborigines of Australia mourn in white, and, their clothing being of the scantiest, they plaster their foreheads, the tips of their noses, and the lower parts of the orbit of their eyes with pipe-clay. As long as the people of Europe represented the Devil in human form they represented him in black. In Africa the natives of the Guinea coast paint him in the whitest colors.

To Northern nations Hell was a cold place, a dreary region of snow and frost; to Eastern nations, and those who derive their notions from the East, the place of torment was ablaze with fire and flame. Who shall tell which is right?

And now, after we have gone through these few samples, ancient and modern, of barbarous and refined customs, we are afraid that we have given but a very incomplete idea of what may be found in Mr. Tylor's book on the early history of mankind. We have endeavored to point out the importance of the subject which he has treated, but we have hardly done justice to the careful yet pleasing manner in which he has treated it. There are in the beginning four chapters on the various ways in which man utters his thoughts in gestures, words, pictures, and writing. Of these we have not been able to say anything, though they contain much that is new, and the result of thoughtful observation. Then there is a chapter on images and names, where an attempt is made to refer a great part of the beliefs and practices included under the general name of magic to one very simple mental law, namely, the taking the name for the thing, the idol for the deity, the doll for the living child. There is an excellent essay on flints and celts, in which it is shown that the transition from implements of stone to those of metal took place in almost every part of the globe, and a progress from ruder to more perfect modes of making fire and boiling food is traced in many different countries. Here Mr. Tylor expresses his obligations to Mr. Henry Christie, whose great collection of the productions of the lower races has few rivals in Europe, and whose lucid Paper on the "Different Periods of the Stone

Age," lately published, is, we hope, but the first instalment of a larger work. Lastly, there are several chapters in which a number of stories are grouped together as "Myths of Observation," *i. e.* as stories invented to account, somehow or other, for actual facts, the real origin of which was unknown. Every one of these subjects would well deserve a separate review. But, having already overstepped the proper limits of a literary article, we will not anticipate any further the pleasure of those who want to have an instructive book to read during their leisure hours.

April, 1865.

XXVI.

OUR FIGURES.[1]

THE two words "cipher" and "zero," which are in reality but one, would almost in themselves be sufficient to prove that our figures are borrowed from the Arabs. "Cipher" is the Arabic "cifron," which means empty, a translation of the Sanskrit name of the nought, "sûnya." The same character, the nought, is called "zephiro" in Italian, and has by rapid pronunciation been changed into "zero" — a form occurring as early as 1491, in a work of Philip Calander on Arithmetic, published at Florence. "Cipher" — originally the name of the tenth of the numerical figures, the nought — became in most European languages the general term for all figures, "zero" taking its place as the technical name of the nought; while in English "cipher" retained its primitive sense, and is thus used even in common parlance, as, for instance, "He is a mere *cipher*."

The Arabs, however, far from claiming the discovery of the figures for themselves, unanimously ascribe it to the Indians; nor can there be much doubt that the Brahmans were the original inventors of those numerical symbols which are now used over the whole

1 *Mémoire sur la Propagation des Chiffres Indiens.* Par M. F. Woepcke. Paris, 1863.

civilized world. But although this has long been admitted as true, there is considerable difficulty when we come to trace the channels through which the figures could have reached, and did reach the nations of Europe. If these numerical symbols had been unknown in Europe before the invasion of Spain by the Mohammedans, or before the rise of Mohammedanism, all would be easy enough. We possess the work through which the Arabs, under the Khalif Almâmûn, in the ninth century, became initiated into the science of Indian ciphering and arithmetic. This work of Abu Jafar Mohammed Ben Mûsâ Alkhârizmî was founded on treatises brought from India to Bagdad in 773, and was translated again into Latin during the Middle Ages, with the title of "Algoritmi de numero Indorum." It was generally supposed, therefore, that the Mohammedans brought the Indian figures into Spain; and that Gerbert, afterwards Pope Sylvester II., who died 1003, acquired a knowledge of them at Seville or Cordova, where he was supposed (though wrongly) to have lived as a student. Unfortunately, the figures used in the principal countries of Europe during the Middle Ages, and, with some modifications, to the present day, differ considerably from the figures used in the East; and while they differ from these, they approach very near to the figures used by the Arabs in Africa and Spain. This is the first point that has to be explained. Secondly, there is at the end of the first book of the "Geometry" of Boëthius a passage where, in describing the *Mensa Pythagorea*, also called the *Abacus*, Boëthius mentions nine figures which he ascribes to the Pythagoreans or Neo-Pythagoreans, and which, to judge from the best MSS., are curiously like the figures used in Africa, Syria, and the principal countries of Europe. To increase the difficulty of our problem, this very important passage of Boëthius is wanting in some MSS., is considered spurious by several critics, and is now generally ascribed to a continuator of Boëthius, who drew, however, not from Eastern, but, as it would seem, from Greek sources. We have, therefore, in MSS. of the eleventh century, figures which are supposed to have been used, if not by Boëthius himself, at least by his continuators and successors in the sixth and following centuries — figures strikingly like those used by the Arabs in Africa and Spain, and yet not to be traced directly to an oriental source, but to the school of the Neo-Pythagoreans. The Neo-Pythagoreans, however, need not therefore be the inventors of these figures, any more than the Arabs. All that can be claimed for them is, that they were the first teachers of ciphering among the Greeks and Romans; that they, at Alexandria or in Syria, became acquainted with the Indian figures, and adapted them to the Pythagorean Abacus; that Boëthius, or his continuator, made these figures generally known in Europe by means of mathematical hand-books; and that thus, long before the time of Gerbert, who probably never went to Spain, and long before the influence of the Arabs could be felt in the literature of Europe, these same figures had found their way from Alexandria into our schools and monasteries. The names by which these nine figures are called in some of the MSS. of Boëthius, though extremely obscure, are supposed to show traces of that mingling of Semitic and Pythagorean ideas which could well be accounted for in the schools of Alexandria.

Yet all these considerations do not help us in tracing with any certainty the first appearance in Europe of our own figures beyond the eleventh century. The MSS. of Boëthius, which contain the earliest traces of them, belong to the eleventh century; and, strictly speaking, they cannot be made to prove that such figures as we there see existed in the time of Boëthius, *i. e.* the sixth century, still less that they were known to the Neo-Pythagorean philosophers. All that can be conceded is that Boëthius, or rather his continuator, knew of nine figures; but that they had in his time the same form which we find in the MSS. of the eleventh century, is not proven.

It is at this stage that M. Woepcke, an excellent Arabic scholar and mathematician, takes up the problem in his "Mémoire sur la Propagation des Chiffres Indiens," just published in the "Journal Asiatique." He points out, first of all, a fact which had been neglected by all previous writers, namely, that the Arabs have two sets of figures, one used chiefly in the East, which he therefore calls the "Oriental;" another used in Africa and Spain, and there called "Gobar." "Gobar" means "dust," and these figures were so called because, as the Arabs say, they were first introduced by an Indian who used a table covered with fine dust for the purpose of ciphering. Both sets of figures are called Indian by the Arabs. M. Woepcke then proceeds to show that the figures given in the MSS. of Boëthius coincide with the earliest forms of the Gobar figures, whilst they differ from the Oriental figures; and, adopting the view of Prinsep[1] that the Indian figures were originally the initial letters of the

[1] *Journal of the Asiatic Society of Bengal*, April, 1838.

Sanskrit numerals, he exhibits in a table the similarity between the Gobar figures and the initial letters of the Sanskrit numerals, giving these letters from Indian inscriptions of the second century of our era. Hereby an important advance is made, for, as the Sanskrit alphabet changes from century to century, M. Woepcke argues very plausibly, though, we must add, not quite convincingly, that the *apices* given in Boëthius, and ascribed by him to the Neo-Pythagoreans, could not have been derived from India much after the third or fourth centuries. He points out that these nine figures were of less importance to the Greeks, who used their letters with numerical values, and who had in the Abacus something approaching to a decimal system; but that they would have been of the greatest value to the Romans as replacing their V, X, L, C, D, M. In Italy, therefore, and in the Roman provinces, in Gaul and Spain, the Indian figures, which were adopted by the Neo-Pythagoreans, and which resemble the Gobar figures, began to spread from the sixth century, so that the Mohammedans, when arriving in Spain in the eighth, found these figures there already established. The Arabs themselves, when starting on their career of conquest, were hardly able to read or to write; they certainly were ignorant of ciphering, and could not therefore be considered as the original propagators of the so-called Arabic figures. The Khalif Walid, who reigned at Damascus from 705 to 715 A. D., prohibited the use of Greek in public documents, but was obliged to make an exemption in favor of Greek figures, because it was impossible to write them in Arabic. In Egypt, the Arabs adopted the Coptic figures. In 773 an Indian embassy arrived at Bagdad, at the court of the Khalif Almansur, bringing among other things a set of astronomical tables. In order to explain these tables, the ambassadors had naturally to begin with explaining their figures, their arithmetic, and algebra. Anyhow, the astronomical work, the Siddhânta of Brahmagupta, which that astronomer had composed in 628 A. D.,[1] at the court of king Vyâghra, was then and there translated into Arabic by Mohammed Ben Ibrâhim Alfâzâri, under the title of the "Great Sindhind." This work was abridged in the first half of the ninth century by a contemporary of the Khalif Almâmûn, Mohammed Ben Mûsâ Alkhârizmî, the same who afterwards wrote a manual of practical arithmetic, founded likewise on an Indian original (Woepcke, p. 58). We can well understand, therefore, that the Arabs, on arriving in Spain, without, as yet, any considerable knowledge of arithmetic, should have adopted there, as they did in Greece and Egypt, the figures which they found in use, and which had travelled there from the Neo-Pythagorean schools of Egypt, and originally from India; and likewise that when, in the ninth or tenth century, the new Arabic treatises on arithmetic arrived in Spain from the East, the Arabs of Spain should have adopted the more perfect system of ciphering, carried on without the Abacus, and rendering, in fact, the columns of the Abacus unnecessary by the judicious employment of the nought. But while dropping the Abacus, there was no necessity for their discontinuing or changing the figures to which the Arabs as well as the Spaniards had then been accustomed for centuries; and hence we find that the ancient figures

[1] Dr. Bhao Daji, "On the Age of Âryabhatta," etc., in the *Journal of the Royal Asiatic Society*, 1865, p. 410.

were retained in Spain, only adapted to the purposes of the new Indian arithmetic by the more general use of the nought. The nought was known in the Neo-Pythagorean schools, but with the columns of the Abacus it was superfluous, while, with the introduction of ciphering in fine powder, and without columns, its use naturally became very extensive. As the system of ciphering in fine powder was called "Indian," the Gobar figures, too, were frequently spoken of under the same name, and thus the Arabs in Spain brought themselves to believe that they had received both their new arithmetic and their figures from India; the truth being, according to M. Woepcke, that they had received their arithmetic from India directly, while their figures had come to them indirectly from India through the mediation of the Neo-Pythagorean schools.

M. Woepcke would therefore admit two channels through which the Indian figures reached Europe — one passing through Egypt about the third century of our era, when not only commercial but also philosophical interests attracted the merchants of U*gg*ayinî (Ὀζήνη) towards Alexandria, and thinkers such as Plotinus and Numenius toward Persia and India; another passing through Bagdad in the eighth century, and following the track of the victorious Islam. The first carried the earlier forms of the Indian figures from Alexandria to Rome and as far as Spain, and, considering the active social, political, and commercial intercourse between Egypt, as a Roman province, and the rest of the Roman Empire, we must not look upon one philosophical school, the Neo-Pythagorean, as the only agents in disseminating so useful an invention.

The merchant may have been a more active agent than the philosopher or the schoolmaster. The second carried the later forms from Bagdad to the principal countries conquered by the Khalifs, with the exception of those where the earlier or Gobar figures had already taken firm root. M. Woepcke looks on our European figures as modifications of the early Neo-Pythagorean or Gobar forms, and he admits their presence in Europe long before the science and literature of the Arabs in Spain could have reacted on our seats of classical learning. He does not pronounce himself distinctly on the date and the authorship to be assigned to the much controverted passage of Boëthius, but he is evidently inclined to ascribe, with Boeckh, a knowledge of the nine Indian figures to the Western mathematicians of the sixth century. The only change produced in the ciphering of Europe by the Arabs was, according to him, the suppression of the Abacus, and the more extended use of the cipher. He thinks that our own figures are still the Gobar figures, written in a more cursive manner by the Arabs of Spain; and that Adelard of Bath, Robert of Reading, William Shelley, David Morley, Gerard of Cremona, and others who, in the twelfth century, went to Spain to study Arabic and mathematics, learnt there the same figures, only written more cursively, which Boëthius or his continuator taught in Italy in the sixth. In MSS. of the thirteenth and fourteenth centuries the figures vary considerably in different parts of Europe, but they are at last fixed and rendered uniform by the introduction of printing.

It will be admitted by everybody who has taken an interest in the complicated problem of the origin and the migrations of our figures, that the system proposed by M. Woepcke would remove many difficulties. It is quite clear that our figures could not have come to us from the Arabs of Bagdad, and that they are the same as those of the Arabs of Spain. But it might still be questioned whether it is necessary to admit that the Arabs found the Gobar figures on their arrival in Spain established in that country. Is there really any evidence of these Gobar figures being in common use anywhere in the West of Europe before the eleventh century? Could not the Gobar figures represent one of the many local varieties of the Indian figures of which Albirûni speaks in the eleventh century, nay, which existed in India from the earliest to the present time? It should be borne in mind that the Gobar figures are not entirely unknown among the Eastern Arabs, and there are traces of them in MSS. as early as the middle of the tenth century (p. 150). How could this be explained, if the Arabs became acquainted with the Gobar figures only after their arrival in Spain? Could not the mathematicians of the Meghrab have adopted one kind of Indian figures, the Gobar, and brought them to Spain, just as they brought their own peculiar system of numerical letters, differing slightly, yet characteristically, from the numerical alphabet of the Eastern Mohammedans? Once in Spain, these Gobar figures would naturally find their way into the rest of Europe, superseding the Eastern figures which had been adopted in the mathematical works of Neophytus, Planudes, and other Byzantine writers of the fourteenth century. There is, no doubt, that passage of Boëthius, or of his continuator. But to a skeptical mind that passage can carry no conviction. We do not know who wrote it, and, strictly speaking, the figures which it contains can only prove that the writer of the MS. in the eleventh century was acquainted with the Gobar figures, which at that time were known, according to M. Woepcke's own showing, both at Shiraz and at Toledo. But though M. Woepcke has not driven away all our doubts, he has certainly contributed greatly to a final settlement of this problem, and he has brought together evidence which none but a first rate Arabic scholar and mathematician could have mastered. M. Woepcke, before grappling with this difficult subject, has even taken the trouble to familiarize himself with Sanskrit, and he has given, in his Essay, some valuable remarks about the enormous numbers used by the Buddhists in their sacred writings. Whether these enormous numbers necessitate the admission that the nine figures and the use of the cipher were known to the Buddhists in the third century B. C. is again a more doubtful point, particularly if we consider that the numbers contained in the Bactro-Pali inscriptions, in the first or second century B. C., show no trace, as yet, of that perfect system of ciphering. They either represent the numerals by a corresponding number of upright strokes, which is done up to five in the Kapurdi-giri inscription, or they adopt a special symbol for four — namely, a cross — and then express five by a cross and one stroke, eight by two crosses,[1] and ten, twenty, and a hundred by other special symbols. Thus seventy-eight is written in the Taxila inscription by three twenties, one ten, and two fours. This is a late discovery due to the ingenious

[1] It would be very desirable if the origin of the numerical figures in the Hieratic inscriptions could be satisfactorily explained. If the Hieratic figures for one, two, and three are mere corruptions of the hieroglyphic signs, the similarity between them and the Indian figures would certainly be startling. Writing the eight by two fours is likewise a strange coincidence between the Hieratic and the Indian system, and the figures for nine are almost identical in both.

researches of Professor Dowson, Mr. Norris, and General A. Cunningham, as published in the last numbers of the "Journals of the Royal Asiatic Society," and of the "Asiatic Society of Bengal." We also beg to call attention to a list of ancient Sanskrit numerals collected by Dr. Bhao Daji, and published in the last number of the "Journal of the Asiatic Society of Bengal." They are of a totally different character, and place the theory of Prinsep, that the Indian figures were originally the initial letters of the numerals in Sanskrit, beyond all doubt. Yet here too, we see no trace, as yet, of decimal notation, or of the employment of the cipher. We find nine letters, the initials of the Sanskrit numerals, employed for 1 to 9 — a proceeding possible in Sanskrit, where every numeral begins with a different letter; but impossible in Greek, where four of the simple numerals began with *e*, and two with *t*. We then find a new symbol for ten, sometimes like the *d*, the initial letter of the Sanskrit numeral; another for twenty, for a hundred, and for a thousand; but these symbols are placed one after the other to express compound numerals, very much like the letters of the Greek alphabet, when employed for numerical purposes; they are never used with the nought. It would be highly important to find out at what time the nought occurs for the first time in Indian inscriptions. That inscription would deserve to be preserved among the most valuable monuments of antiquity, for from it would date in reality the beginning of true mathematical science, impossible without the nought — nay, the beginning of all the exact sciences to which we owe the discoveries of telescopes, steam-engines, and electric telegraphs.

December, 1863.

XXVII.

CASTE.[1]

WHAT is caste? The word is used everywhere and by everybody. We have heard it of late in Parliament, at public meetings, in churches and chapels. It has found its way into English, and into most of the modern languages of Europe. We hear of caste not only in India, and in ancient Egypt, and among the Persians; but in England, in London, in the very drawing-rooms of Belgrave Square we are told by moralists and novel writers that there is caste. Among the causes assigned for the Sepoy mutiny, caste has been made the most prominent. By one party it is said that too much, by another that too little regard was paid to caste. An Indian colonel tells us that it was impossible to keep up military discipline among soldiers who, if their own officers happened to pass by while the privates were cooking their dinner, would throw their mess into the fire, because it had been defiled by the shadow of a European. An Indian civil-

1 *Original Sanskrit Texts on the Origin and Progress of the Religion and Institutions of India*, collected, translated into English, and illustrated by notes, chiefly for the use of students and others in India. By J. Muir, Esq., D. C. L., late of the Bengal Civil Service. Part First, "The Mythical and Legendary Accounts of Caste." London, 1858. Williams & Norgate.

ian assures us with equal confidence that the Sepoys were driven mad by the greased cartridges; that they believed they were asked to touch what was unclean in order to lose their caste, and that, rather than lose their caste, they would risk everything. Missionaries have been preaching against caste as the chief obstacle to conversion. Philanthropists have seen in the constant attacks of the missionaries upon caste the chief obstacle to the spreading of Christianity among the Hindus. Among the Hindus themselves some patriots have represented caste as the cause of India's humiliation and weakness, while their priests maintain that the dominion of the barbarians, under which India has been groaning for so many centuries, was inflicted as a divine vengeance for the neglect of the old and sacred distinctions of caste.

Where such different effects are attributed to the same cause, it is clear that different people must ascribe very different meanings to the same word. Nor is this at all extraordinary. In India caste, in one form or other, has existed from the earliest times. Words may remain the same, but their meaning changes constantly; and what was meant by caste in India a thousand years B. C., in a simple, healthy, and patriarchal state of society, was necessarily something very different from what is called caste nowadays. M. Guizot, in his "History of Civilization," has traced the gradual and hardly perceptible changes which the meaning of such words as liberty, honor, right, has undergone in different periods of the history of Europe. But the history of India is a longer history than the history of Europe; and creeds, and laws, and words, and traditions had been growing, and changing, and decaying on the borders of the Sarasvatî and the Ganges, before the Saxons had reached the borders of the Elbe and their descendants had settled on the coast of Kent. There may have been less change in India than in Europe, but there has been considerable change in India too. The Brahmans of the present day are no longer the Brahmans of the Vedas, and the caste of the Sepoys is very different from the caste of the old Kshatriya warriors. Yet we call it all caste, — a word not even Indian in its origin, but adopted from the Portuguese, — and the Brahmans themselves do very much the same. They use, indeed, different words for what we promiscuously call caste. They call it "var*n*a" and "*g*âti," and they would use "kula" and "gotra," and "pravara" and "*k*ara*n*a," in many cases where we promiscuously use the word "caste." But on the whole they also treat the question of caste as if caste had been the same thing at all times. Where it answers their purpose they admit, indeed, that some of the old laws about caste have become obsolete, and are no longer applicable to a depraved age. But in the same breath they will appeal to the Veda as their most ancient and most sacred authority in order to substantiate their claim to a privilege which their forefathers enjoyed some thousand years ago. It is much the same as if the Archbishop of Canterbury were to declare the ninth commandment, "Thou shalt not bear false witness against thy neighbor," was antiquated, because it had never been reënacted since the time of Moses; and were to claim at the same time the right of excommunicating the Queen, or flogging the nobility, because, according to the most ancient testimonies of

Cæsar and Tacitus, the Druids and the ancient priests of Germany enjoyed the same privilege.

The question of caste in India has, however, assumed too serious an aspect to be treated any longer in this vague manner. New measures will soon have to be adopted with regard to it, and these measures must be such as will be approved by the more enlightened among the natives. Whatever the truth may be about the diabolical atrocities which are said to have been committed against women and children, a grievous wrong has been done to the people of India by making them responsible for crimes committed or said to have been committed by a few escaped convicts and raving fanatics; and, in spite of the efforts now making to counteract the promiscuous hatred against Hindus and Mohammedans, it will be long before the impression once created can be effaced, and before the inhabitants of India are treated again as men, and not as monsters. It is now perceived that it will never answer to keep India mainly by military force, and that the eloquent but irritating speeches of Indian reformers must prove very expensive to the tax-paying public of England. India can never be held or governed profitably without the good-will of the natives, and in any new measures that are to be adopted it will be necessary to listen to what they have to say, and to reason with them as we should reason with men quite capable of appreciating the force of an argument. There ought to be no idea of converting the Hindus by force, or of doing violence to their religious feelings. They have the promise, and that promise, we know, will never be broken, that their religion is not to be interfered with, except where it violates the laws of humanity. Hinduism is a decrepit religion, and has not many years to live. But our impatience to see it annihilated cannot be pleaded as an excuse for employing violent and unfair means to hasten its downfall. If, therefore, caste is part of the Hindu religion, it will have to be respected as such by the Government. If it is not, it may be treated in the same spirit as social prejudices are treated at home.

Now, if we ask the Hindus whether their laws of caste are part of their religion, some will answer that they are, others that they are not. Under these circumstances we must clearly decide the question for ourselves. Thanks to the exertions of Sir William Jones, Colebrook, Wilson, and others, we possess in this country a nearly complete collection of the religious and legal works of the Brahmans. We are able to consult the very authorities to which the Hindus appeal, and we can form an opinion with greater impartiality than the Brahmans themselves.

The highest authority for the religion of the Brahmans is the Veda. All other works, — the "Laws of Manu," the six orthodox systems of philosophy, the Purâ*n*as, or the legendary histories of India, — all derive their authority from their agreement with the Veda. The Veda alone is called *S*ruti, or revelation; everything else, however sacred, can only claim the title of Sm*r*iti, or tradition. The most elaborate arguments have been framed by the Brahmans to establish the divine origin and the absolute authority of the Veda. They maintain that the Veda existed before all time, that it was revealed by Brahman, and seen by divine sages, who themselves were free from the taint of humanity. "For what authority," the Brahmans say, "could we claim for a revelation which had been revealed by Brahman to fallible mortals? It might have been perfect truth as seen by Brahman, but as seen by men it would have been affected by their faulty vision. Hence revelation, in order to be above all suspicion, must be handed down by inspired *R*ishis, till at last it reaches in its perfect form the minds of the common believers, and is accepted by them as absolute truth." This is a curious argument, and not without some general interest. It is one of the many attempts to alleviate the responsibility of the believer in his own belief, to substitute a faith in man for a faith in God, to get something external to rest on instead of trying to stand on that which alone will last — a man's own faith in his own God. It is the story of the tortoise and the elephant and the earth over again, only in a different form; and the Brahmans, in order to meet all possible objections, have actually imagined a series of sages — the first quite divine, the second three fourths divine and one fourth human, the third half divine and half human, the fourth one fourth divine and three fourths human, the last human altogether. This Veda then, as handed down through this wonderful chain, is the supreme authority of all orthodox Brahmans. To doubt the divine origin and absolute authority of the Veda is heresy. Buddha, by denying the authority of the Veda, became a heretic. Kapila, an atheistic philosopher of the purest water, was tolerated by the Brahmans, because however much he differed from their theology, he was ready to sign the most important article of their faith — the divine origin and infallibility of scripture.

At the present day there are but few Brahmans who can read and understand the Veda. They learn portions of it by heart, these portions consisting of hymns and prayers, which have to be muttered at sacrifices, and which every priest must know. But the language and grammar of the Veda being somewhat different from the common Sanskrit, the young priests have as much difficulty in understanding those hymns correctly as we have in translating old English. Hence arguments have not been wanting to prove that these hymns are really more efficacious if they are not understood, and all that the young student is required to learn is the pronunciation, the names of the metre, of the deity to whom the hymn is addressed, and of the poet by whom it was composed. In order to show that this is not an exaggerated account we quote from an article in the "Calcutta Review," written by a native and a real Sanskrit scholar: "The most learned Pandit in Bengal," he says, "has need to talk with diffidence of what he may consider to be the teaching of the Vedas on any point, especially when negative propositions are concerned. It may be doubted whether a copy of the entire Vedas is procurable in any part of Hindostan; it is more than probable that such a copy does not exist in Bengal. It would scarcely be modest or safe, under such circumstances, to say that such and such doctrines are not contained in the Vedas." In the South of India the Veda is perhaps studied a little more than in Bengal, yet even there the Brahmans would be completely guided in their interpretation by their scholastic commentaries; and when the Pandits near Madras were told by Dr. Graul, the director of the Lutheran Missions in India, that a countryman of his had been intrusted by the East India Company with the publication of the Veda, they all declared that it was an impossible task.

Instead of the Veda, the Brahmans of the present day read the "Laws of Manu," the six systems of philosophy, the Purâ*n*as, and the Tantras. Yet, ignorant as they are of the Veda, they believe in it as implicitly as the Roman Catholic friar believed in the Bible, though he had never seen it. The author of the so-called "Laws of Manu" is but a man, and he has to produce his credentials before the law which he teaches can be acknowledged as an authority. Now, what are his credentials, what is the authority of Manu? He tells us himself: "The root of the law," he says, "is the whole Veda and the tradition and customs of those who knew the Veda." Exactly the same words, only not yet reduced to a metrical form, occur in the old Sûtras or law-books which were paraphrased by the author of the "Laws of Manu." Towards the end of the law-book the author speaks of the Veda in still stronger terms: —

"To the departed, to gods and to men, the Veda is an imperishable eye; the Veda is beyond the power and beyond the reason of man: this is certain. Traditional codes of law, not founded on the Veda, and all the heterodox theories of man, produce no good fruit after death; they are all declared to rest on darkness. Whatever they are, they will rise and perish; on account of their modern date they are vain and false. The four classes of men, the three worlds, the four stages of life, all that has been, is, and will be, is known from the Veda. The imperishable Veda supports all creatures, and therefore I think it is the highest means of salvation for this creature — man. Command of armies, royal authority, power of inflicting punishment, and sovereign dominion over all nations, he only will deserve who perfectly understands the Veda. As fire with augmented force burns up even humid trees, thus he, who well knows the Veda, burns out the taint of sin in his soul which arose from evil works. He who completely knows the sense of the Veda, while he remains in any one of the four stages of life, approaches the divine nature, even though he sojourn in this low world."

Again, whatever system of philosophy we open, we invariably find in the very beginning that as for right behavior ("dharma"), so for right knowledge, the Veda is to be considered as the highest authority. In the Vedânta philosophy the beginning of all wisdom is said to be a desire to know God, who is the cause of the Universe, and that he is the cause of the Universe is to be learnt from the scripture. The Nyâya philosophy acknowledges four sources of knowledge; and the fourth, which follows after perception, induction, and analogy, is the Word, or the Veda. The Vaiseshika philosophy, an atomistic system, and looked upon with no very favorable eye by the orthodox Brahmans, is most emphatic in proclaiming the absolute authority of the Veda. And even the "Sânkhya," the atheistic "Sânkhya," which maintains that a personal God cannot be proved, conforms so far as to admit the received doctrine of the Veda as evidence in addition to perception and induction. At the time when these systems were originally composed, the Veda was still studied and understood; but in later times the Veda was superseded by more modern works, particularly the Purâ*n*as, and the less its real contents were known, the more easily could its authority be appealed to by the Brahmans in support of anything they wished to establish as a divine ordinance. In their controversies with the Mohammedans, and in more recent times with the missionaries, the Brahmans, if they were hard pressed, invariably fell back upon the Veda. The "Laws of Manu" and other law-books were printed and translated. Some of their Purâ*n*as, also, had been rendered into English and French. With regard to these, therefore, the missionaries could ask for chapter and verse. But the Veda was unknown to either party, and on the principle of *omne ignotum pro magnifico*, the Brahmans maintained and the missionaries had to believe that everything which was to be found nowhere else was to be found in the Veda. There was no commandment of the Old Testament which, according to the Brahmans, might not be matched in the Veda. There was no doctrine of Christianity which had not been anticipated in the Veda. If the missionaries were incredulous and called for the manuscripts, they were told that so sacred a book could not be exposed to the profane looks of unbelievers, and there was an end to all further argument.

Under these circumstances it was felt that nothing would be of greater assistance to the missionaries in India than an edition of the Veda. Prizes were offered to any Sanskrit scholar who would undertake to edit the work, but after the first book, published by the late Dr. Rosen in 1838, no further progress was made. The Directors of the East India Company, always ready to assist the missionaries by any legitimate means, invited the Pandits, through the Asiatic Society at Calcutta, to undertake the work, and to publish a complete and authentic edition of their own sacred writings. The answers received only proved what was known before, that in the whole of Bengal there was not a single Brahman who could edit the Veda. In spite of all these obstacles, however, the Veda is now being published in this country under the patronage of the East India Company. The missionaries have already derived great assistance from this edition of the Veda and its commentary, and constant applications are being made by various missionary societies for copies of the original and its English translation. The Brahmans, though they did not approve the publication of their sacred writings by a Mle*kkh*a, have been honest enough to admit that the edition is complete and authentic. One of their most learned representatives, when speaking of this edition, says, "It will furnish the Vaidic Pandits with a complete collection of the Holy Sanhitâs, only detached portions of which are to be found in the possession of a few of them." And again, "It is surely a very curious reflection on the vicissitudes of human affairs that the descendants of the divine *R*ishis should be studying on the banks of the Bhâgîrathî, the Yamunâ, and the Sindhu, their Holy Scriptures, published on the banks of the Thames by one whom they regard as a distant Mle*kkh*a."

If, then, with all the documents before us, we ask the question, Does caste, as we find it in Manu and at the present day, form part of the most ancient religious teaching of the Vedas? we can answer with a decided "No." There is no authority whatever in the hymns of the Veda for the complicated system of castes; no authority for the offensive privileges claimed by the Brahmans; no authority for the degraded position of the *S*ûdras. There is no law to prohibit the different classes of the people from living together, from eating and drinking together; no law to prohibit the marriage of people belonging to different castes; no law to brand the offspring of such marriages with an indelible stigma. All that is found in the Veda, at least in the most ancient portion of it, the hymns, is a verse, in which it is said that the priest, the warrior, the husbandman, and the serf, formed all alike part of Brahman. Rv. x. 90, 6, 7: "When they divided man, how many did they make him? What was his mouth? what his arms? what are called his thighs and feet? The Brâhma*n*a was his mouth, the Râ*g*anya was made his arms, the Vaisya became his thighs, the *S*ûdra was born from his feet." European critics are able to show that even this verse is of later origin than the great mass of the hymns, and that it contains modern words, such as *S*ûdra and Râ*g*anya, which are not found again in the other hymns of the Rig-veda. Yet it belongs to the ancient collection of the Vedic hymns, and if it contained anything in support of caste, as it is now understood, the Brahmans would be right in saying that caste formed part of their religion, and was sanctioned by their sacred writings. But, as the case now stands, it is not difficult to prove to the natives of India that, whatever their caste may be, caste, as now understood, is not a Vedic institution, and that in disregarding the rules of caste, no command of the real Veda is violated. Caste in India is a human law, a law fixed by those who were most benefited by it themselves It may be a venerable custom, but it has no authority in the hymns of the *R*ishis. The missionaries, if they wish to gain the ear and confidence of the natives, will have to do what the Reformers did for the Christian laity. The people in the sixteenth century, no doubt, believed that the worship of the Virgin and the Saints, auricular confession, indulgences, the celibacy of the clergy, all rested on the authority of the Bible. They could not read the Bible in the original, and they were bound to believe what they were taught by the priests. As our own Reformers pointed out that all these were institutions of later growth, that they had become mischievous, and that no divine law was violated in disregarding them, it should be shown to the natives of India that the religion which the Brahmans teach is no longer the religion of the Veda, though the Veda alone is acknowledged by all Brahmans as the only divine source of faith. A Hindu who believes only in the Veda would be much nearer to Christianity than those who follow the Purâ*n*as and the Tantras. From a European point of view there is, no doubt, even in the Veda a great deal that is absurd and childish; and from a Christian point of view there is but little that we can fully approve. But there is no trace in the Veda of the atrocities of *S*iva and Kali, nor of the licentiousness of K*r*ish*n*a, nor of most of the miraculous adventures of Vish*n*u. We find in it no law to sanction the blasphemous pretensions of a priesthood to divine honors, or the degradation of any human being to a state below the animal. There is no text to countenance laws which allow the marriage of children and prohibit the remarriage of child-widows, and the unhallowed rite of burning the widow with the corpse of her husband is both against the spirit and the letter of the Veda. The great majority of those ancient hymns are mere prayers for food, health, and wealth; and it is extraordinary that words which any child might have uttered should ever have seemed to require the admission of a divine author. Yet there are passages scattered about in these hymns which, apart from their interest as relics of the earliest period in the history of the human mind, are valuable as expressions of a simple faith in God, and of a belief in the moral government of the world. We should look in vain in Sanskrit works for hymns like the following: —

1. Wise and mighty are the works of him who stemmed asunder the wide firmaments (heaven and earth). He lifted on high the bright and glorious heaven; he stretched out apart the starry sky and the earth.

2. Do I say this to my own self? How can I get unto Varu*n*a? Will he accept my offering without displeasure? When shall I, with a quiet mind, see him propitiated?

3. I ask, O Varu*n*a, wishing to know this my sin. I go to ask the wise. The sages all tell me the same: Varu*n*a it is who is angry with thee.

4. Was it an old sin, O Varu*n*a, that thou wishest to destroy thy friend, who always praises thee? Tell me, thou unconquerable lord, and I will quickly turn to thee with praise, freed from sin.

5. Absolve us from the sins of our fathers, and from those which we committed with our own bodies. Release Vasish*t*ha, O king, like a thief who has feasted on stolen oxen; release him like a calf from the rope.

6. It was not our own doing, O Varu*n*a, it was necessity (or temptation), an intoxicating draught, passion, dice, thoughtlessness. The old is there to mis lead the young; even sleep brings unrighteousness.

7. Let me without sin give satisfaction to the angry

god, like a slave to the bounteous lord. The lord god enlightened the foolish; he, the wisest, leads his worshipper to wealth.

8. O lord Varu*n*a, may this song go well to thy heart! May we prosper in keeping and acquiring! Protect us, O gods, always with your blessings!

It would be a mistake to suppose that the educated classes in India are unable to appreciate the argument which rests on a simple appeal to what, from their very childhood, they have been brought up to consider as the highest authority in matters of religion. They have seen the same argument used repeatedly by their own priests. Whenever discussions about right and wrong, about true and false doctrine, arose, each party appealed to the Veda. Decided heretics only, such as the Buddhists, objected to this line of argument. Thus, when the question was mooted whether the burning of widows was an essential part of the Hindu religion, the Brahmans were asked to produce an authority for it from the Veda. They did so by garbling a verse, and as the Veda was not yet published, it was impossible at that time to convict them of falsification. They tried to do the same in defense of the law which forbids the marriage of widows. But they were met by another party of more enlightened Brahmans, who, with the support of the excellent President of the Sanskrit College at Calcutta, Eshvar Chandra Vidyasagar, and several enlightened members of the government, carried the day.

The following correspondence, which passed between an orthodox Brahman and the editor of one of the most influential native newspapers at Madras, may serve as a specimen of the language used by native divines in arguments of this kind.

The pious correspondent begins with a prayer to Vish*n*u:—

"O thou heavenly Boar, Vish*n*u, residing in Seitripötti (in the neighborhood of Madras), which place, rising like a mountain, is brilliant in its fullness, bless the inhabitants of the sea-girt Earth by knowledge which alone leads to virtue!"

Then comes an address to the editor:—

"Among the followers of the six religions by which the four castes have been divided, there are but few to whom sound knowledge and good conduct have been granted. All the rest have been robbed of these blessings by the goddess of mischief. They will not find salvation either in this life or in the life to come. Now in order to benefit those miserable beings, there appears every Sunday morning your excellent paper, bearing on its front the three forms of *S*iva, and rising like the sun, the dispeller of darkness. Please to vouchsafe in that paper a small place to these lines. It is with that confident hope that I sharpen my pen and begin:—

"For some time I have harbored great doubts within myself, and though I always intended to place them before the public in your newspaper, no opportunity seemed hitherto to offer itself. But you have yourself pronounced an opinion in one of your last numbers about infanticide, and you remark that it reveals a depravation more depraved than even the passion of lust. This seems a small saying, and yet it is so full of meaning that I should fain call it a drop of dew poised on the top of a blade of grass in which a mighty tree is fully reflected. It is true there is on earth no greater bliss than love. This is proved by the word of the poet: 'Say, is the abode of the lotus-eyed god sweeter than a dream on the shoulders of the beloved?' No intoxication is so powerful as the intoxication of love. This is proved by another verse of the same poet: 'Not the palm-wine, no, it is love which runs through the veins, and enraptures even by sight.' Nay, more, love is a fire beyond all fires. And this also is proved by a verse of the poet: 'If I fly, there is fire; if I am near her, there is refreshing coolness. Whence did she take that strange fire?'

"And love leaves neither the high nor the low without temptation. Even the curly-haired *S*iva could not resist the power of love, as you may read in the story of Pandya and his Fish-flag, and in many other legends. Nor are women less moved by passion than men. And hence that secret criminal love, and, from fear of shame, the most awful of all crimes, infanticide! The child is killed, the mother frequently dies, and bad gossip follows; and her relations have to walk about with their heads bent low. Is it not all the consequence of that passion? And such things are going on among us, is it not so? It is said, indeed, that it is the fault of the present generation, and that good women would never commit such atrocities. But even in the patriarchal ages, which are called the virtuous ages, there was much vice, and it is owing to it that the present age is what it is. As the king, so the subjects. Where is chastity to be found among us? It is the exception, and no longer the rule. And what is the chief cause of all this misery?

"It is because people are married in their tender in

fancy. If the husband dies before the child grows into a woman, how much suffering, how much temptation, will come upon her. The poet says: 'A woman that faithfully serves her husband, even though she serve not the gods, if she prays, Send us rain, it will rain.' Women who heed this will no doubt walk the path of virtue. Yet it is a sad thought. There is much that is good and true and beautiful in our poet; people read it, but they do not act according to it. Most men follow another verse of the poet, — 'I swim about on the wild sea of love; I see no shore; the night also I am tossed about.'

"Alas, my dear editor! All this hellish sin is the fault of father and mother who do not prevent it. If, *in accordance with the Vedas, and in accordance with the sacred codes that are based on them*, women were allowed to marry again, much temptation and shame would be avoided. But then the world calls out, 'No, no, widow-marriage is against all our rules; it is low and vulgar.' Forsooth, tell me, are the four holy Vedas, which sprang from the lotus-born god, books of lies and blasphemy? If we are to believe this, then our sacred laws, which are all ordained in the Vedas, are branded as lies. If we continue in this path, it will be like a shower of honey running down from a roof of sugar to the heathen, who are always fond of abusing us. Do we read in the Vedas that a man only may marry two, three, or four times? Do we not read in the same place that a woman may marry at least twice? Let our wise masters ponder on this. Really we are shamed by the lowest castes. They follow the holy Vedas on this point, and we disregard them. O marvel of marvels! This country is full already of people who do not scruple to murder the sacred cow! Should murder of infants be added thereto, as though the murder of cows was not yet enough? My dear editor, how long is our god likely to bear this?"

There is a good deal more in the same style, which is not quite adapted for publication in a more northern climate. At the end, the editor is exhorted not to follow the example of other editors, who are afraid of burning their fingers, and remain silent when they ought to speak.

After some weeks, the editor published a reply. He fully agrees with the arguments of his correspondent, but he says that the writer does not sufficiently appreciate the importance of universal custom. Universal custom, he continues, is more powerful than books, however sacred. For books are read, but customs are followed. He then quotes the instance of a learned Brahman, a great Sanskrit scholar. His daughter had become a child-widow. He began to search in the sacred writings in order to find whether the widow of a Brahman was really forbidden to marry again. He found just the contrary, and was determined to give his daughter in marriage a second time. But all his relations came running to his house, entreating him not to do a thing so contrary to all etiquette, and the poor father was obliged to yield.

At the end, however, the editor gives his correspondent some sensible advice. "Call a great meeting of wise men," he says. "Place the matter before them, and show the awful results of the present system. If some of them could be moved, then they might be of good cheer. A few should begin allowing their widowed children to marry. Others would follow, and the new custom would soon become general etiquette."

The fact is that even now the Brahmanic law has by no means gained a complete ascendency, and in Malabar, where a list has been drawn up of sixty-four offenses tolerated or even sanctioned in Kerala, the fifty-fourth offense is described as follows: "The Vedas say that the widow of a Brahman may marry again. This is not the law in Kerala or elsewhere."

We must be prepared, no doubt, to find the Brahmans standing up for their traditional law as equally sacred as the Veda. They will argue even against their own Veda in the same spirit in which the Church of Rome argued against the Bible, in order to defend the hierarchical and dogmatic system which, though it had no sanction in the Bible, was said to be but a necessary development of the spirit of the Bible. The Brahmans maintain, first of all, that there are four Vedas, each consisting of two portions, the hymns or Mantras, and theological tracts or Brâhma*n*as. Now, with regard to the hymns, it can easily be shown that there is but one genuine collection, the so-called Rig-veda, or the Veda of Praise. The Sâma-veda is but a short extract from the Rig-veda, containing such hymns as had to be chanted during the sacrifice. The Ya*g*ur-veda is a similar manual intended for another class of priests, who had to mutter certain hymns of the Rig-veda, together with invocations and other sacrificial formulas. The fourth, or Atharva-veda, is confessedly of later origin, and contains, besides a large number of hymns from the Rig-veda, some interesting specimens of incantations, popular rhymes, and mystical odes. There remains, therefore, the Rig-veda only which has a right to be called the Veda.

As to the theological tracts attached to each Veda, the Brahmans stoutly maintain that the arguments by which they have established the divine origin of the hymns apply with equal force to these tracts. It is in these Brâhma*n*as that they find most of the passages by which they support their priestly pretensions; and this is but natural, because these Brâhma*n*as were composed at a later time than the hymns, and when the Brahmans were already enjoying those very privileges which they wish to substantiate by a primeval revelation. But even if we granted, for argument's sake, that the Brâhma*n*as were as ancient as the hymns, the Brahmans would try in vain to prove the modern system of caste even from those works. Even there, all we find is the division of Indian society into four classes, — priests, warriors, husbandmen, and serfs. A great distinction, no doubt, is made between the three higher castes, the Âryas, and the fourth class, the *S*ûdras. Marriages between Âryas and *S*ûdras are disapproved of, but we can hardly say that they are prohibited (Vâj. Sanhitâ 23, 30); and the few allusions to mixed castes which have been pointed out, refer only to special professions. The fourth class, the *S*ûdras, is spoken of as a degraded race whose contact defiles the Aryan worshipper while he is performing his sacrifice, and they are sometimes spoken of as evil spirits; but even in the latest literary productions of the Vedic age, we look in vain for the complicated rules of Manu.

The last argument which a Brahman would use under these circumstances is this: "Though at present we find no authority in the Veda for the traditional rules about caste, we are bound to admit that such an authority did exist in portions of the Veda which have been lost; for Manu and other ancient lawgivers are known to be trustworthy persons, and they would not have sanctioned such laws unless they had known some divine authority in support of them. Therefore, unless it can be proved that their laws are contrary to the Veda, we are bound to believe that they are based on lost portions of the Veda." However, there are few people, even in India, who do not see through this argument, which is ironically called the appeal to the dead witness.

The Brahmans themselves have made this admission, that when the Veda, the Law-books, and the Purâ*n*as differ, the Veda is the supreme authority; and that where the Purâ*n*as differ from the Law-books, the Purâ*n*as are overruled. According to this decision of Vyâsa, the fallibility of the Law-books and the Purâ*n*as is admitted. They may be respected as the works of good and wise men; but what was ruled by men may be overruled by men. And even Manu, after enumerating the various sources of law — the Veda, the traditions and customs of those who knew the Veda and the practice of good men, — adds as the last, man's own judgment ("âtmanas tush*t*is"), or the approval of conscience.

As the case now stands, the government would be perfectly justified in declaring that it will no longer consider caste as part of the religious system of the Hindus. Caste, in the modern sense of the word, is no religious institution; it has no authority in the sacred writings of the Brahmans, and by whatever promise the government may have bound itself to respect the religion of the natives, that promise will not be violated, even though penalties were inflicted for the observation of the rules of caste.

It is a different question whether such a proceeding would be either right or prudent; for, although caste cannot be called a religious institution, it is a social institution, based on the law of the country. It has been growing up for centuries, and the whole frame of Hindu society has been moulded in it. On these grounds the question of caste will have to be treated with great caution: only it is right that the question should be argued on its real merits, and that religious arguments should not be dragged in where they would only serve to make confusion worse confounded. If caste is tolerated in India, it should be known on both sides that it is not tolerated on religious grounds. If caste is to be put down, it should be put down as a matter of policy and police. How caste grew up as a social institution, how it changed, and how it is likely to change still further, these are questions which ought to be carefully considered before any decision is taken that would affect the present system of caste.

Mr. Muir, therefore, seems to us to have undertaken a very useful work at the present moment in collecting and publishing a number of extracts from Sanskrit works bearing on the origin and history of caste. In his first part he treats on the mythical and legendary accounts of caste, and he tries to discover in them the faint traces of the real history of that extraordinary institution.

As soon as we trace the complicated system of caste, such as we find it in India at the present day, back to its first beginnings, we find that it flows from at least three different sources, and that accordingly we must distinguish between *ethnological*, *political*, and *professional* caste.

Ethnological caste arises wherever different races are brought in contact. There is and always has been a mutual antipathy between the white and the black man, and when the two are brought together, either by conquest or migration, the white man has invariably asserted his superiority, and established certain social barriers between himself and his dark-skinned brother. The Âryas and the *S*ûdras seem to have felt this mutual antipathy. The difference of blood and color was heightened in ancient times by difference of religion and language; but in modern times also, and in countries where the negro has learnt to speak the same language and to worship the same God as his master, the white man can never completely overcome the old feeling that seems to lurk in his very blood, and makes him recoil from the embrace of his darker neighbor. And even where there is no distinction of color, an analogous feeling, the feeling of race, asserts its influence, as if inherent in human nature. Between the Jew and the Gentile, the Greek and the barbarian, the Saxon and the Celt, the Englishman and the foreigner, there is something — whether we call it hatred, or antipathy, or mistrust, or mere coldness — which in a primitive state of society would necessarily lead to a system of castes, and which, even in more civilized countries, will never be completely eradicated.

Political caste arises from the struggles of different parties in the same state for political supremacy. The feeling between the patrician and the plebeian at Rome was a feeling of caste, and for a long time marriage between the son of a plebeian and the daughter of a patrician was as distasteful at Rome as the marriage between a *S*ûdra and the daughter of a Brahman in India. In addition to these two classes of society, the governing and the governed, the nobility and the people, we find a third class starting into existence at a very early period, and in almost all countries, the priests ; and if we look at the history of the ancient world, particularly among Eastern nations, it chiefly consists in contests between the nobility and the priesthood for political supremacy. Thus, whereas ethnological caste leads generally only to one broad division between the white and the black man, between the conquering and the conquered race, between the freeman and the slave, political caste superadds a threefold division of the superior race, by separating a military nobility and a priestly hierarchy from the great body of the citizens.

Professional caste is in reality but a continuation of the same social growth which leads to the establishment of political caste. After the two upper classes have been separated from the main body of the people, the gradual advancement of society towards a more perfect organization takes place, chiefly by means of new subdivisions among the middle classes. Various trades and professions are established, and privileges once granted to them are defended by guilds and corporations, with the same jealousy as the political privileges of the nobility and the priesthood. Certain trades and professions become more respectable and influential than others, and, in order to keep up that respectability, the members of each bind themselves by regulations which are more strictly enforced and more severely felt than the laws of the people at large. Every nation must pass through this social phase, which in Europe was most completely realized during the Middle Ages. And though, in later times, with the progress of civilization and true religion in Europe, all the barriers of caste became more and more leveled, the law being the same for all classes, and the services of Church and State being opened to the intellectual aristocracy of the whole nation, yet within smaller spheres the traditional feeling of caste, in its threefold character, lingers on; and the antipathy between Saxon and Celt, the distinction between nobility and gentry, the distance between the man who deals in gold and silver and the man who deals in boots and shoes, are still maintained, and would seem almost indispensable to the healthy growth of every society.

The first trace of caste which we find in India is purely ethnological. India was covered by a stratum of Turanian inhabitants before the Âryas, or the people who spoke Sanskrit, took possession of the country. Traces of these aboriginal inhabitants are still to be found all over India. The main body of these earlier settlers, however, was driven to the South, and to the present day all the languages spoken in the south of India, Tamil, Telugu, Canarese, etc., are perfectly distinct from Sanskrit and the modern Sanskrit dialects, such as Hindustani, Bengali, and Mahratti. At the time of the great Aryan immigration the differences in the physical appearance of the conquered and the conquering races must have been considerable, and even at present a careful observer can easily distinguish the descendants of the two. "No sojourner in India," Dr. Stevenson remarks, "can have paid any attention to the physiognomy of the higher and lower orders of natives, without being struck with the remarkable difference that exists in the shape of the head, the build of the body, and the color of the skin between the higher and the lower castes into which the Hindu population is divided. The high forehead, the stout build, and the light copper color of the Brahmans, and other castes allied to them, appear in strong contrast with the somewhat low and wide heads, slight make, and dark bronze of the low castes." Time, however, has worked many changes, and there are at present Brahmans, particularly in the South of India, as black as Pariahs.

The hymns of the Veda, though they never mention the word *S*ûdra, except in the passage pointed out before, allude frequently to these hostile races, and call them "Dasyus," or enemies. Thus one poet says (Rv. III. 34, 9): —

"Indra gave horses, Indra gave the sun, he gave the earth with food for many, he gave gold, and he gave wealth; destroying the Dasyus, Indra protected the Âryan color."

The word which is here translated by color, "var*n*a," is the true Sanskrit name for caste. Nor can there be any doubt that there was a distinction of color between the Âryas and the Dasyus, and that the name "var*n*a" — meaning originally color — was afterwards used in the more general sense of caste.[1] Mr. Muir has quoted a passage from the Mahâbhârata, where it is said that the color of the Brahmans was white; that of the Kshatriyas, red; that of the Vaisyas, yellow, and that of the *S*ûdras, black. But this seems to be a later allegory, and the colors seem to be chosen in order to express the respective character of the four castes. At the time when this name of "var*n*a" was first used in the sense of caste, there were but two castes, the Âryas

[1] See page 176.

and the non-Âryas, the bright and the dark race. This dark race is sometimes called by the poets of the Veda "the black skin." Rig-veda I. 130, 8: "Indra protected in battle the Aryan worshipper, he subdued the lawless for Manu, he conquered the black skin." Other names given to them by their Aryan conquerors are "goat-nosed and noseless," whereas the Aryan gods are frequently praised for their beautiful noses. That those people were considered as heathen and barbarians by the Vedic poets we may conclude from other passages where they are represented as keeping no sacred fires and as worshipping mad gods. Nay, they are even taunted with eating raw flesh, — as in the Dekhan some of the low castes are called Puliyars, or Poliars, *i. e.* flesh eaters, — and with feeding on human flesh. How they were treated by the Brahmans, we may conclude from the following invocation: —

"Indra and Soma, burn the devils, destroy them, throw them down, ye two Bulls, the people that grow in darkness! Hew down the madmen, suffocate them, kill them; hurl them away, and slay the voracious.

"Indra and Soma, up together against the cursing demon! May he burn and hiss like an oblation in the fire! Put your everlasting hatred upon the villain who hates the Brahman, who eats flesh, and whose look is abominable.

"Indra and Soma, hurl the evil-doer into the pit, even into unfathomable darkness! May your strength be full of wrath to hold out, that no one may come out again!"

This ancient division between Aryan and non-Aryan races, based on an original difference of blood, was preserved in later times as the primary distinction between the three twice-born castes and the *S*ûdras. The word "âryа" (noble) is derived from "ărya," which means a householder, and was originally used as the name of the third caste, or the Vai*s*yas. These Aryas or Vai*s*yas formed the great bulk of the Brahmanic society, and it is but natural that their name, in a derivative form, should have been used as a common name of the three classes into which these Aryas became afterwards divided. How these three upper castes grew up we can see very clearly in the hymns, in the Brâhma*n*as, and in the legendary stories contained in the epic poems. The three occupations of the Aryas in India were fighting, cultivating the soil, and worshipping the gods. Those who fought the battles of the people would naturally acquire influence and rank, and their leaders appear in the Veda as Rajahs or kings. Those who did not share in the fighting would occupy a more humble position; they were called "Vi*s*," "Vai*s*yas," or householders, and would no doubt have to contribute towards the maintenance of the armies. "Vi*s*pati," or "lord of the Vi*s*," became the usual name for king, and the same word is found in the old Persian "Vi*s*paiti," and the modern Lithuanian "wiêszpatis," king. But a third occupation, that of worshipping the gods, was evidently considered by the whole nation to be as important and as truly essential to the well-being of the country as fighting against enemies or cultivating the soil. However imperfect and absurd their notions of the Deity may seem to us, we must admit that no nation was ever so anxious to perform the service of their gods as the early Hindus. It is the gods who conquer the enemy, it is the gods who vouchsafe a rich harvest. Health and wealth, children, friends, flocks, and gold, all are the gifts of the gods. And these are not unmeaning phrases with those early poets. No, the poet believes it; he not only believes, but he knows it, that all good things come from above. "Without thee, O Varu*n*a!" the poet says, "I am not the master even of a twinkling of the eye. Do not deliver us unto death, though we have offended against thy commandment day by day. Accept our sacrifice, forgive our offenses, let us speak together again, like old friends." Here it is where the charm of these old hymns lies. There is nothing in them as yet about a revelation to be believed in, because it was handed down by sages three fourths divine and one fourth human. They believe in one great revelation, and they require no one to answer for its truth, and that revelation is that God is wise, omnipotent, the Lord of heaven and earth; that he hears the prayers of men, and forgives their offenses. Here is a short verse containing every one of these primitive articles of faith (Rig-veda I. 25, 19): —

"Hear this my calling, O Varu*n*a, and bless me now; I call upon thee, desirous of thy help.

"Thou, O wise God, art the king of all, of heaven and earth, hear me on thy path."

Among a nation of this peculiar stamp the priests were certain to acquire great influence at a very early period, and, like most priests, they were as certain to use it for their own advantage, and to the ruin of all true religious feeling. It is the life-spring of all religion that man feels the immediate presence of God, and draws near to God as a child to his father. But the priests maintained that no one should approach the gods without their intercession, and that no sacrifices should be offered without their advice. Most of the Indo-European nations have resisted these claims, but in India the priests were successful, and in the Veda, already, though only in some of the latest hymns, the position of the priest, or the Purohita, is firmly established. Thus we read (Rv. IV. 50, 8): —

"That king before whom marches the priest, he alone dwells well-established in his own house; to him the earth yields at all times, to him the people bow by themselves.

"The king who gives wealth to the priest that implores his protection, he will conquer unopposed the treasures, whether of his enemies or his friends; him the gods will protect."

This system of Purohitî, or priestly government, had gained ground in India before the first collection of the Vedic hymns was accomplished. These very hymns were the chief strength on which the priests relied, and they were handed down from father to son as the most valuable heir-loom. A hymn by which the gods had been invoked at the beginning of a battle, and which had secured to the king a victory over his enemies, was considered an unfailing spell, and it became the sacred war-song of a whole tribe. Thus we read, —

Rv. VII. 33, 3. "Did not Indra preserve Sudâs in the battle of the ten kings through your prayer, O Vasish*th*as?"

Rv. III. 53, 12. "This prayer of Visvâmitra, of one who has praised heaven and earth and Indra, preserves the people of the Bhâratas."[1]

[1] J. Muir, *On the Relations of the Priests*, p. 4.

But the priests only were allowed to chant these songs, they only were able to teach them, and they impressed the people with a belief that the slightest mistake in the words, or the pronunciation of the words, would rouse the anger of the gods. Thus they became the masters of all religious ceremonies, the teachers of the people, the ministers of kings. Their favor was courted, their anger dreaded, by a pious but credulous race.

The following hymn will show that at an early time the priests of India had learned, not only to bless, but also to curse (Rv. VI. 52): —

1. No, by heaven! no, by earth! I do not approve of this; no, by the sacrifice! no, by these rites! May the mighty mountains crush him! May the priest of Atiyâ*g*a perish! [1]

2. Whosoever, O Maruts, weans himself above us, or scoffs at the prayer ("bráhma") which we have made, may hot plagues come upon him, may the sky burn up that hater of Brahmans ("brahma-dvísh")!

3. Did they not call thee, Soma, the guardian of the Bráhman? did they not say that thou didst shield us against curses? Why dost thou look on when we are scoffed at? Hurl against the hater of the Brahman the fiery spear!

4. May the coming dawns protect me, may the swelling rivers protect me! May the firm mountains protect me! May the Fathers protect me at the invocation of the gods!

5. May we always be happy, may we see the rising

[1] See J. Muir, *On the Relations of the Priests*, p. 33; and Wilson, *Translation of the Rig-veda*, vol. iii. p. 490.

sun! May the Lord of the Vasus order it thus, he who brings the gods, and is most ready with his help; —

6. Indra who comes nearest with his help; Sarasvatî, the swelling, with the rivers; Par*g*anya who blesses us with plants; the glorious Agni who, like a father, is ready to hear when we call; —

7. All ye gods, come hither! hear this my prayer! Sit down on this altar!

8. To him, O gods, who honors you by an oblation flowing with butter, to him ye come all.

9. May they who are the sons of the Immortal, hear our prayers, may they be gracious to us!

10. May all the righteous gods who hear our prayers, receive at all seasons this acceptable milk!

11. May Indra, with the host of the Maruts, accept our praise; may Mitra with Tvash*t*ar, may Aryaman receive these our oblations!

12. O Agni, carry this our sacrifice wisely, looking for the divine host.

13. All ye gods, hear this my call, ye who are in the air, and in the sky, ye who have tongues of fire,[1] and are to be worshipped; sit down on this altar and rejoice!

14. May all the holy gods hear, may Heaven and Earth, and the Child of the waters (the Sun) hear my prayer! May I not speak words which you cannot approve, may we rejoice in your favors, as your nearest friends!

15. May the great gods, who are as strong as the enemy, who sprang from the earth, from heaven, and

[1] This means the gods who receive sacrifice offered on the fire of the altar.

from the conflux of the waters, give us gifts according to our desire, all our life, day and night!

16. Agni and Par*g*anya, accept my prayer, and our praise at this invocation, ye who are well invoked. One made the earth, the other the seed: give to us here wealth and progeny!

17. When the grass is spread, when the fire is kindled, I worship with a hymn with great veneration. Rejoice to-day, ye adorable Vi*s*ve Devas, in the oblation offered at this our sacrifice!

The priests never aspired to royal power. "A Brahmin," they say, "is not fit for royalty." (*S*atapatha-brâhma*n*a, V. 1, 1, 12). They left the insignia of royalty to the military caste. But woe to the warrior who would not submit to their spiritual guidance, or who would dare to perform his sacrifice without waiting for his Samuel! There were fierce and sanguinary struggles between the priests and the nobility, before the king consented to bow before the Brahmin. In the Veda we still find kings composing their own hymns to the gods, royal bards, Râ*g*arshis, who united in their person the powers both of king and priest. The family of Vi*s*vâmitra has contributed its own collection of hymns to the Rig-veda, but Vi*s*vâmitra himself was of royal descent; and if in later times he is represented as admitted into the Brahmanic family of the Bh*r*igus, — a family famous for its sanctity as well as its valor, — this is but an excuse invented by the Brahmans, in order to explain what would otherwise have upset their own system. King *G*anaka of Videha is represented in some of the Brâhma*n*as as more learned than any of the Brahmans at his court. Yet, when instructed by Yâ*g*ñavalkya as to the real nature of the soul and its identity with Brahma, or the divine spirit, he exclaims, "I will give thee, O Venerable, the kingdom of the Videhas, and my own self, to become thy slave."

As the influence of the Brahmans extended, they became more and more jealous of their privileges, and, while fixing their own privileges, they endeavored at the same time to circumscribe the duties of the warriors and the householders. Those of the Âryas who would not submit to the laws of the three estates were treated as outcasts, and they are chiefly known by the name of "Vrâtyas," or tribes. They spoke the same language as the three Aryan castes, but they did not submit to Brahmanic discipline, and they had to perform certain penances if they wished to be readmitted into the Aryan society. The aboriginal inhabitants again, who conformed to the Brahmanic law, received certain privileges, and were constituted as a fourth caste, under the name of "*S*ûdras," whereas all the rest who kept aloof were called "Dasyus," whatever their language might be (Manu, X. 45). This Brahmanic constitution, however, was not settled in a day, and we find everywhere in the hymns, in the Brâhma*n*as, and in the epic poems, the traces of a long continued warfare between the Âryas and the aboriginal inhabitants, and violent contests between the two highest classes of the Âryas striving for political supremacy. For a long time the three upper classes continued to consider themselves as one race, all claiming the title of Ârya, in contradistinction from the fourth caste, or the *S*ûdras. In the Brâhma*n*as it is stated distinctly: Âryas are only the Brahmans, Kshatriyas, and Vaisyas, for they are admitted to the sacrifices. They shall not speak with everybody, for the gods did not speak with everybody, but only with the Brahman, the Kshatriya, and the Vai*s*ya. If they should fall into a conversation with a *S*ûdra, let them say to another man, "Tell this *S*ûdra so." In several passages of the Purâ*n*as, where an account of the creation is given, we hear of but one original caste, which, by the difference of works, became afterwards divided into three. Professor Wilson says: —

"The existence of but one caste in the age of purity, however incompatible with the legend which ascribes the origin of the four castes to Brahmâ, is everywhere admitted. Their separation is assigned to different individuals, whether accurately to any one may be doubted; but the notion indicates that the distinction was of a social or political character."

In some places the threefold division of caste is represented to have taken place in the Tretâ age, and Mr. Muir quotes a passage from the Bhâgavatapurâ*n*a, where it is said, —

"There was formerly only one Veda, only one God, one fire, and one caste. From Purûravas came the triple Veda, in the beginning of the Tretâ age."

A similar idea is expressed in the account of the creation given in the B*r*ihad-âra*n*yaka-upanishad. It is there stated that in the beginning there was but One, which was Brahman; that Brahman created the warlike gods, such as Indra, Varu*n*a, Soma, Rudra, Par*g*anya, Yama, M*r*ityu, and I*s*âna. That after that, he created the corporations of gods, the Vasus, Rudras, Âdityas, Vi*s*ve Devas, and Maruts; and at last he created the earth, which supports all things. This creation of the gods is throughout treated as a prelude to the creation of man. And as Brahman was the first god, so the Brâhman is the first man. As the warlike gods came after, so after the Brâhman comes the Kshatriya. As the corporations of gods came third, so the corporations of men, the Vaisyas, occupy the third place, whereas the fourth order, the *S*ûdra color, is represented as the earth or Pûshan, this being one of their ancient gods, who is called Pûshan because he nourishes all beings. Practical conclusions are at once drawn from this passage. "Brahman," it is said, "is the birthplace of the Kshatriya; therefore, although the king obtains the highest dignity, he at last takes refuge in Brahman as in his birthplace. Whosoever despises him, destroys his own birthplace; he is a very great sinner, like a man who injures his superior."

Even the name of gods is claimed for the Brâhmans as early as the Brâhma*n*a period. In the *S*atapatha-brâhma*n*a (II. 2, 2, 6), we read: "There are two kinds of gods: first the gods, then those who are Brâhmans, and who have learnt the Veda and repeat it; they are human gods ('manushya-devâ*h*'). And this sacrifice is twofold: oblations for the gods, gifts for the human gods, the Brâhmans, who have learnt the Veda and repeat it. With oblations he appeases the gods, with gifts the human gods, the Brâhmans, who have learnt the Veda and repeat it. Both gods when they are pleased, place him in bliss."

Nevertheless, the Brahman knew how to be humble where it was necessary. "None is greater," he says, "than the warrior, therefore the Brâhman under the warrior worships at the royal sacrifice."

After long and violent struggles between the Brâhmans and the Kshatriyas, the Brâhmans carried the day, and, if we may judge from the legends which they themselves have preserved of these struggles, they ended with the total destruction of most of the old Kshatriya families and the admission of a few of them to the privileges of the first caste. Parasurâma is the great hero of the Brahmans: —

"He cleared the earth thrice seven times of the Kshatriya caste, and filled with their blood the five large lakes of Samanta, from which he offered libations to the race of Bh*r*igu. Offering a solemn sacrifice to the king of the gods, Parasurâma presented the earth to the ministering priests. Having given the earth to Kasyapa, the hero of immeasurable prowess retired to the Mahendra mountain, where he still resides; and in this manner was there enmity between him and the race of the Kshatriyas, and thus was the whole earth conquered by Parasurâma."

The destruction of the Kshatriyas by Parasurâma had been provoked by the cruelty of the Kshatriyas. We are told that there had been a king K*r*itavîrya, by whose liberality the Bh*r*igus, who officiated as his priests, had been greatly enriched with corn and money. After he had gone to heaven his descendants were in want of money, and came to beg for a supply from the Bh*r*igus, of whose wealth they were aware. Some of the latter hid their money under ground, others bestowed it on Brâhmans, being afraid of the Kshatriyas, while others again gave these last what they wanted. It happened, however, that a Kshatriya, while digging the ground, discovered the money concealed in the house of a Bh*r*igu. The Kshatriyas then assembled and saw this treasure, and slew in consequence all the

Bh*r*igus down to the children in the womb. One of them concealed her unborn child. The Kshatriyas, hearing of its existence, sought to kill it; but it issued forth with a lustre which blinded the persecutors. They now humbly supplicated the mother of the child for the restoration of their sight; but she referred them to her wonderful infant, Aurva, into whom the whole Vedas had entered, as the person who had robbed them of their sight, and who alone could restore it. Aurva did restore their sight, and, admonished by the spirits of his ancestors, he abstained from taking vengeance on the Kshatriyas; but vengeance was to come from the Bh*r*igus upon the Kshatriyas. Parasurâma, the scourge of the Kshatriyas, was, through his father *G*amadagni and his grandfather *Rik*îka, a descendant of the Bh*r*igus, though, through his grandmother, the daughter of Gâdhi, the king of Kanyâkub*g*a, he belonged to the royal race of the Kusikas.

This royal race of the Kusikas, which produced the avenger of the Brahmans, the destroyer of all Kshatriyas, Parasurâma, counts among its members another equally remarkable person, Visvâmitra. He was the son of the same Gâdhi whose daughter, Satyâvatî, became the mother of *G*amadagni and the grandmother of Parasurâma. Though of royal extraction, Visvâmitra conquered for himself and his family the privileges of a Brahman. He became a Brahman, and thus broke through all the rules of caste. The Brahmans cannot deny the fact, because it forms one of the principal subjects of their legendary poems. But they have spared no pains to represent the exertions of Visvâmitra, in his struggle for Brahmahood, as so superhuman that no one would easily be tempted to follow his example. No mention is made of these monstrous penances in the Veda, where the struggle between Visvâmitra, the leader of the Kusikas or Bharatas, and the Brahman Vasish*tha*, the leader of the white-robed Tritsus, is represented as the struggle of two rivals for the place of Purohita, or chief priest and minister at the court of king Sudâs, the son of Pi*g*avana. In the epic poems this story is frequently alluded to, and we give the following extracts from Mr. Muir's book, as likely to throw some light on the history of caste in India: —

"Saudâsa was king of the race of Ikshvâku. Visvâmitra wished to be employed by him as his officiating priest, but the king preferred Vasish*tha*. It happened, however, that the king had gone out to hunt, and meeting *S*aktri, the eldest of Vasish*tha*'s hundred sons, on the road, he ordered him to get out of his way. The priest civilly replied, 'The path is mine, O king; this is the immemorial law; in all observances the king must cede the way to the Brahman.' In later times he would have quoted a less civil sentence from the Brahma-vaivarta: 'He who does not immediately bow down when he sees his tutor, or a Brahman, or the image of a god, becomes a hog on earth.' The king struck the priest with a whip; the priest cursed the king to become a cannibal. Visvâmitra, who happened to be near, took advantage of this *fracas*, prevented the king from imploring the priest's mercy, and the priest himself, the son of Vasish*tha*, fell as the first victim of Saudâsa's cannibalism. The same fate befell all the other sons of Vasish*tha*. Vasish*tha*, on hearing of the destruction of his sons by Visvâmitra, supported his affliction as the great mountain sustains the earth.

He meditated his own destruction, and never thought of exterminating the Kau*s*ikas. In spite of repeated efforts, however, Vasish*th*a failed in depriving himself of his life, and when returning to his hermitage he discovered that the wife of his eldest son was pregnant, and that there was hope of his lineage being continued. A son was born, and he was called Parâ*s*ara. The king Saudâsa was going to swallow him also, when Vasish*th*a interfered, exorcised the king, and delivered him from the curse by which he had been affected for twelve years. Vasish*th*a resumed his duties as priest, and the king remained a patron of the Brahmans, but he is always quoted as an instance of a Kshatriya, hostile to the Brahmans, and punished for his hostility."

The most important point in the eyes of the later Brahmans was how Vi*s*vâmitra, being born a Kshatriya, could have become a Brahman, and it is for the solution of this difficulty that they invented the most absurd fables. The object of his ambition is said to have been the cow of Vasish*th*a, a most wonderful animal, and, though in the end he did not obtain that cow, yet he obtained by penance, performed during thousands of years, a share in the benefits of the priesthood. Mr. Muir has carefully collected all the passages from the Purâ*n*as and the epic poems, which illustrate the contest for the milk-cow of the priest, and the chief passages from the Râmâya*n*a may be read in Chevalier Gorresio's excellent Italian translation of that epic poem.

Another difficulty for the later Brahmans was the case of their own most famous legislator, Manu. He, too, was by birth, a Râ*g*anya or Kshatriya, and his father Vivasvat is called "the seed of all the Kshatriyas" (Madhusûdana, Bhagavadgîtâ, IV. 1). For a Kshatriya to teach the law was a crime ("svadharmâtikrama"), and it is only by a most artificial line of argument that the dogmatic philosophers of the Mîmâ*m*sâ school tried to explain this away. The Brahmans seem to have forgotten that, according to their own Upanishads, A*g*âta*s*atru, the king of Kâ*s*î, possessed more knowledge than Gârgya, the son of Balâka, who was renowned as a reader of the Veda,[1] and that Gârgya desired to become his pupil, though it was not right, as the king himself remarked, that a Kshatriya should initiate a Brahman. They must have forgotten that Pravâhana *G*aivali, king of the Pañ*k*âlas, silenced *S*vetaketu Aru*n*eya and his father, and then communicated to them doctrines which Kshatriyas only, but no Brahmans, had ever known before.[2] That king *G*anaka of Videha possessed superior knowledge is acknowledged by one of the most learned among the Brahmans, by Yâ*g*ñavalkya himself; and in the *S*atapatha-brâhma*n*a, which is believed to have been the work of Yâ*g*ñavalkya, it is said that king *G*anaka became a Brahman.[3]

Whatever we may think of the historical value of such traditions, one thing is quite clear, namely, that the priests succeeded in establishing, after a time, a lucrative supremacy, and that it was worth fighting for to be admitted to their caste. When the supremacy of the Brahmans was once firmly established, the rules

[1] Kaushîtaki-brâhma*n*a-upanishad, cap. 4, ed. Cowell, p. 167. In the *S*atapatha-brâhma*n*a, XIV. 5, 1, nearly the same story is told of D*r*iptabalâki Gârgya.

[2] *Kh*ândogya-upanishad, V. 3, 7, translated by Dr. Roër, p. 85. In the *S*atapatha-brâhma*n*a, XIV. 9, 1, read *G*aivali.

[3] *S*atapatha-brâhma*n*a, XI. 6, 2, 5.

about caste became stricter than ever, and the prohibition of marriage, not only between Âryas and *S*ûdras, but between the different castes of Âryas, became essential for the maintenance of those privileges for which the Brahmans and Kshatriyas had been fighting their sanguinary battles. It is, indeed, only in the very latest works of the Vedic period of literature that we meet with the first traces of that intolerant spirit of caste which pervades the "Laws of Manu." But that the oppressiveness of the system and the arrogant tyranny of the Brahmans were felt by the people at an earlier period we may guess from that reaction which called forth the opposite system of Buddha, and led to the adoption of Buddhism as the state religion of India in the third century B. C. Buddha himself was a Kshatriya, a royal prince, like *G*anaka, like Vi*s*vâmitra, and the secret of his success lies in his disregard of the privileges of the priestly caste. He addressed himself to all classes; nay, he addressed himself to the poor and the degraded rather than to the rich and the high. He did not wish to abolish caste as a social institution, and there is no trace of social leveling or democratic communism in any of his sermons. His only attacks were leveled against the exclusive privileges claimed by the Brahmans, and against their cruel treatment of the lowest castes. He was met by the Brahmans with the same arguments with which they had met former reformers: "How can a Kshatriya take upon himself the office of a priest? He breaks the most sacred law by attempting to interfere in religious matters." Buddha, however, having no views of personal aggrandizement like Vi*s*vâmitra, and abstaining from all offensive warfare, simply went on preaching and teaching, that "all that is born must die, that virtue is better than vice, that passions must be subdued, till a man is ready to give up everything, even his own self." These doctrines would hardly have possessed so great a charm in the eyes of the people if they had not been preached by a man of royal extraction, who had given up his exalted position and mixed with the lowest classes as his friends and equals.

"As the four rivers which fall in the Ganges lose their names as soon as they mingle their waters with the holy river, so all who believe in Buddha cease to be Brahmans, Kshatriyas, Vai*s*yas, and *S*ûdras."

This was the teaching of Buddha. Or again, —

"Between a Brahman and a man of another caste there is not the same difference as between gold and a stone, or between light and darkness. The Brahman is born of a woman, so is the *K*andâla. If the Brahman is dead, he is left as a thing impure, like the other castes. Where is the difference?" "If the Brahmans were above the law, if for them there were no unhappy consequences of sins committed, then, indeed, they might be proud of their caste." "My law is a law of grace for all." "My doctrine is like the sky. There is room for all without exception — men, women, boys, girls, poor, and rich."

Such a doctrine, preached in a country enthralled under the rules of caste, was sure to conquer. At the bidding of Buddha the evil spirit of caste seems to have vanished. Thieves and robbers, beggars and cripples, slaves and prostitutes, bankrupts and sweepers gathered around him. But kings also came to confess their sins and to perform public penance, and the most learned among the Brahmans confessed their ignorance before Buddha. Hindu society was changed. The dynasties which reigned in the chief cities of India were *S*ûdras. The language used in their edicts is no longer Sanskrit, but the vulgar dialects. The Brahmanic sacrifices were abolished, and buildings rose over the whole of India, sacred through the relics of Buddha which they contained, and surrounded by monasteries open to all ranks, to Brahmans and *S*ûdras, to men and women. How long this state of things lasted it is difficult to say. Towards the end of the fourth century, when Fahian, the Chinese pilgrim, travelled through India, a Brahmanic reaction had already commenced in some parts of the country. At the time of Hiouen-thsang, in the middle of the seventh century, Buddhism was losing ground rapidly, and some of its most sacred places were in ruins. The Brahmans had already gained back much of their former influence, and they soon grew strong enough to exterminate forever the heresy of Buddha on the soil of India, and to reëstablish orthodoxy under *S*ankara-Â*k*ârya. There are at present no Buddhists left in India; they have migrated to Ceylon in the South, to Nepal, Thibet, and China in the North. After the victorious return of the Brahmans the old laws of caste were reënacted more vigorously than ever, and the Brahmans became again what they had been before the rise of Buddhism — the terrestrial gods of India. A change, however, had come over the system of caste. Though the laws of Manu still spoke of four castes, of Brahmans, Kshatriyas, Vaisyas, and *S*ûdras, the social confusion during the long reign of Buddhism had left but one broad distinction; on the one side the pure caste of the Brahman; on the other, the mixed and impure castes of the people. In many places the pure castes of the Kshatriyas and Vai*s*yas had become extinct, and those who could not prove their Brahmanic descent were all classed together as *S*ûdras. At present we should look in vain for pure Kshatriyas and Vai*s*yas in India, and the families which still claim those titles would find it difficult to produce their pedigree. Nay there are few who could even lay claim to the pure blood of the *S*ûdra. Low as the *S*ûdra stood in the system of Manu, he stood higher than most of the mixed castes, the Var*n*asaṅkaras. The son of a *S*ûdra by a *S*ûdra woman is purer than the son of a *S*ûdra by a woman of the highest caste (Manu, X. 30). Manu calls the *K*andâla one of the lowest outcasts, because he is the son of a *S*ûdra father and a Brahmanic mother. He evidently considered the *mésalliance* of a woman more degrading than that of a man. For the son of a Brahman father and a *S*ûdra mother may in the seventh generation raise his family to the highest caste (Manu, X. 64); while the son of a *S*ûdra father and a Brahman mother belongs forever to the *K*andâlas. The abode of the *K*andâlas must be out of the town, and no respectable man is to hold intercourse with them. By day they must walk about distinguished by badges; by night they are driven out of the city.

Manu represents, indeed, all the castes of Hindu society, and their number is considerable, as the result of mixed marriages between the four original castes. According to him, the four primitive castes, by intermarrying in every possible way, gave rise to sixteen mixed castes, which by continuing their intermarriages produced the long list of the mixed castes. It is extremely doubtful, however, whether Manu meant to say that at all times the offspring of a mixed marriage had to enter a lower caste. He could not possibly maintain that the son of a Brahman father and a Vaisya mother would always be a physician or a Vaidya, this being the name given by Manu to the offspring of these two castes. At present the offspring of a *S*ûdra father and a Brahman mother would find no admission in any respectable caste. Their marriage would not be considered marriage at all. The only rational explanation of Manu's words seems to be that originally the caste of the Vaidyas or physicians sprang from the union of a Brahman father and a Vaisya mother, though this, too, is of course nothing but a fanciful theory. If we look more carefully, we shall find that most of these mixed castes are in reality the professions, trades, and guilds of a half-civilized society. They did not wait for mixed marriages before they came into existence. Professions, trades, and handicrafts had grown up without any reference to caste in the ethnological or political sense of the word. Some of their names were derived from towns and countries where certain professions were held in particular estimation. Servants who waited on ladies were called "Vaidehas," because they came from Videha, the Athens of India, just as the French called the "porteur d'eau" a "Savoyard." To maintain that every member of the caste of the Vaidehas, in fact, every lady's maid, had to be begotten through the marriage of a Vaisya and a Brâhma*n*î, is simply absurd. In other cases the names of Manu's castes were derived from their occupations. The caste of musicians, for instance, were called "Ve*n*as," from "vî*n*â," the lyre. Now, it was evidently Manu's object to bring these professional corporations in connection with the old system of the castes, assigning to each, according to its higher or lower position, a more or less pure descent from the original castes. The Vaidyas, for instance, or the physicians, evidently a respectable corporation, were represented as the offspring of a Brahman father and a Vai*s*ya mother, while the guild of the fishermen, or Nishâdas, were put down as the descendants of a Brahman father and a *S*ûdra mother. Manu could hardly mean to say that every son of a Vai*s*ya father and Kshatriya mother was obliged to become a commercial traveller, or to enter the caste of the Magadhas. How could that caste have been supplied after the extinction in many places of the Kshatriya and Vai*s*ya castes? But, having to assign to the Magadhas a certain social position, Manu recognized them as the descendants of the second and third castes, in the same manner as the Herald office would settle the number of quarters of an earl or a baron.

Thus, after the political caste had become nearly extinct in India, leaving nothing behind but the broad distinction between the Brahmans and mixed castes, a new system of caste came in of a purely professional character, though artificially grafted on the rotten trunk of the ancient political castes. This is the system which is still in force in India, and which has exercised its influence on the state of Indian society for good and evil. During periods of history when public opinion is weak, and when the administration of justice is precarious, institutions analogous to these Indian castes must necessarily spring into existence. Men who have the same interests, the same occupations, the same principles, unite in self-defense, and after acquiring power and influence they not only defend their rights, but claim important privileges. They naturally impose upon their members certain rules which are considered essential to the interest of their caste or company. These rules, sometimes of apparently the most trifling character, are observed by individual members with greater anxiety than even the laws of religion, because an offense against the latter may be pardoned, while a disregard of the former would lead to instant exclusion or loss of caste. Many a Hindu carrier would admit that there was no harm in his fetching water for his master. But he belongs to a caste of carriers who have bound themselves not to fetch water, and it would be dishonorable if he, for his own personal convenience, were to break that rule. Besides it would interfere with the privileges of another caste, the water-carriers. There is an understanding in most parts of India that certain trades should be carried on by certain castes, and the people no doubt have the same means of punishing interlopers as the guilds had during the Middle Ages. The more lucrative the trade, the more jealously it was guarded, and there was evidently no trade in India so lucrative as that of the priests. The priests were therefore the strongest advocates of the system of caste, and after investing it with a sacred character in the eyes of the people, they expanded it into an immense spider's web, which separated class from class, family from family, man from man, and which, while it rendered all united public action impossible, enabled the watchful priests to pounce upon all who dared to disturb the threads of their social tissue, and to wither them to death. But although much harm was done by allowing the priests to gain too great an influence, much good also was achieved by the system of caste with regard to public morality. A man knew that he might lose caste for offenses of which the law would take no cognizance. Immorality and drunkenness might be punished by degradation or loss of caste. In fact, if caste could be divested of that religious character which the priests for their own advantage succeeded in fastening upon it, thereby giving an unnatural permanence and sanctity to what ought to be, like all social institutions, capable of change and growth, it would probably be found that the system of caste was well adapted to that state of society and that form of government which has hitherto existed in India; and that if it were suddenly destroyed, more harm than good would follow from such a change.

The great objections against the system of castes as it exists at present, are, that it prevents people from dining with whom they please, from marrying whom they please, and from following what profession they please. The mere prohibition of dining together is no very serious inconvenience, particularly in Eastern countries; and people belonging to different castes, and abstaining from mutual hospitality, may entertain, nevertheless, the most friendly relations. Dining together among oriental nations has a different meaning from what it has with us. It is more than our social feeding together. It is dining *en famille.* No one invites, and no one wishes to be invited. At all events there is something mutual in caste. It is not that the rich may visit the poor, but that the poor must not visit the rich. It is not that the Brahman may invite the Sûdra to dinner, but must not be invited in turn. No one in India is ashamed of his caste, and the lowest Pariah is as proud and as anxious to preserve his own caste as the highest Brahman. The Turas, a class of *S*ûdras, consider their houses defiled, and throw away their cooking utensils, if a Brahman visit them. Another class of *S*ûdras throw away their cooking vessels if a Brahman comes upon their boat. Invite one of the lowest orders of *S*ûdras to a feast with a European of the highest rank, and he turns away his face with the most marked disgust.

The prohibition of certain marriages, again, is less keenly felt in an Eastern country than it would be among ourselves. Nor is the prohibition of marriages the result of caste alone. People belonging to the same caste are prohibited from marrying on account of their pedigree. Kulins, *S*rotriyas, and Va*m*sa*g*as, though all of them Brahmans, will freely dine together, though they have scruples about allowing their children to marry. The six divisions of the caste of the Tatis, or weavers, will neither visit nor intermarry with each other. These are social prejudices which exist in half-civilized countries, and which even in Europe are not quite extinct. Nay, it is doubtful whether an absolute prohibition of certain marriages is more cruel than a partial prohibition. It is certainly a curious fact, which psychologists have still to explain, that people very seldom fall in love when marriage is absolutely impossible. Now, there never has been, and there never will be, any state of society without the distinctions of birth, position, education, and wealth; and, in order to keep up these distinctions, marriages between high and low, educated and uneducated, rich and poor people, must to a certain extent be discouraged and prohibited. In England, where women occupy so different a position in society from what they do in the East, where they are conscious of their own worth and of their own responsibility, exceptions will no doubt occur. A young lord may imagine that a poor governess is more beautiful, more charming, more ladylike, more likely to make him truly happy than any rich heiress that happens to be in the market; the daughter of an earl may imagine that the young curate of the village is more manly, more cultivated, more of a gentleman, than any of the young scions of the nobility; yet such is the power of society, such is the hidden influence of caste, that these marriages are violently opposed by fathers and mothers, by uncles and aunts. In countries where such marriages are altogether impossible, much shedding of tears and breaking of hearts are avoided, and the hardship in reality is not greater than what every commoner in England endures in abstaining from falling in love with the most charming of the princesses of the Royal Family.

As to the choice of a profession being circumscribed by caste, it may seem to be a great grievance. We read but lately in a very able article on caste in the "Calcutta Review:" —

"The systems by which a person's studies and profession are made dependent on his birth can never be sufficiently execrated. The human mind is free, it will not submit to restraints; it will not succumb to the regulations of freakish legislators. The Brahman or the Kshatriya may have a son whose mind is ill adapted to his hereditary profession; the Vaisya may have a son with a natural dislike for a counting-house, and the

*S*ûdra may have talents superior to his birth. If they be forced to adhere to their hereditary professions their minds must deteriorate."

Now, this is language applicable to England in the nineteenth century, but hardly to India. Where there is a well organized system of public education, a boy may choose what profession he likes. But where this is not the case, the father most likely will be the best teacher of his son. Even in England the public service has but very lately been thrown open to all classes, and we heard it stated by one of the most eminent men that the Indian Civil Service would no longer be fit for the sons of gentlemen. Why? Because one of the elected candidates was the son of a missionary. The system of caste, no doubt, has its disadvantages, but many of them are inherent in human society, and are felt in England as well as in India.

There may seem to be an essential distinction between caste in India and caste in Europe, the one being invested with a sacred character and supposed to be unchangeable, the other being based merely on traditional prejudices and amenable to the pressure of public opinion. But that sacred character of caste is a mere imposition of the priests, and could be removed without removing at the same time those necessary social distinctions which are embodied in India in the system of caste. In a country governed, if not politically, at least intellectually, by priests, the constant appeal to divine right, divine grace, divine institutions, loses much of its real meaning. Though the Brahmans may appeal to the "Laws of Manu," these Laws of Manu, like the Canon Law of the Church of Rome, are not unchangeable. The Brahmans themselves violate these laws daily. They accept gifts from *S*ûdras, though Manu declares that a Brahman shall not accept gifts from a *S*ûdra. They will bow before a rich banker, however low his caste, and they will sit on the same carpet and at the feet of a *S*ûdra, though Manu declares (VIII. 281), "A man of the lowest class anxious to place himself on the same seat with one of the highest, is to be banished with a mark branded on his back," etc. In fact, however unchangeable the laws of caste may seem in the eyes of the Brahmans, they have only to open their eyes, to read their ancient works, and to look at the society around them, in order to convince themselves that caste is not proof against the changes of time. The president of the Dharma-sabhâ at Calcutta is a *S*ûdra, while the secretary is a Brahman. Three fourths of the Brahmans in Bengal are the servants of others. Many traffic in spirituous liquors, some procure beef for the butchers, and wear shoes made of cow leather. Some of the Brahmans themselves are honest enough to admit that the Laws of Manu were intended for a different age, for the mythical Satyayuga, while the Laws of the Kaliyuga were written by Parâ*s*ara. In places like Calcutta and Bombay the contact with English society exercises a constant attrition on the system of castes, and produces silently and imperceptibly a greater effect than can ever be produced by violent declamation against the iniquity of caste. As soon as the female population of India can be raised from their present degradation; as soon as a better education and a purer religion will have inspired the women of India with feelings of moral responsibility and self-respect; as soon as they have learned — what Christianity alone can teach —

that in the true love of a woman there is something far above the law of caste or the curses of priests, their influence will be the most powerful, on the one side, to break through the artificial forms of caste, and on the other, to maintain in India, as elsewhere, the true caste of rank, manners, intellect, and character.

With many of the present missionaries, the abolition of caste has become a fixed idea. Some of the early Roman Catholic missionaries, no doubt, went too far in their toleration of caste, but some of the most efficient Protestant missionaries, men of the school of Schwarz, have never joined in the indiscriminate condemnation of caste, and have allowed their Christian converts to keep up, under the name of caste, those social distinctions which in European countries are maintained by public opinion, by the good feeling and the self-respect of the lower classes, and, where necessary, by the power of the law. As regards the private life of the natives, their match-making, their hospitality, their etiquette, and their rules of precedence, it would be unwise for missionaries as well as for the Government to attempt any sudden interference. What would people say in England if Parliament, after admitting the Jews, were to insist on Mr. Newdegate shaking hands with Baron Rothschild, or asking the Jewish members to his dinner parties? How would the fashionable occupants of our church pews in their crisp muslin dresses like it if the bishops were to require that they should sit side by side with men in oily fustian jackets? How would our bankers and Quakers bear any interference with their system of marrying, if possible, within their own families?

There are, however, certain points where the Government will have to interfere with caste, and where it may do so without violating any pledge and without rousing any serious opposition. If any of its Indian subjects are treated with indignity on account of their caste, the law will have to give them protection. In former times a Pariah was obliged to carry a bell — the very name of Pariah is derived from that bell — in order to give warning to the Brahmans, who might be polluted by the shadow of an outcast. In Malabar, a Nayadi defiles a Brahman at a distance of seventy-four paces; and a Nayer, though himself a *S*ûdra, would shoot one of these degraded races if they approached too near. Here the duty of the Government is clear.

Secondly, no attention should be paid to caste in any contract which the Government makes with the natives. Where natives are to be employed, whether in the civil or military service, no concession should be made to the punctilio of caste. Soldiers must not only fight together, but they must live and mess together. Those who have any conscientious objections must stay away.

Thirdly, caste must be ignored in all public institutions, such as schools, hospitals, and prisons. Railway companies cannot provide separate carriages for each of the fifty castes that may wish to travel by themselves, nor can Government provide separate forms, or wards, or cells for Brahmans and *S*ûdras. Firmness on the part of the Government is all that is required. At Madras a few Pariah boys were admitted at the High-school. The other boys rebelled, and forty left the school. After a time, however, twenty returned, and the spell was broken.

The missionaries are not obliged to act with the same rigor. Their relation to the natives, and particularly to their converts, is a private relation, and much of their success will depend on their discretion in dealing with native prejudices. A Hindu who embraces Christianity loses caste, and is cut off from all his friends. But if he was brought up as a gentleman, it is not fair that, as a Christian, he should be forced to mix with other converts, his inferiors in birth, education, and manners. Much offense has been given by the missionaries by maintaining that no one can be a true convert who refuses to eat and drink with his fellow-converts. "The kingdom of God is not meat and drink." The social position of the converts in India will be for a long time a stumbling-block. Native converts are not admitted to English caste, and it is the dread of this isolated position which acts most powerfully against conversion. The Mohammedans admit Hindu converts into their own society, and treat every Mussulman on terms of equality. Christian society in India is hardly able to do this, and it is a question whether even the purest religion will be able to overcome that deep-rooted feeling of caste which divided the Ârya from the Dasyu, and which still divides the white European from the dark Asiatic. Measures must be adopted to give to the Hindus who accept Christianity something in place of the caste which they lose. In a certain sense no man ought to be without caste, without friends who take care of him, without companions who watch him, without associates whose good opinion he values, without companions with whom he can work for a common cause. The healthy life of a political body can only be supported by means of associations, circles, leagues, guilds, clans, clubs, or parties; and in a country where caste takes the place of all this, the abolition of caste would be tantamount to a complete social disorganization. Those who know the Hindus best are the least anxious to see them without caste. Colonel Sleeman remarks: —

"What chiefly prevents the spread of Christianity is the dread of exclusion from caste and all its privileges, and the utter hopelessness of their ever finding any respectable circle of society of the adopted religion, which converts, or would be converts, to Christianity now everywhere feel. Form such circles for them; make the members of these circles excel in the exertion of honest and independent industry. Let those who rise to eminence in them feel that they are considered as respectable and important in the social system as the servants of Government, and converts will flock around you from all parts and from all classes of the Hindu community. I have, since I have been in India, had, I may say, at least a score of Hindu grass-cutters turn Mussulmans, merely because the grooms and the other grass-cutters of my establishment happened to be of that religion, and they could neither eat, drink, nor smoke with them. Thousands of Hindus, all over India, become every year Mussulmans from the same motive, and we do not get the same number of converts to Christianity, merely because we cannot offer them the same advantages. I am persuaded that a dozen such establishments as that of Mr. Thomas Ashton, of Hyde, as described by a physician of Manchester, and noticed in Mr. Baines' admirable work on the cotton manufactures of Great Britain (page 447), would do more in the way of conversion among the people of India than has ever yet been done by all the religious establishments, or ever will be done by them, without some such aid."

Caste, which has hitherto proved an impediment to the conversion of the Hindus, may in future become one of the most powerful engines for the conversion not merely of individuals, but of whole classes of Indian society. Caste cannot be abolished in India, and to attempt it would be one of the most hazardous operations that was ever performed on a living political body. As a religious institution caste will die; as a social institution it will live and improve. Let the *S*ûdras, or, as they are called in Tamil, the Petta Pitteï, the children of the house, grow into free laborers, the Vai*s*yas into wealthy merchants, the Kshatriyas into powerful barons, and let the Brahmans aspire to the position of that intellectual aristocracy which is the only true aristocracy in truly civilized countries, and the four castes of the Veda will not be out of date in the nineteenth century, nor out of place in a Christian country. But all this must be the work of time. "The teeth," as a native writer, says, "fall off themselves in old age, but it is painful to extract them in youth."

April, 1858.

INDEX.

The numerals i. and ii. refer to the volumes; the figures to the pages.
Pr. = Preface.

www.ingramcontent.com/pod-product-compliance
Lightning Source LLC
LaVergne TN
LVHW020059110826
845151LV00001B/20

9781425544805